Religion and the Bush Presidency

THE EVOLVING AMERICAN PRESIDENCY SERIES

Series Foreword:

The American Presidency touches virtually every aspect of American and world politics. And the presidency has become, for better or worse, the vital center of the American and global political systems. The Framers of the American government would be dismayed at such a result. As invented at the Philadelphia Constitutional Convention in 1787, the Presidency was to have been a part of a government with shared and overlapping powers, embedded within a separation-of-powers system. If there was a vital center, it was the Congress; the Presidency was to be a part, but by no means, the centerpiece of that system.

Over time, the Presidency has evolved and grown in power, expectations, responsibilities, and authority. Wars, crises, depressions, industrialization, all served to add to the power of the presidency. And as the United States grew into a world power, presidential power also grew. As the United States became the world's leading superpower, the presidency rose in prominence and power, not only in the United States, but on the world stage.

It is the clash between the presidency as invented and the presidency as it has developed that inspired this series. And it is the importance and power of the modern American presidency that makes understanding the office so vital. Like it or not, the American Presidency stands at the vortex of power both within the United States and across the globe.

This Palgrave series, recognizing that the Presidency is and has been an evolving institution, going from the original constitutional design as a Chief Clerk, to today where the president is the center of the American political constellation. This has caused several key dilemmas in our political system, not the least of which is that presidents face high expectations with limited constitutional resources. This causes presidents to find extra-constitutional means of governing. Thus, presidents must find ways to bridge the expectations/power gap while operating within the confines of a separation-of-powers system designed to limit presidential authority. How presidents resolve these challenges and paradoxes is the central issue in modern governance. It is also the central theme of this book series.

Michael A. Genovese
Loyola Chair of Leadership
Loyola Marymount University
Palgrave's **The Evolving American Presidency**, Series Editor

The Second Term of George W. Bush
>   edited by Robert Maranto, Douglas M. Brattebo, and Tom Lansford

The Presidency and the Challenge of Democracy
>   edited by Michael A. Genovese and Lori Cox Han

Religion and the American Presidency
>   edited by Mark J. Rozell and Gleaves Whitney

Religion and the Bush Presidency
>   edited by Mark J. Rozell and Gleaves Whitney

Religion and the Bush Presidency

Edited by Mark J. Rozell and Gleaves Whitney

RELIGION AND THE BUSH PRESIDENCY
© Mark J. Rozell and Gleaves Whitney, 2007.

First published in 2007 by
PALGRAVE MACMILLAN™
175 Fifth Avenue, New York, N.Y. 10010 and
Houndmills, Basingstoke, Hampshire, England RG21 6XS
Companies and representatives throughout the world.

PALGRAVE MACMILLAN is the global academic imprint of the Palgrave Macmillan division of St. Martin's Press, LLC and of Palgrave Macmillan Ltd. Macmillan® is a registered trademark in the United States, United Kingdom and other countries. Palgrave is a registered trademark in the European Union and other countries.

ISBN-13: 978–1–4039–8007–6
ISBN-10: 1–4039–8007–1

Library of Congress Cataloging-in-Publication Data

Religion and the Bush presidency / edited by Mark J. Rozell and Gleaves Whitney.
    p. cm.—(Evolving American presidency series)
    Includes bibliographical references.
    ISBN 1–4039–8007–1 (alk. paper)
    1. Bush, George W. (George Walker), 1946—Religion. 2. Bush, George W. (George Walker), 1946—Political and social views. 3. United States—Politics and government—2001– 4. Religion and politics—United States. I. Rozell, Mark J. II. Whitney, Gleaves.

E903.3.R45 2007
973.931092—dc22   2006036621

A catalogue record for this book is available from the British Library.

Design by Newgen Imaging Systems (P) Ltd., Chennai, India.

First edition: September 2007

10 9 8 7 6 5 4 3 2 1

Printed in the United States of America.

Contents

Illustrations   vii

Introduction: Religion and the Bush Presidency   1
    Mark J. Rozell

1 Bush and the Christian Right: The Triumph
   of Pragmatism   11
   Mark J. Rozell

Part I   Religion and the 2004 Election

2 "What Does the Lord Require?" Evangelicals
   and the 2004 Presidential Vote   31
   Corwin Smidt, John C. Green, Lyman Kellstedt,
   and James Guth

3 Catholics and the Politics of Change: The
   Presidential Campaigns of Two JFKs   51
   John Kenneth White and William D'Antonio

4 The Mainline Protestant Vote   69
   Laura R. Olson and Adam L. Warber

5 The Politics of the Religious Minorities
   Vote in the 2004 Elections   95
   Paul A. Djupe, Eric McDaniel, and Jacob R. Neiheisel

Part II   Religion and the Policies of the Bush Administration

6 Keeping the Charge: George W. Bush,
   the Christian Right, and the New Vital
   Center of American Politics   129
   John W. Wells and David B. Cohen

7   The Politics of Faith-Based Initiatives   155
     Amy E. Black and Douglas L. Koopman

8   Buying Black Votes? The GOP's
     Faith-Based Initiative   177
     Michael K. Fauntroy

9   Life Issues: Abortion, Stem-Cell
     Research, and the Case of Terry Schiavo   197
     Ted G. Jelen

10 Evangelical "Internationalists" and U.S.
     Foreign Policy during the Bush Administration   213
     Kevin R. den Dulk

11 President George W. Bush and Judicial
     Restraint: Accommodating Religion   235
     Nina Therese Kasniunas and Jack E. Rossotti

Notes on Contributors   255

Index   259

Illustrations

Figure

10.1 Evangelical Attention to Global Issues, 1998–2004   226

Tables

2.1 Frequency Distribution of Religious
Traditions, 2004   36
2.2 Turnout in 2004 Presidential Election
by Religious Tradition   37
2.3 Turnout among Evangelicals in 2004
Presidential Election   38
2.4 Two-Party Vote in 2004 Presidential
Election by Religious Tradition   39
2.5 Issue Priorities in 2004 Presidential Election
by Religious Tradition   40
2.6 Issue Positions in 2004 Presidential Election
by Religious Tradition   41
2.7 Proximity to Bush and Party Identification by
Religious Tradition, 2004   43
2.8 Evangelicals and Political Behavior:
Within-Tradition Variation   46
3.1 Catholic Vote for President, 1976–2004   57
4.1 Religion and Ideology, 2004   78
4.2 Religion and Level of Egalitarianism, 2004   80
4.3 Religion and Level of Moral Traditionalism, 2004   81
4.4 Religion and Opinions about Same-Sex
Marriage, 2004   82
4.5 Religion and Opinions about Abortion, 2004   83
4.6 Religion and Opinions about Privatizing Social
Security, 2004   83

4.7	Religion and Disapproval of President George W. Bush's Handling of Public Policy Issues, 2004	84
4.8	Religion and Partisanship, 2004	85
4.9	Religion and Presidential Vote, 2004	85
4.10	Religion and Political Participation Beyond Voting, 2004	87
5.1	The Estimated Effects of Biblical Literalism for Whites and Blacks on Candidate Affect, Support for Gay Marriage, and Presidential Vote	109
5.2	American Muslims and Social Issues, 2004	113
5.3	A More Personal Agenda: American Muslim Foreign Affairs Opinions and Reports of Discrimination	114
5.4	Vote Switching from 2000 to 2004 among American Muslims	117
11.1	Religious Composition of the Roberts, Rehnquist, Burger, and Warren Courts	239
11.2	Religious Cases before the Supreme Court during the Bush Administration	243
11.3	Supreme Court Cases in which the United States Filed Amicus Briefs during the Merits Phase	245
11.4	Supreme Court Cases in which the United States Filed Amicus Briefs during the Petitions Phase	246

Introduction: Religion and the Bush Presidency

Mark J. Rozell

Even before he first took the oath of office as president in 2001, a debate raged over the role of faith in forming George W. Bush's views on politics and policy. It is easy to understand why. Although Bush certainly was not the first serious presidential contender of the modern era to speak openly about his faith, when he did so during his first national campaign his comments pleased religious conservatives and at the same time invited strongly negative reactions from many liberal and moderate commentators. Most famously, when asked in a candidate forum in 1999 to name his favorite philosopher, Bush immediately answered, "Christ, because he changed my heart." Bush's opponents seized on this comment as evidence of a flaccid mind (because he did not name Plato or Aristotle perhaps), or at least proof that he was a religious fanatic. But these charges did not matter, because what Bush had said resonated with a core constituency in the Republican Party and gave him a lift over other candidates who tried to court the Christian Right.

Bush's comment of course was not an isolated one, but rather a reflection of a viewpoint that he had expressed for a number of years. The story of Bush's undisciplined young adulthood and battles with alcoholism is well known. At the urging of a friend some years ago, Bush joined a Bible class and he ultimately found the path that changed his life for the better. Bush was nearly 40 years of age at the time when he decided to devote his life to Jesus. Bush gave up alcohol and he became for the first time a disciplined and determined man.

During his first campaign for the presidency, Bush did not hesitate to tell his personal faith story. For many religious conservatives, the experience of the fall from grace, finding religion, and then charting a new life path is a familiar and powerful one. When Bush spoke, he thus connected with a significant portion of the population that could relate to his story. Bush's personal faith and his manner of expressing it became an asset in his campaign for the GOP nomination in 2000, and they have helped to sustain a certain level of intense support for him during his presidency, even in difficult times.

As important to the story of Bush's faith is how that has affected his policy positions and governing. In this regard, sharply divided opinions in the country over Bush's religiosity tend to exaggerate its actual effects. Some of the president's strongest detractors believe that he is deeply committed to imposing a rigid moralistic agenda on both domestic and foreign policies. But at the same time, many in the religious conservative community have expressed disappointment that Bush has not effected major social policy change in his presidency.

The essays that follow tell a much more nuanced story of the impact of religion on George W. Bush and his presidency. The opening essay, for example, reviews and analyzes the impact of religious conservative voters in both of Bush's elections. The story is a mixed one indeed. These voters were the key to Bush's GOP nomination campaign victory over Senator John McCain (R-AZ) in 2000, yet their mobilization in the general election was a serious disappointment to the GOP that year. Election turnout among conservative evangelicals dropped significantly from Senator Robert Dole's losing 1996 campaign to Bush's ultimately victorious one in 2000. Bush made a great deal of effort in his first term to reach these key potential GOP supporters, and the evidence suggests that the effort paid off in 2004. Significant attention in chapter one is given to the so-called "values election" in 2004 and the role of the Christian Right. The essay makes the case that Bush is the most genuinely social conservative president ever, that he has rewarded the Christian Right in some tangible and symbolic ways, and that indeed this constituency was a key to his reelection in 2004. Nonetheless, many of the postelection analyses in 2004 overreached in evaluating the role played by religious conservatives in Bush's victory and the extent to which he "owed" the movement in his second term.

The rest of the volume is divided into two parts. The first examines the impact of various religious voting groups to the 2004 presidential campaign. The second reviews and assesses the impact of religion on the policies of the George W. Bush presidency.

Part 1 opens with an analysis of the impact of the evangelical vote in 2004 by scholars Corwin Smidt, John C. Green, Lyman Kellstedt, and James Guth. The authors maintain in chapter two that evangelical Protestants played an important, though not necessarily a determinative, role in securing the reelection of George Bush. The evangelical contribution to the Bush victory stemmed from three factors: their relatively large numbers within the American electorate, their continuing strong loyalty to Bush, and the increased level of voting turnout within their ranks. The support that evangelical Protestants gave to

Bush never wavered during the course of the campaign; they were committed to him from the beginning of the primary season to Election Day. This loyalty was based on the conjunction of several factors. First, given his religious faith and willingness to employ religious language in public, Bush was personally attractive to many evangelicals. Second, the issue positions of evangelical Protestants across issue domains have converged over the past several elections, as their policy positions have become more strongly inter-correlated and fewer wedge issues have become available for opposing candidates to exploit. In other words, Kerry had fewer issues to exploit by which to try to "peel off" evangelical votes from George W. Bush than either Dukakis or Clinton did from George H.W. Bush. Finally, the growth in Republican partisan identification among evangelicals over time also meshed with their support for Bush in 2004.

Evangelical Protestants entered the 2004 campaign as the primary base from which the GOP and Bush could build in order to forge a winning electoral coalition; at the end of that campaign, the party solidified that position. For at least the near future, the GOP cannot win solely on the basis evangelical support but neither can they win without it.

In chapter three, scholars John Kenneth White and William D'Antonio assess the impact of the Catholic vote on the 2004 presidential campaign. In so doing, they first tell the tale of two JFKs: John F. Kennedy and John F. Kerry. Both were Massachusetts Catholics who received the Democratic presidential nomination. But the receptions they received among American Catholics could not have been more different. John F. Kennedy was nominated at a time when there was a strong sense of Catholic voter identification and remembrance of a time of anti-Catholic discrimination. Catholic versus white Protestant was the prevailing axial principle of U.S. politics. Depending on what side of that divide voters were on often determined the presidential ballot.

John F. Kerry was nominated when another axial principle was beginning to take shape. Instead of Catholic versus white Protestant, a new values divide, partly based on religiosity and church attendance, began to emerge. Frequent church attenders, whether Catholic or Protestant, were strong supporters of George W. Bush. Those who attended church less often were strong supporters of John F. Kerry.

In chapter four, scholars Laura R. Olson and Adam L. Warber examine the often overlooked but important mainline Protestant vote in 2004. Indeed, they argue that mainline Protestants constitute a significant swing constituency in American politics. During the 2004 presidential election, mainline Protestants divided their votes evenly between George W. Bush and John F. Kerry. While they may not receive as much press as evangelical Protestants and Catholics, mainline Protestants are almost as numerous—and at least as civically engaged—as either of these other religious traditions.

Skeptics might say that the influence of "old-line" Protestant voting has become less relevant in recent years as these denominations have declined in membership and political visibility. However, Olson and Warber argue that despite these challenges, mainline Protestant voters retain electoral significance due to their relatively high socioeconomic status and long-standing commitment to civic participation. Although mainline Protestants traditionally have favored *economic* conservatism, they are by no means a natural component of the religious right because they do not emphasize strict moral conservatism.

In 2004, mainline Protestant laity drifted ever closer to the Democratic Party, which marks their rejection of the alliance between the Republican Party and evangelical Protestants. In particular, mainline Protestants seem to be questioning the Republicans' emphasis on morality politics under George W. Bush.

In chapter five, Paul Djupe, Eric McDaniel, and Jacob R. Neiheisel explore the politics of "religious minorities," specifically of American blacks, Jews, and Muslims, in the 2004 election. These groups were at times at the center of politics in the first Bush term, showcasing how religion sometimes acts to maintain group solidarity and sometimes to undermine it. Muslims, in particular, show how drastically voter commitments can shift from election to election.

For many years, political observers have puzzled at the voting behavior of American Jews, united behind the Democratic Party when their economic interests might suggest another option. The 2004 campaign did not alter that pattern significantly, as Jewish commitments to social welfare, nondiscrimination, and civil rights and liberties remained intact. But with the gradual disappearance of discrimination from society, the Jewish community is generating new and distinct interests along its fault lines of religion, social context, and status. The authors observe that socially conservative and staunchly pro-Israel Orthodox Jews are starting to forge tentative links to the Republican Party that are likely to grow over time.

The Republican Party has held out the possibility that religiously observant and socially conservative African Americans would switch affiliations if the issues were right. 2004 might have fit the bill, with antigay marriage initiatives on the ballot in many states. However, African Americans clearly do not vote social issues as much as the host of civil rights and economic issues that have tied them to the Democratic Party for years. In fact, ties to the Black Church only serve to maintain traditional ties to the Democratic Party and any slim gains for Bush in 2004 seem to have come from outside of the black religious establishment.

Muslims were a divided community in 2000, on balance supporting Bush. That all changed in the political aftermath from September 11, 2001. By 2004, a once mildly supportive community was united against Bush. Although Muslims are socially conservative, they are almost united in their support for the welfare state, and fragmented along class and ethnic lines. For these reasons and until Muslims are better integrated into society—and until heated political issues dissipate—the community is unlikely to have strong partisan moorings. For now, it seems unlikely that Muslims will back a Republican candidate, especially one with ties to Bush.

Part 2 of the volume turns to the topic of religion and the policies of the Bush administration. Beginning with chapter six, John W. Wells and David B. Cohen explore the impact of the Christian Right movement on the policies of the Bush administration. They maintain that whereas the Christian Right forms a key element in the pro-Bush coalition, the administration has acted independently of this movement. In fact, far from attempting to use religion as a means of isolating the left culturally and solidifying his claim to right-leaning voters, George W. Bush has skillfully used religion and issues of importance to conservative people of faith as a means of creating a new vital center in American politics.

In several domestic issue areas, the Bush White House has sought to carve out a unique center-right position that appeals to social conservatives without alienating Bush's more secular constituency. This new "vital center" situates the administration's agenda in such a fashion that it avoids the ideological excesses of the base while at the same time shifts the national conversation in a direction that is more favorable to social conservatives. Bush's success in maintaining high levels of support with these constituencies demonstrates the continuing willingness of the American people to respond to religious appeals as long as they appear as manifestations of a middle-of-the-road civil religion and not the agenda of the theological fringe. Among the policy areas that Bush addressed in his first term, this chapter examines abortion, stem-cell research, same-sex marriage, and the faith-based initiative to illustrate the Bush administration's center-right strategy.

On the issue of abortion, Bush portrays Democrats as being outside the mainstream, an effect that is achieved by constant reference to late-term or "partial-birth" abortion. Thus, Bush has afforded himself more room to maneuver without alienating his most fervent supporters. On the issue of stem-cell research, Bush articulates a strategy that purports to prevent the wanton use of stem cells for research while guaranteeing that such research will continue via the use of existing lines. Bush has also found the middle ground on the controversy surrounding same-sex marriage. His earlier pronouncements against the practice were balanced by a late election decision to support civil unions. Finally, Bush's faith-based initiative was almost exclusively packaged in terms of the public policy benefits to be derived. By stressing the objectives of the Christian Right while refusing to use the most partisan and jingoistic language available, Bush struck middle ground, at least in the first term.

In chapter seven, Amy E. Black and Douglas L. Koopman examine the twists and turns of President Bush's faith-based initiative during the first term of the administration and speculate on its future. The initial strategic decision by Capitol Hill and White House Republicans to coordinate the faith-based legislative proposal with the "purist" faction of faith-based interest groups harmed its legislative prospects in the House and did so in the Senate. But the administration's rule-making efforts to change executive agency cultures concerning faith-based groups were quieter and, ultimately, more successful. Aided by a mixed lot of related federal judicial decisions, this high presidential priority is slowly if inexorably changing the relationship between government and faith-based service providers.

In light of key strategic mistakes and inside the beltway's conflicted view of religion, the faith-based initiative has shown remarkable resiliency, mostly because of the president's personal interest in these efforts and the apparent belief in eventual policy and political success. This chapter provides a balanced policy analysis and political assessment of this issue and looks ahead to its future.

In chapter eight, Michael K. Fauntroy explores efforts by the Bush administration to use faith-based initiatives to win political support from African American religious leaders. The relationship between African Americans and the Republican Party is one of trust and distrust, friendship and antagonism, and support and opposition. Many contemporary observers do not understand why African Americans are so resistant to the Republicans, particularly given the history of the party during the abolition movement and Reconstruction. These observers overlook the long history of Republican public policy initiatives, political strategies, and other actions that have repelled black voters and created an environment of hostility toward African Americans.

Demographic and other political changes have put the Republican Party in a position where it needs more African American support to continue its electoral success. The party has used a combination of political rhetoric and policy changes in a renewed effort to win a larger share of the African American vote. The faith-based initiative is the most significant attempt in this regard. It has changed federal regulations to allow church-based organizations to receive government grants. These organizations had previously been precluded from accessing such federal funding. The change has granted millions of dollars to church-based organizations to provide a range of social services. This change is seen as a political winner for Republicans, who believe that the high religiosity of African Americans can make government funding of church-based organizations a vehicle to woo black voters.

Fauntroy examines the GOP's use of the federal faith-based initiative to overcome its perennial poor standing in the black community and to maintain its political success. He situates the initiative in the context of other Republican attempts in recent decades to use public policy to attract African American voters. He also explores the extent to which these policies have borne any fruit in terms of increased numbers of black voters. While the initiative is relatively new, it does have the potential to win black voters in certain segments of the country.

In chapter nine, Ted G. Jelen takes on the most overheated issues concerning religion and the Bush presidency: abortion, stem-cell research, and the Terry Schaivo case. As part of his appeal to cultural and religious conservatives, President Bush has consistently endorsed what he (following John Paul II) has characterized as a "culture of life." This concept has applied mainly to domestic issues sometimes and has its most obvious manifestation with respect to legal abortion.

Jelen first examines Bush's approach to the abortion issue. In addition, the "pro-life" frame has expanded to include the issue of stem-cell research, and this chapter contains an analysis of the Bush administration's attempts to subsume this issue under the pro-life agenda and also details attempts to distinguish the moral issues involved in medical research on fetal tissue from those involved in abortion. Finally, the chapter analyzes the administration's approach to the Terry Schaivo case (involving "the right to die" of a terminally comatose patient), and the political ramifications of the attempt to apply the life-affirming gestalt to this case. Jelen concludes by exploring the implications for the future of pro-life politics.

Although most debate over the impact of religion on policy in the United States focuses on domestic issues, during the Bush years there has been considerable discussion and controversy over the role of evangelical internationalists in the administration. In chapter ten, Kevin R. den Dulk explores the complicated linkage of religion and foreign policy in the Bush years.

As den Dulk explains, the foreign policy agenda of evangelical Protestants during the Bush administration has been ambitious, but their efforts have met with mixed success. On the one hand, he argues that evangelicals have developed a range of foreign policy goals rooted in a variety of theological beliefs; they have also been aided by increasing sophistication in terms of political strategy, partly because of their experience of battling on domestic issues since the 1980s. On the other hand, with some notable exceptions, he finds that foreign policy remains a largely elite-driven phenomenon; it has not captured the attention of the grassroots in quite the same way as the domestic agenda. In addition, those elites have often disagreed on priorities and tactics.

The chapter examines four areas of evangelical international engagement: the Israeli-Palestinian conflict; human rights abroad, which has focused especially on religious persecution; the "War on Terror" overseas; and global population issues, including abortion and AIDS/HIV. In each of these areas den Dulk argues that evangelicals have rejected isolationism, though their "internationalism" is complex, unconventional, and varied. As a result, the Bush administration, which is also cross-pressured by other foreign policy interests, has had and will continue to have an uneasy relationship with evangelicals on international affairs.

Finally, in chapter eleven, Nina Therese Kasniunas and Jack E. Rossotti examine the religious factor in President Bush's appointments to the federal courts. They note that Bush is the first president in over a century to seemingly disregard the balance of religions represented on the U.S. Supreme Court. On the surface this seems puzzling, as Bush is widely viewed as a leader who gives ample voice to the conservative Christian wing of his party. Nonetheless, the only concern of President Bush is that his appointees maintain a posture of judicial restraint. This has been a prime consideration in his nominations, not only for the courts but for the Department of Justice as well.

President Bush has not been disregarding religion; in fact, appointing judicial restraintists has been his strategy to provide more accommodation for religion in this country. Placing restraintists on the federal courts enables more conservative interpretations of the establishment and free exercise clauses as well as on other moral issues such as abortion, affirmative action, and homosexuality. Selecting solicitors general from the growing pool of Federalist Society members ensures his administration will pursue litigation that enables restraintist decisions. It also enables them to file amicus curiae briefs in cases that could render such decisions.

Religion thus was not disregarded at all, when Bush chose his judicial nominees. He astutely chose judicial restraint as a guiding consideration fully realizing that such jurisprudence would render decisions most accommodating to the role of religion. He is advancing the interests of conservative Christians without appearing to do so, keeping the religious sector of his party gratified while at the same time not unsettling moderates.

In all, the essays in this volume showcase the importance of the religion factor to the elections and the policies of the George W. Bush presidency. It is clear that in his national campaigns and as president, Bush has skillfully courted the support of religious conservatives while at the same time he has not alienated more moderate segments of the population with these efforts. Bush has promoted the interests of religious conservative constituencies, but he has not used his presidency to effect wide-scale social policy changes, as had been feared by his most vocal opponents. Nonetheless, when compared to his Republican predecessors, George H. W. Bush and Ronald Reagan, George W. Bush has delivered far more to the religious conservative community and that legacy will continue well beyond his presidency through his judicial appointments.

Bush's presidency also has heightened broader interest in the topic of the "faith factor" in U.S. politics. Many observers attributed Bush's 2004 reelection to the impact of the "values voters," and some prominent aspirants for the presidency are talking more openly than ever about the importance of faith to their lives and policy views. Even many Democratic candidates for public office who were previously known to be very reluctant to discuss religion now eagerly profess their faith and describe its impact on their role in public life. It seems that near the end of the George W. Bush era, "God talk" pervades public life in America, and there is little evidence at this time that this trend will abate.

Acknowledgments

The impetus for this book was a November 2004 conference on Religion and the Presidency sponsored by the Hauenstein Center for Presidential Studies at Grand Valley State University in Grand Rapids, Michigan. For that conference a group of leading scholars in history, political science, and sociology presented research papers on the impact of religion on the U.S. presidency. Scholarly panels examined various presidencies from George Washington to George W. Bush.

Two of the panels focused on the Bush presidency and the role of religion in the election of 2004. Thus, chapters one, two, three, seven, and ten are revised and updated versions of essays originally presented at the conference. The remaining essays were commissioned for this volume. The other essays presented at the conference are collected in the volume *Religion and the American Presidency* (New York: Palgrave Macmillan, 2007).

Chapter One

Bush and the Christian Right: The Triumph of Pragmatism

Mark J. Rozell

> The Christian Right has infiltrated and taken over the White House—in the person of the President of the United States. If Jerry Falwell and Pat Robertson had sat down some 15 years ago and created the profile of their perfect president—a born-again Christian from the Bible Belt, flagrantly open about his faith—George W. Bush would fit it almost to a T.
> —Rich Lowry, editor of *National Review*,
> writing in the *Washington Post* (August 10, 2003)

The above statement is an exaggeration, but it largely fits the conventional wisdom about the Bush presidency and the Christian Right. To be sure, Bush may be the best president the Christian Right movement has ever had. Yet to say that the movement has "taken over the White House" does not dovetail with reality. The story is much more complicated, as Bush has been a friend to the movement but has frustrated social conservatives at the same time.

Many of the analyses of the 2004 election have been similarly stark, suggesting that the Christian Right delivered victory to the president and that the movement would be cashing in its earnings in the second Bush term. In fact, although Bush indeed prevailed among the "moral issues" voters in the election, he also achieved a broad-based victory that could be attributed to a variety of voting groups, not just the Christian Right.

Nonetheless, there is no denying that Bush owes a large debt of gratitude to the Christian Right, especially for how the movement rescued his tough GOP nomination battle against Senator John McCain in 2000 and successfully mobilized its base in the 2004 general election. The following analysis examines the relationship between Bush and the Christian Right movement. It begins with Bush's initial quest for the presidency and then covers his first term and reelection campaign. It concludes with some speculation about the impact of the Bush presidency and the future prospects for the Christian Right.

The 2000 Presidential Election

The early conventional wisdom regarding the role of the Christian Right in the Republican presidential contest in 2000 was that the movement would play a minor role. At most, many assumed, it would influence the vice presidential nomination and some party platform positions. Although wrong, there were credible reasons for this assessment.

First, the Christian Right lacked a standard bearer. Throughout 1999 then Missouri senator John Ashcroft appeared to be both in the running for the nomination, and he was clearly the favored candidate of the movement. When he announced his intention not to seek the presidency, there was no obvious candidate to unify the Christian Right.

Second, the Christian Coalition was in serious trouble. Its fundraising and membership were declining substantially. It was beset with infighting, resignations of staff and of state and local chapter chairs, and some of its state- and local-based chapters either disappeared or merely continued to exist on paper. Some scholars suggested that the organization's decline reflected the waning influence of the Christian Right.[1]

Third, without a standard bearer, numerous candidates appealed to the Christian Right, thus splintering the movement. George W. Bush uniquely among them emphasized socially conservative views couched in the liberal rhetoric of compassion and tolerance. Many leading Christian Rightists, particularly Pat Robertson and Ralph Reed, signed on early to back Bush. Yet their support was not initially matched by grassroots Christian Right enthusiasm.

The Republican nomination race quickly became a bitter contest between Bush and McCain, with the Christian Right taking central stage in the drama and ultimately delivering victory to Bush. Amid predictions of the movement's political irrelevancy, Christian Right activists became the kingmakers in the GOP contest (Rozell 2000).

The Republican Primary Campaign

The New Hampshire primary effectively narrowed the GOP field to Bush and McCain. McCain stunned the GOP establishment with a 49 to 30 percent victory over Bush. The exit polls showed a GOP fissure that would become problematic for McCain later on. While McCain did exceptionally well among Independents, Democrats, and some Republicans, Bush showed his greatest strength among Christian social conservatives.[2] The social conservative voting base in the New England states is quite small. The exit polls therefore provided encouraging news for Bush as the campaign moved toward South Carolina.

Among the 53 percent Republican identifiers who voted in the GOP primary in New Hampshire, 41 percent chose Bush and 38 percent McCain. The Arizona senator overwhelmingly won among Independents (62 to 19 percent), who comprised 41 percent of the vote, and Democrats (78 to 13 percent), who comprised 4 percent. Liberals and moderates also overwhelmingly backed McCain, whereas he and Bush almost evenly split the conservative vote. Those who identified themselves as "very conservative" backed Bush 33 to 21 percent.

Among "Religious Right" voters, Bush prevailed 36 percent to 26 percent over McCain. Yet these voters were only 16 percent of the GOP primary electorate, suggesting that Bush had strong vote-getting potential in the more culturally conservative states outside of the northeast. Bush also won among those voters who said that they attend church more than once per week (10 percent of the voters) and those who oppose abortion in all circumstances (12 percent of the voters).

McCain had thus become the candidate of the moderate wing of the GOP and Bush the candidate of the Christian Right. Both candidates were strongly pro-life, and it was almost impossible to detect any differences between them in their views on social issues. Bush's gubernatorial record and McCain's 18-year voting record in Congress gave each an equally valid claim to support from the Christian Right. Yet Robertson's attacks at times were personal. He suggested that McCain lacked the temperament and emotional stability to be president. Focus on the Family Director James Dobson criticized McCain's personal fitness as a moral leader because of the senator's earlier admitted adultery and then divorce from his first marriage.

The leaders of the nation's most prominent social conservative organizations put forth a major effort to stop McCain's candidacy in South Carolina, backed by extensive independent spending efforts. Robertson in particular made numerous appearances on television news and commentary shows denouncing McCain and asserting that social conservatives would sit out the general election if the Arizona senator were nominated by the GOP.

Christian Right attacks on McCain's credibility centered on four factors. First, McCain's suggestion that the GOP should soften the language of the party's antiabortion platform plank to make the party more inclusive. Second, the senator's vote to allow fetal tissue research for combating Parkinson's disease. Third, his suggestion, later retracted, that he would not support a repeal of the *Roe v. Wade* decision.

Fourth, his statement that if his daughter became pregnant he would leave the abortion decision up to her. These factors hardly justified the severe attacks on McCain, given his consistently pro-life voting record in Congress. The National Right to Life (NRTL) Committee in fact had consistently given McCain nearly 100 percent ratings for his votes in Congress. The NRTL Committee nonetheless led the attack on McCain with mass mailings (one with a picture of a baby and the words, "This little guy wants you to vote for George Bush"), radio ads, and voter telephone calls throughout the state (Edsall and Neal 2000).

Robertson was a highly visible spokesperson during the primary, targeting his energies against McCain. So while the NRTL Committee did the grassroots campaigning, Robertson commanded attention on the national airwaves.

The role of religion in the campaign took center stage when McCain attacked Bush's decision to speak at Bob Jones University— a fundamentalist institution that prohibited interracial dating and characterized Catholicism as "a satanic counterfeit." The university's founder had made disparaging comments about the pope and referred to the Catholic Church as a "satanic cult." Bush ultimately expressed regret for his appearance at the university. In a letter to the former cardinal John O'Connor, Bush referred to his own visit at the university and failure to address its anti-Catholic views as "a missed opportunity causing needless offense, which I deeply regret." Bush admitted that "[o]n reflection, I should have been more clear in disassociating myself from the anti-Catholic sentiments and racial prejudice."[3]

Bush won South Carolina 53 percent to 42 percent. The Christian Right carried the state for Bush. Among the 61 percent who said in exit polls that they were *not* members of the Religious Right, McCain won 52 percent to 46 percent. Among the 34 percent Religious Right voters, Bush won overwhelmingly 68 percent to 24 percent. Bush once again prevailed heavily among the voters who said that abortion never should be legal (67 percent to 19 percent). Forty-three percent of the voters chose either moral values or abortion as the most important issue in their voting decision. Bush overwhelmingly won those voters.[4]

Two major factors boosted Bush's showing in South Carolina. First, Bush's margin over McCain among Religious Right voters went from a mere 10 percent in New Hampshire to 44 percent in South Carolina. Second, the percentage of socially conservative voters in the South Carolina primary was substantially higher than in New Hampshire.

Most analysts suggested that a loss in South Carolina would have ended Bush's candidacy. If true, the Christian Right vote surely could lay claim to having saved his presidential bid. With each candidate claiming one major state primary victory, the campaign focus shifted to the crucial Michigan contest. With a heavy Catholic population the McCain campaign counted on anger at Bush's appearance at Bob Jones University to aid the senator's candidacy.

Once again, Christian Right and pro-life groups became involved in the race. The powerful Michigan Right to Life Committee sent pro-Bush, anti-McCain mailings to 400,000 Michigan voters and followed up with phone calls to those same voters. The mailing featured a picture of a smiling baby with the words "George W. Bush, A Prolife Vote." The inside featured statements favorable toward Bush's views on social issues and statements critical of McCain's alleged views (Edsall 2000a).

Robertson taped an anti-McCain phone message for social conservative Michigan voters. He lambasted McCain's New Hampshire campaign manager, former GOP senator Warren Rudman, as "a vicious bigot" who once made disparaging comments about the Christian Right. The taped calls became a national news story about the tactics of the Christian Right, and even the Bush campaign privately urged Robertson to tone down his rhetoric.

McCain's campaign targeted Catholic voters. The candidate himself denied knowledge of efforts by an independent group to conduct mass phone calls to Catholics to alert them to Bush's appearance at Bob Jones University. Eventually McCain admitted that he knew of the plan to target those voters, and he too came under criticism for playing the "religion card" too heavily in the campaign. McCain won the Michigan primary 51 percent to 43 percent. Much the same pattern held: McCain won Independent and Democrat votes in the open primary, Bush won the Republican identifiers. Among the two-thirds of voters who were *not* members of the Religious Right, 60 percent voted for McCain, 36 percent for Bush. Bush again overwhelmed McCain among Religious Right voters (but only 27 percent of the Michigan GOP primary voters) 66 percent to 25 percent. Bush's numbers declined among pro-life voters, suggesting that although he lost nothing in Religious Right appeal, he lost some Catholic pro-life voters. Among pro-life voters, Bush won 54 percent, although his numbers were strongest among those who said that abortion "never" should be legal (62 percent for Bush, 27 percent for McCain).[5]

Most of the following key states held "closed" primaries—open only to formally registered Republicans. The next major contest was Virginia—home to the Christian Coalition, the former Moral Majority, and fertile territory for Christian Right candidates in the GOP.

Although an "open" primary state, the Virginia GOP instituted a requirement that all voters in the primary must sign a "loyalty oath" as a condition for voting. The oath was a nonbinding statement in which the voter, in signing, affirms that he or she will be loyal to the party and vote for its nominee in November. Not all voters understood the purpose of the oath, and many believed that it was legally binding. The effect was to substantially lower participation among non-Republican-identifying voters. That was the goal of the state GOP leaders, all of whom backed Bush.

Polls showed McCain running behind Bush, but still competitive. For months Bush had been spending heavily in the state on mass mailings and television ads. McCain initially appeared not to be contesting the state. But once the polls showed McCain had moved within a single digit margin behind Bush, the senator took a remarkable gamble that some likened to a political "hail Mary" pass.

The day before the February 29 primary, McCain went to Virginia Beach, the hometown of Pat Robertson, to make a speech laced with stinging criticism of the Christian Coalition founder and of the former Moral Majority founder Jerry Falwell. McCain drew a clear distinction between Christian social conservatives and their values on the one hand and the political tactics of certain Christian Right leaders on the other. He also drew a distinction between a number of widely admired Christian Right leaders on the one hand and Robertson and Falwell on the other. These distinctions were lost on the media and the electorate—especially supporters of the Christian Right who widely interpreted McCain's remarks as an attack on people of faith being involved in politics. McCain angered many social conservatives when he equated Robertson and Falwell with Louis Farrakhan and Al Sharpton. The McCain speech precipitated an emotionally charged national debate over the role of the Christian Right in the GOP, with many social conservatives outraged and others seeing an act of political courage.

McCain lost Virginia 53 percent to 44 percent and once again the Christian Right delivered the victory to Bush. Among the one in five voters who were self-described members of the Religious Right, 80 percent supported Bush, 14 percent McCain. McCain prevailed 52 percent to 45 percent over Bush among the nearly four in five voters who said that they were *not* members of the Religious Right. McCain overwhelmingly won the pro-choice vote; Bush overwhelmingly won the pro-life vote.[6]

McCain's strategists thought they saw an opportunity in the senator's attack on Robertson and Falwell. Although the strategy hurt McCain in Virginia, the GOP contest soon turned to more progressive states with smaller Christian Right voting blocs, among them New York and California. Perhaps it was McCain's intention all along to try to look principled by denouncing the Christian Right leaders in their home state.

There would not be an electoral payoff for McCain. His attacks sank his candidacy. After the Virginia loss, a reporter asked McCain about his strong language against Robertson and Falwell. McCain rhetorically replied, "You're supposed to tolerate evil in your party in the name of party unity?" (Gibbs 2000). He later backtracked from the comment, but the damage to his candidacy had been done. Commentators lambasted McCain for crossing the line of allowable criticism.

The Super Tuesday primaries took place one week after the Virginia primary. Among the crucial states were New York, California, Maryland, Georgia, Mississippi, and Ohio. Pro-life groups stepped up their attacks on the senator's campaign. The National Right to Life Committee alone spent over $200,000 on anti-McCain phone calls in the Super Tuesday states. "For the children's sake, please vote for George Bush," said the phone message (Lardner 2000, A8).

The Committee's spending to defeat McCain was extraordinary. In all, the organization spent over $500,000 against McCain in the primaries, more than one-half of its total spending on all races in the 1998 election cycle. Their spending about equaled the organization's total budget reported at the beginning of 2000 (Lardner 2000).

McCain's standing among key religious constituencies began a precipitous decline in the wake of his "evil" comment. Super Tuesday ended his candidacy. Although the senator won several New England states with low Christian Right populations, he lost all the important contests. His attacks on Robertson and Falwell backfired. One-third of the voters in New York and Ohio said that McCain's comments had influenced their voting decisions, and those voters opposed the senator by a 4 to 1 margin (Associated Press 2000).The Christian Right delivered the key votes to Bush in most of the states. For example, in Ohio McCain won the three in four voters who said that they were *not* members of the Religious Right (52 percent to 44 percent). Among the one in four who were members, Bush won strongly (74 percent to 19 percent) (Associated Press 2000). In New York, only 15 percent of the voters were self-described members of the Religious Right, and they backed Bush over McCain 62 percent to 28 percent. The rest of the GOP vote was split evenly between Bush and McCain (47 percent each).

McCain again took the pro-choice vote, and Bush overwhelmingly won the pro-life vote. The New York vote was 50 percent Catholics, and those voters favored Bush over McCain 52 percent to 43 percent, lending credibility to the argument that there was a backlash against McCain's efforts to link Bush with anti-Catholic bigotry.[7]

2000 GOP Contest in Retrospect:
Christian Right Kingmakers

McCain had a long record as a conservative vote in Congress, including on the social issues. Yet he was anathema to the conservative movement in 2000, especially the Christian Right. Social conservative opposition cost him the nomination. An ABC News poll in late February underscored McCain's challenge running for the GOP nomination. Seven in ten Americans believed that McCain was either a liberal, a moderate, or could not place him ideologically.[8] Christian Right groups effectively distorted his record. Exit poll data from the primary states show that in every contest GOP voters ranked moral values as the most important issue facing the country. Among those voters Bush prevailed heavily.

The early decision to back Bush seems the ultimate act of pragmatism. Bush was the candidate of the establishment wing of the GOP and was widely hailed as the one with the best chance for uniting the party and winning the general election. There were many more genuinely social conservative candidates, but Robertson, Reed, and others early on jumped on the Bush bandwagon hoping to become players in the next GOP administration.

The case for Christian Right pragmatism is less easily made with regard to the Bush-McCain race. All of the polls suggested that McCain had a much stronger chance than Bush to win the general election. One possible explanation is that once the Christian Right leaders so strongly backed Bush, they had to protect their own credibility and stay loyal to their candidate. Nobody anticipated McCain's strong challenge for the nomination. Yet not only did the Christian Right leaders stand behind Bush, but they also launched an extraordinary offensive against McCain.

It is plausible that some Christian Right opposition to McCain was of a more personal than political nature. Dobson was candid about his view that past adultery, divorce, and a tolerant attitude toward gays made McCain unacceptable. Bush clearly was more comfortable than McCain in the role of articulating "family values" issues. Throughout his congressional career, McCain had never shown much interest in the intersection of religion and politics. By contrast, Bush spoke very openly of his faith, his own personal redemption from an undisciplined youth and early adulthood, and he made much of his own belief in the value of faith-based institutions in solving social problems. The risk in backing Bush was that the Christian Right might have borne the brunt of criticism for consigning the GOP to defeat. Bush's electoral college victory spared the Christian Right from this potential criticism.

The 2000 General Election Campaign

The general election campaign in 2000 highlighted one of the continuing dilemmas for the Christian Right: how to deliver campaign energy and enthusiasm in both GOP nomination contests *and* general election campaigns. The Christian Right energy for Bush against McCain was substantial. The movement's general election activity was significantly lower than even in 1996 when Bob Dole ran a futile campaign against Bill Clinton.

The percentage of the 2000 electorate who identified as Religious Right members was only 14 percent, a decline of more than 3 percentage points from the 1996 elections. Voting by the evangelical core constituency of the Christian Right also declined in 2000. The National Election Studies (NES) show that turnout among white evangelicals dropped by 6 percentage points from 1996 to 2000, whereas turnout among white Catholics dropped by 1 percent, and white mainline Protestants by 2 percent. Furthermore, the NES data show a decline in national support for the Christian Coalition, from 15.5 percent in 1996 to 13.7 percent in 2000 (Wilcox 2001).

Other forms of political activity than voting also declined among white evangelicals. Fewer white evangelicals reported that they were contacted by a religious or moral group in 2000 than in 1996. Fewer reported receiving information about candidates in churches. An Annenberg Public Policy Center study found that pro-choice groups spent heavily in television advertising in 2000, whereas Christian conservative organizations spent relatively little (Slass 2001). Wilcox (2001) reports that Christian Right groups nonetheless actively used their radio programs to communicate with targeted audiences and that this type of activity has the advantage of reaching its intended audiences much more cost-effectively than television.

The Christian Coalition was practically invisible in key primary states and in the general election. Many of its election voters' guides went undelivered. Whether good or bad for the Christian Right, Robertson was a constant presence in the news during the 2000 elections, especially during the GOP nomination contest.

Some Christian Right PACs such as Gary Bauer's Campaign for Working Families were active. Bauer's PAC reported receipts of $2.7 million and made significant contributions to a number of GOP candidates and engaged in independent expenditures (Wilcox 2001).

Though Christian Right political activity declined in 2000, the movement was more united for Bush than it had been for Dole in 1996. Although the Religious Right component of the electorate had declined, exit poll data reported that 80 percent of that group backed Bush in 2000 whereas 65 percent backed Dole in 1996. Thus, the strongly united vote of the Christian Right was crucial to Bush's victory. Moreover, the Christian Right was more prevalent voting in some states than in others. In Al Gore's home state of Tennessee, for example, the Religious Right vote was 27 percent of the electorate, and among those voters 78 percent backed Bush.

Furthermore, even at just 14 percent of the electorate the Christian Right in 2000 was on a par with labor union household vote and slightly larger than the African American vote. As both labor and civil rights groups have shown in the past, strongly united groups of such size in the electorate can be the key difference to the electoral fortunes of a political party.

Bush's First Term: Mixed Record for the Christian Right

Having delivered the nomination to Bush, the Christian Right had a strong claim to a "place at the table" in the Bush administration. But Bush's first term record on social issues was somewhat mixed. Among actions that pleased the Christian Right were the nomination of John Ashcroft as attorney general, the executive order prohibiting federal funding for international agencies that provide abortions and abortion counseling, the creation of a faith-based initiatives office in the White House, the president's initial support for an education vouchers program, and, most importantly, his signing the ban on late-term abortions. The president also endorsed the idea of a constitutional amendment to prohibit same-sex marriage, though most observers said that he realized there was little chance of it ever passing. Nonetheless, with the country in the midst of a contentious debate over gay unions, the president affirmed his strong support for "traditional marriage," a key position of the Religious Right.

The administration's most significant effort to integrate faith into policy was the creation of the Office of Faith-Based Initiatives. Nonetheless, prominent Christian Right leaders strongly criticized elements of this initiative, especially the proposal that the federal government take the lead in funding certain church-based programs. Bush appointed a Democrat and university professor John DiIulio to head this office. DiIulio incensed Christian Right critics of the faith-based initiative when he said that their opposition revealed that they did not care enough about the plight of inner-city poor minorities eventually quit, and Bush appointed a less high-profile repla(run the downgraded office.

Christian conservatives also expressed dismay at some of Bush's appointments, in particular an openly gay leader of the Log Cabin Republicans to become director of the Office of National AIDS Policy and another gay activist to the job of screening civilian applicants for Pentagon jobs. Several Christian Right leaders criticized these appointments as out of character for an administration that pledges to uphold moral values in government (Hallow 2001).

Bush's most difficult first term social issue was whether to allow federal support for the continuation of stem-cell research. The controversy deeply divided his administration, and many social conservatives saw his handling of the issue as the major test of his commitment to moral values. Bush mostly sided with his religious conservative base when he decided to severely limit the federal role in stem-cell research, although he presented his decision as striking a reasonable middle position. In his major speech on the controversy, the religious emphasis was clear. Bush referred twice to prayer in the speech. He said, "I believe that human life is a sacred gift from our creator" (Mayer and Rozell 2005).

Nonetheless, Bush constantly courted the support of conservative evangelicals during his first term, and the evidence suggests that his efforts paid off. As scholars Black, Koopman, and Ryden (2004) point out, even though the faith-based initiative was beset by failures, in many ways this effort by Bush was primarily about political competition: seeking the loyalty and political support of key religious constituencies that could bolster his agenda and help him to win a second term. By this standard, the strategy worked.

There is evidence of the growing identification of evangelical Protestants with the Republican Party, a trend that began with the Reagan administration but that became even more pronounced during Bush's first term. A 2004 Pew survey found that while 38 percent of the public identified Republican, the number went up to 56 percent for evangelicals. Sixty-eight percent of respondents said it is important for a president to be a person with strong religious beliefs, a position held by 87 percent of evangelicals. In 2003, at a time when merely 47 percent supported Bush's reelection, 69 percent of evangelicals backed the president (www.pewcenter.org). But despite this support, the tepid turnout among conservative evangelicals in 2000 became the wildcard of the 2004 presidential campaign (Rozell 2004).

The 2004 Election: A "Moral Values" Campaign?

During the 2004 campaign, many observers suggested that the country had become unusually divided and that supporters of Bush and Democratic nominee John Kerry shared little in common. There is some evidence to support the divided electorate thesis. A Zogby International poll found that while two-thirds of Kerry's supporters had watched the controversial film *Fahrenheit 911*, only 3 percent of Bush's supporters had done so. Half of Bush's supporters said they had seen the film *The Passion of the Christ*, while only 15 percent of Kerry's supporters had done so. To the statement "We were better off in the old days when everyone just knew how they were expected to behave" 61 percent of Bush's supporters agreed, while only 18 percent of Kerry's supporters agreed. Seventy-five percent of Bush's supporters said that a president should emphasize his religious values, and 96 percent of Kerry's supports said that religion is a private matter that does not belong in public discourse (Zogby International).

Some observers also said that 2004 would be a "values" election, and the same Zogby poll confirmed that assessment. When asked to name their most important voting criterion, 54 percent said having a president who shares their values, 29 percent said having a president who can best provide for their safety, and only 13 percent said having a president who will improve their personal finances.

Exit polling data confirm the importance of moral values to the 2004 election outcome. For example, the leading factor cited by voters was moral values, at 22 percent of the electorate. Among these voters, 80 percent backed Bush, 18 percent Kerry. By contrast, in 2000, when only 14 percent of voters were self-identified as belonging to the Religious Right, 72 percent of them voted for Bush and 27 percent for Al Gore. Although the exit poll questions in 2000 and 2004 were not the same, the evidence suggests that there was a much stronger turnout in 2004 among white evangelical conservatives and that these voters were more solidly Republican than in 2000. White evangelical and born-again Protestants were 23 percent of the electorate and favored Bush over Kerry by 78 percent to 21 percent. Bush won all 15 states with the largest evangelical populations, for a total of 121 electors toward the 270 needed for victory. More importantly, in some of the crucial swing states, the evangelical margin for Bush was far more than his margin of victory. For example, in Iowa, one-third of the voters were white evangelicals. In Colorado, one-fourth were evangelicals, and they voted 86 percent for Bush (Waldman and Green 2004). In all of the swing states combined, the moral values voters supported Bush over Kerry by 84 percent to 15 percent of the vote, even larger than the national average.

A good indictor of voter preferences in 2004 was church attendance. Among those who attend services more than once per week (16 percent of the electorate), two-thirds of these voters supported Bush. Among those who attend weekly (26 percent), 58 percent went for Bush and 41 percent for Kerry. But Bush broke about even with Kerry among voters who attended services a few times per month (14 percent). Kerry prevailed strongly among nonchurchgoers and those who merely attend a few times per year (43 percent of voters). Among the 42 percent of the electorate that said abortion should be illegal in most or all cases, these voters favored Bush over Kerry by a 3 to 1 margin.

The gay marriage issue helped mobilize the Christian Right in 2004. Among those who say that there should be no legal recognition of same-sex relationships (37 percent of voters), this group voted 70 percent to 29 percent for Bush over Kerry. The result reversed among those who favor legal recognition of gay marriage (25 percent), with Kerry prevailing 77 percent to 22 percent. In Ohio, the state that decided the presidential election outcome, 62 percent favored the referendum banning gay marriage, and this number rose to 86 percent among evangelicals (2004 exit polls at www.beliefnet.com). Nonetheless, it is important not to overstate the impact of the antigay marriage referenda across the country. Although all 11 states that had these bans on the ballot passed them by significant margins, there was not a higher voter turnout rate in these states than in the rest of the country. Some postelection analyses suggested that these referenda were responsible for higher Christian Right turnouts, but the evidence is not so clear that this was the case.

It is also evident that Bush's victory was not merely a Christian Right triumph and that many voting groups contributed to his defeat of John Kerry. Bush had also devoted considerable effort to courting regular Church-attending Catholics in his first term, and there is evidence that this effort also paid off. Bush increased his vote share among all Catholics from about 47 percent in 2000 to 52 percent in 2004. Much of his improvement was expectedly among white Churchgoing Catholics. Bush's improvement in the Catholic vote in Ohio from 2000 to 2004 was about 172,000, larger than his approximately 130,000 vote margin in that decisive state. Thus, it is plausible to argue that the Catholic vote just as much as the Religious Right vote delivered victory to the president. Bush also improved his showing among Jews (17 percent in 2000, 25 percent in 2004). In the end, Bush won a broad-based victory, with all religious groups showing a significant improvement for him in 2004, with the exception of "other faiths" that went more heavily for Kerry in 2004 than for Gore in 2000, largely due to the switching allegiances of Muslims who were included in this category in the exit polls. Kerry won two-thirds of voters who identified their religious affiliation as "none," an improvement over Gore's 61 percent with this group in 2000.

A key to Bush's success was his ability to both reach out to conservative evangelicals, while also appealing to Churchgoing Catholics and many moderate voters. Indeed, while Bush won a commanding margin among conservative voters, he also received 45 percent of the moderate vote. Bush evidenced an ability to speak to different audiences at the same time. Rather than discuss abortion directly, he used such phrases as "the culture of life" to appeal to social conservatives while not appearing threatening to moderates at the same time. And this strategy has fit a pattern of his presidential rhetoric, as he has frequently used language that connects deeply with coreligionists while flying under the radar of nonreligious Americans (e.g., his use of such phrases as "wonder working power," his references to "evil" and "evildoers").

Another key was the grassroots mobilization of social conservative voters that seemed to take off largely on its own, rather than being directed by any interest group organization such as the Christian Coalition. Indeed, whereas many previous studies of the Christian Right have emphasized the top-down nature of the mobilization of religious conservative voters, the 2004 election may be the best evidence yet that locally directed grassroots efforts around the country added up to a large-scale political mobilization without any national group or campaign coordinating the strategy. Reports in the campaign made it clear that the same-sex marriage issue was a major factor in mobilizing grassroots activists—a Massachusetts court decision sanctioning same-sex marriage and then the defiant act by San Francisco's mayor of illegally marrying thousands of same-sex couples planting the seeds of a major mobilization by evangelical Protestants and conservative Catholics. Although Bush had initially wavered about whether to support a constitutional ban on gay marriage, a few weeks after the action of the San Francisco mayor the president stated his support. "A few judges and local authorities are presuming to change the most fundamental institution of civilization. Their actions have created confusion on an issue that requires clarity," he implored (Cooperman and Edsall 2004).

Indeed, the Bush campaign caused a stir when reports revealed that it had requested thousands of churches to turn over membership directories for the purpose of political contacting. But the evidence suggests that this effort was not needed, as evangelical clergy across the country were discussing the election from the pulpit and prominent evangelical leaders also expressed their preferences and urged supporters to vote moral values in the election. Focus on the Family Chairman James Dobson personally endorsed Bush, even though he had never made a public endorsement of a presidential candidate before (Cooperman and Edsall 2004).

Given this successful organizing by the Christian Right, the movement can lay claim to being a major player in Bush's win. Thus, many in the movement have been quick to assert that they could also lay legitimate claim to a significant portion of Bush's second-term agenda.

Conclusion: The Christian Right in Bush's Second Term

The Christian Right has more to be pleased with in the second Bush term. The largest victory for the movement is the appointments of two conservative jurists to the Supreme Court, thus raising the possibility that *Roe v. Wade* will be revisited and perhaps so will the Texas sodomy decision. Because of these appointments, it is likely that there will be a number of significant cases in the future decided more favorable to the interests of social conservatives.

Yet other victories for the movement are not so certain. Bush is likely to continue to give support to a constitutional ban on same-sex marriages, although the chances for such an amendment remain remote. It is doubtful that the president will change his stand on stem-cell research and there is even the possibility that some in the Congress will try to pass legislation restricting the right of states (such as California) to finance such research. Nonetheless, passage of such a law appears elusive. Christian Right groups are hoping to push such agenda items as education vouchers for students in parochial schools, perhaps government aid and deregulation of home-schooling, and also policies restricting gambling. None of these initiatives appears likely to succeed.

Indeed, it may be that the victory of the Christian Right in the Bush years is more of a defensive one than anything. That is, Bush's elections ensured that—at least until 2009—the push for civil unions or gay marriage is stopped, pro-choice judges are less likely to be appointed to the federal courts, the ban on federal funding of family-planning services overseas is maintained, late-term or "partial-birth" abortions continue to be prohibited, and the federal government will not fund broader stem-cell research than is currently allowed.

Finally, there is the potential of a future splintering of the Republican Party if the Christian Right pushes its agenda too hard. Bush won a second term on the strength of a broad-based coalition that included moderates and social libertarians. After years of intense fighting within the GOP over the growing role of the Christian Right, these groups seemed to reconcile having a social conservative base in the party. But this peace within the party could be a temporary one, as seen in the highly charged national debate over the Terry Schiavo controversy (see Ted Jelen's essay in this volume [chapter nine]). That controversy displayed the real consequences of the Christian Right pushing too hard. National opinion polls for years had shown that a strong majority of Americans consider the Christian Right a fairly benign influence on society. But after the extraordinary intervention in this controversy by President Bush and the GOP Congress, polls showed a shift in public perceptions with a majority saying that the Christian Right poses a threat to our values.

Thus, to be successful the Christian Right may have to scale back some of its aspirations and accept only incremental change. If true, that suggests that there are real limits to how far the movement can go in the future.

Notes

1. See, e.g., the analysis in Rosin (2000).
2. Exit polling data from http://cnn.com/ELECTION/2000/primaries/NH/poll.rep.html.
3. Text of Bush letter quoted in "Bush Regrets Visit to anti-Catholic School" (2000).
4. http://cnn.com/ELECTION/2000/primaries/SC/poll.rep.html.
5. http://cnn.com/ELECTION/2000/primaries/MI/poll.rep.html.
6. http://cnn.com/ELECTION/2000/primaries/VA/poll.rep.html.
7. http://cnn.com/ELECTION/2000/primaries/NY/poll.rep.html.
8. See Langer 2004.

Sources

Associated Press. 2000. "GOP Conservatives Give Bush the Edge." *Washington Times*, March 8, A12.

Black, Amy, Douglas Koopman, and David Ryden. 2004. *Of Little Faith: The Politics of George W. Bush's Faith-Based Initiatives*. Washington, DC: Georgetown University Press.

Bruce, Steve. 1988. *The Rise and Fall of the New Christian Right*. Oxford: Oxford University Press.

"Bush Regrets Visit to Anti-Catholic School." 2000. *Washington Times*, February 8, A8.

Cooperman, Alan, and Thomas B. Edsall. 2004. "Evangelicals Say They Led Charge for the GOP." *Washington Post*, November 8, A1, 7.

Edsall, Thomas B. 2000a. "Powerful Anitabortion Lobby Targets McCain." *Washington Post*, February 22, A6.

——— 2000b. "Senator Risking Key Constituency." *Washington Post*, February 29, A14.

Edsall, Thomas B., and Terry M. Neal. 2000. "Bush, Allies Hit McCain's Conservative Credentials." *Washington Post*, February 15, A1, 10.

Gibbs, Nancy. 2000. "Fire and Brimstone." *Time*, March 13, 33.

Green, John C., Mark J. Rozell, and Clyde Wilcox, eds. 2000. *Prayers in the Precincts: The Christian Right in the 1998 Elections*. Washington, DC: Georgetown University Press.

Hallow, Ralph Z. 2000. "McCain's Religion Gambit Draws Quick Backlash in New York." *Washington Times*, March 1, A1.

——— 2001. "Religious Right Loses Its Political Potency." *Washington Times*, May 30, A1.

Langer, Gary. 2004. "A Question of Values". Available at www.nytimes.com/2004/11/06/opinion/06langer.html (accessed April 19, 2004).

Lardner, George, Jr. 2000. "Abortion Foes Spend $200,000 to Beat McCain." *Washington Post*, March 7, A8.

Mayer, Jeremy, and Mark J. Rozell. 2005. "A President Transformed: Bush's Pre- and Post-September 11 Rhetoric and Image". In *In the Public Domain: Presidents and the Challenges of Public Leadership*. Albany, NY: State University of New York Press.

Moen, Matthew. 1989. *The Christian Right and Congress*. Tuscaloosa, AL: University of Alabama Press.

——— 1992. *The Transformation of the Christian Right*. Tuscaloosa, AL: University of Alabama Press.

——— 1997. "The First Generation of Christian-Right Activism." In *Sojourners in the Wilderness: The Christian Right in Comparative Perspective*, edited by James Penning and Corwin Smidt. Lanham, MD: Rowman and Littlefield.

Reed, Ralph. 1993. "What Do Christian Conservatives Really Want?" Paper presented at the Colloquium on the Religious New Right and the 1992 Campaign, Ethics and Public Policy Center, Washington, DC.

Rosin, Hanna. 2000. "Christian Right's Fervor Has Fizzled." *Washington Post*, February 16, A1, 16.

Rozell, Mark J. 1997. "Growing Up Politically: The New Politics of the New Christian Right." In *Sojourners in the Wilderness: The Christian Right in*

Comparative Perspective, edited by James Penning and Corwin Smidt. Lanham, MD: Rowman and Littlefield, 235–248.

Rozell, Mark J. 2000. ". . . Or, Influential as Ever?" *Washington Post*, March 1, A17.

———— 2004. "Bush's Wild Card: The Religious Vote." *USA Today*, September 22, A21.

Rozell, Mark J., and Clyde Wilcox, eds. 1995. *God at the Grass Roots: The Christian Right in the 1994 Elections*. Lanham, MD: Rowman and Littlefield.

———— 1996. *Second Coming: The New Christian Right in Virginia Politics*. Baltimore, MD: Johns Hopkins University Press.

———— 1997. *God at the Grass Roots 1996: The Christian Right in American Elections*. Lanham, MD: Rowman and Littlefield.

Slass, Lorie. 2001. "Spending on Issue Advocacy in the 2000 Cycle." Report. Annenberg Public Policy Center, Washington, DC.

Taylor, Joe. 1992. "Christian Coalition Revamping Image." *Richmond Times-Dispatch*, December 7, B4.

Thomas, Cal. 1996. "Which Way for the Religious Right and the GOP?" *Washington Times*, October 23, A14.

Wald, Kenneth D. 1997. *Religion and Politics in the United States*. 3rd ed. Washington, DC: Congressional Quarterly.

Waldman, Steven and John C. Green. 2004. "It Wasn't Just (Or Even Mostly) the 'Religious Right.'" Available at www.belifnet.com/story/155/story_15598_1.html (accessed on February 6, 2006).

Wilcox, Clyde. 1992. *God's Warriors: The Christian Right in Twentieth-Century America*. Baltimore, MD: Johns Hopkins University Press.

———— 1996. *Onward Christian Soldiers: The Religious Right in American Politics*. Boulder, CO: Westview Press.

———— 2001. "Wither the Christian Right? The 2000 Elections and Beyond." Paper presented at the conference on religion and politics at Rice University, Houston, Texas, November.

Wilcox, Clyde, Mark J. Rozell, and Roland Gunn. 1996. "Religious Coalitions in the New Christian Right." *Social Science Quarterly* 77: 543–558.

Part I

Religion and the 2004 Election

Chapter Two

"What Does the Lord Require?" Evangelicals and the 2004 Presidential Vote

Corwin Smidt, John C. Green,
Lyman Kellstedt, and James Guth

As the 2004 presidential campaign began, some analysts and political strategists pondered whether evangelical Protestants' enthusiasm for political engagement might be waning. After all, during the past century, evangelicals have exhibited a cyclical pattern of political engagement and then withdrawal. And now a quarter-century has passed since the most recent wave of evangelical involvement began.

It was not simply the elapse of time that fostered such speculation. Other developments also suggested some diminution of evangelical political involvement. Organizations that had once brought evangelicals to the polls were in disarray, and evangelical turnout appeared to have declined. Some debate was evident among evangelicals over what the Lord requires related to politics; respected leaders of the community such as Cal Thomas and Ed Dobson (1999) had even called for a "retreat" from the political arena, contending that evangelical efforts to transform American culture through the acquisition of political power had failed and that the church should simply return to "being the church."

This chapter analyzes the role of evangelical Protestants in the 2004 presidential election. First, we assess the size of the evangelical community and its turnout rate, as well as the candidate choices, political priorities, and issue positions that characterize the community. Then we consider the extent to which the campaign energized and politicized evangelicals, and whether evangelicals were drawn to the GOP (Grand Old Party) ticket primarily because of personal affection for President Bush or as a result of their support for the Republican Party. Finally, we examine some fissures within the evangelical camp that might provide some openings for future Democratic candidates.

Historical Context

Over the past century, evangelicals have mounted successive waves of political engagement (Hunter 1987, 117–130; Wilcox 1992). The first such wave emanated from the fundamentalist response to the theological, cultural, and political changes associated with industrialization, urbanization, and immigration during the early decades of the twentieth century. This political activism peaked in the 1920s and centered largely on conflict over three key issues—evolution, prohibition, and (anti-)Catholicism (Hunter 1987, 117–130). Although evangelicals won some critical battles against evolution, demon rum, and "papism," they lost others, and many within their ranks thought the price paid for such gains was excessive, as evangelicalism was popularly linked to anti-intellectualism and bigotry. As a result, many evangelicals, perhaps out of exhaustion, depression, or disillusionment, reacted by simply withdrawing from politics.

For the most part evangelicals did not reenter the political fray until the 1950s. This second wave of activism was sparked largely by the communist threat following World War II. The "loss" of China and the beginning of the cold war alarmed many evangelicals, who perceived communism not only as a threat to the nation but to Christianity as well. As with many other Americans, nationalistic fervor grew among evangelicals, and they too attempted to root out leftists from both the government and even from certain Christian organizations. Yet their participation in the anticommunist crusades of the era was not widespread, and large segments of the evangelical population remained largely apolitical, suspicious of politics, or at least convinced that the Christian's highest task was the preaching of the Word.

Beginning in the late 1970s, a third wave of evangelical political engagement began, attempting to stem the perceived moral decline in the United States. This renewed involvement was symbolized by the election of an evangelical, Jimmy Carter, as president in 1976, as well as by *Time*'s designation of 1976 as "The Year of the Evangelical." Institutionally, the reinvigorated evangelical forces were represented most visibly by the Reverend Jerry Falwell's Moral Majority, formed in 1979. At least in the eyes of some analysts, this third wave also ended in disillusionment, as the Moral Majority and similar organizations disbanded within a few years and as President Ronald Reagan, an evangelical favorite, proved unable or unwilling to enact a conservative social agenda. For other scholars, the almost simultaneous fall of prominent televangelists, such as James Bakker and Jimmy Swaggart, as a result of sexual and financial improprieties, and the collapse of Pat

Robertson's bid for the 1988 GOP presidential nomination ended this phase of evangelical political engagement (e.g., Bruce 1988).

Although one could plausibly argue that a fourth wave of evangelical activism began in the 1990s, it is just as easy to contend that we are still in the third wave of evangelical political involvement discussed above. Whatever may be the case, the evangelical political agenda seems to differ little substantively from previous ones, as the community continues to be preoccupied with a conservative, "pro-family" agenda.

What has changed is the proliferation of Christian interest groups and the growing political sophistication of the evangelical right (Smidt and Penning 1997; Rozell and Wilcox 1997; Green, Rozell, and Wilcox 2003). This political savvy was evidenced most notably by the Christian Coalition, which emerged from the ashes of Robertson's 1988 campaign. The Coalition used the latest communication and organizational techniques to mobilize its members and influence policy makers. Adopting a bottom-up, grassroots approach, the organizations sought to be in politics for the long haul. Under the direction of master strategist Ralph Reed, the Christian Coalition built a grassroots organization designed to parallel and penetrate the local structures of American political parties (Reed 1996).

While Coalition leaders never achieved their lofty goals of establishing at least one local chapter in every county and recruiting at least one activist per precinct nationwide (Berkowitz and Green 1997, 58), they nevertheless attained considerable success politically, making significant inroads into the Republican Party organization and attempting (albeit with limited success) to reach out to many groups outside evangelical ranks, such as Jews, Catholics, and African Americans. The Coalition also sought to broaden its agenda, focusing not only on pro-family social issues but also emphasizing economic policies and social welfare activities (e.g., rebuilding burned African American churches).

Yet, the Christian Coalition left the national political stage almost as quickly as it appeared. By the new millennium the Coalition was only a shell of its former self. There was internal dissension over whether it was better to seek compromise or to take principled, and more prophetic, stances on public policy matters. This dispute and broader personal and political opportunities led the able and pragmatic Ralph Reed to leave the organization. In the absence of his formidable organizational skills, the Coalition has faded from the political scene. Thus, one major organizational vehicle by which many evangelicals had been mobilized in previous elections was no longer as significant electorally—perhaps reflecting a new evangelical withdrawal from politics.

Finally, there was also some evidence that evangelicals were, in fact, less inclined to vote than they had been in previously elections. Of course, turnout had declined among Americans generally over the past several elections, but some thought that the drop among evangelicals was particularly large. In fact, Karl Rove, the chief political strategist for President Bush, contended that four million fewer evangelicals voted in the 2000 presidential election than in the 1996 presidential election, a statement that received massive and repeated coverage in the national media.[1]

Given the call for "political retreat" by some evangelical leaders, the demise of the Christian Coalition, and claims of declining voters turnout, evangelicals entered the 2004 presidential election as a question mark. Of course, few analysts or political strategists doubted the partisan tendencies of evangelicals; after all, by 1994 they had replaced mainline Protestants as the Republican Party's electoral core (Kellstedt et al. 1995). And evangelical Protestants were among the strongest supporters of Bush's Iraq policies and even his tax cuts (Smidt 2005; Guth 2004). What remained unclear was their depth of commitment to the political process and their likelihood of turning out on Election Day.

Data and Methods

To assess the role of evangelicals in the 2004 election, we use data from the Fourth National Survey of Religion and Politics, conducted by the University of Akron and sponsored by the Pew Forum on Religion in Public Life. This survey has two major advantages for studying the role of religion in a presidential campaign; it has a much larger sample (4,000 respondents) and more religious questions than most election polls. The preelection survey was conducted during February and March of 2004, with a postelection "call-back" conducted in the weeks immediately following the presidential election. We also use previous surveys by the University of Akron to address some additional questions.

First, however, it is necessary to discuss briefly the terminology and theoretical approach employed here. Much journalistic and scholarly discussion of evangelical politics suffers from the use of different terms—as if they had identical meanings. For example, the terms fundamentalist, evangelical, born-again, conservative Christian, and Christian Right are used almost interchangeably, even though they refer to distinct, if overlapping, groups of voters. Much greater conceptual clarity is needed.

Our analysis begins with the concept of religious tradition, measured in terms of religious affiliation or belonging. A religious tradition is a set of "religious communities that share a . . . distinctive worldview"; the building blocks of these religious traditions "are the specific religious communities to which individuals typically belong," the most common of which are denominations (Kellstedt et al. 1996, 176). Historically, members of six major religious traditions have dominated American political life: evangelical Protestants, mainline Protestants, black Protestants, Roman Catholics, Jews, and the religiously unaffiliated (the relatively secular component of the American electorate).

The advantage in using the concept of religious traditions is very simple. Rather than employing some categorical entity, whose members are unified only by certain arbitrary criteria specified by the analyst, our approach more fully reflects a sociological reality—members of a religious tradition are likely to interact socially with others in that tradition and are more likely to fall within the same communication and informational networks. Thus, the beliefs and values shared by the religious bodies within a tradition are further reinforced and made more salient through these social factors.

Such a sociological definition of evangelicals does not include most black Protestants—who may share many religious beliefs with evangelical Protestants but belong to socially distinctive religious communities. Similarly, evangelical Protestants are not identical to "born-again" voters. Many evangelicals fall within such ranks but so do people from other religious traditions. For example, three-quarters of all black Protestants, one-third of mainline Protestants, and one-fifth of Roman Catholics claim to be born-again.[2] As a category, then, born-again voters are quite diverse religiously, as evangelicals constitute only a little more than half their number. Similar caveats pertain to the use of "conservative Christians," another categorical entity comprising people from several religious traditions.

Evangelical must also be distinguished from the Christian Right, a social movement dedicated to drawing them and other conservative Christians into politics. However, not all evangelicals support that movement; in our 2004 survey, fewer than half of all evangelicals (49 percent) said they felt close to the Christian Right, joined by smaller number of mainline Protestants, Romans Catholics, and black Protestants. Thus, while the Christian Right may include many evangelicals, the term captures a much more diverse constituency, one united more politically than religiously. With these theoretical concerns classified, we can now turn to the role of evangelicals, defined as a religious tradition, in the 2004 elections.

Analysis

As we suggested above, the size of a religious community is an important factor shaping its political influence. As table 2.1 shows, evangelical Protestants and Roman Catholics are clearly the largest religious traditions within the electorate; evangelicals constitute about quarter of the potential voters, as do Roman Catholics when Hispanic Catholics are combined with non-Hispanics. Mainline Protestants, the religiously unaffiliated, black Protestants, other religions, Jews, and Hispanic Protestants make up the other half of the electorate.[3] Thus, though evangelicals hardly constitute a majority of potential voters, they are the largest single tradition. And, unlike mainline Protestants and white Catholics, evangelicals have held (or perhaps even gained) religious "market shares" over the past several decades (data not shown).

Turnout

The size of a potential electoral bloc means little, however, if its members do not vote. And, in the past, the electoral clout of evangelicals has been limited because they usually voted in lower proportions than those in most other religious traditions. Over the past several decades, however, turnout differences have diminished across the religious landscape. Voting rates among evangelicals still tend to lag behind those of mainline Protestants and Jews, but they are close to those of

Table 2.1 Frequency Distribution of Religious Traditions, 2004

	% of Sample
Evangelical Protestants	25.1
Mainline Protestants	16.4
Black Protestants	9.3
Hispanic Protestants	2.6
Roman Catholics	17.5
Hispanic Catholics	4.5
Jews	1.9
Other faiths	5.4
Unaffiliated	17.3
Entire sample	100.0

Source: Fourth National Survey of Religion and Politics, Bliss Institute of Applied Politics, University of Akron, March–May 2004 ($N = 4,000$).

Roman Catholics and somewhat higher than those of black Protestants and the religiously unaffiliated.

In any case, strong evangelical turnout was critical to the strategy of the Bush campaign in 2004. Karl Rove, Bush's chief political strategist, had focused on the evangelical community as perhaps the most critical element in the GOP base, and he hoped to enhance substantially the turnout among evangelicals. Did this well-publicized effort succeed? Table 2.2 presents estimated turnout figures for major religious traditions in the 2004 presidential election. Clearly evangelicals did turn out at the polls at a higher rate than in previous elections—as almost two-thirds reported voting.[4] In fact, evangelical turnout matched or exceeded that of other religious traditions—except for Jews and mainline Protestants. Thus, in 2004, evangelicals coupled their numerical advantages with a massive march to the polls.

That turnout might be even more impressive if we consider that some political factors worked against it. The many evangelicals who reside in southern states, which went heavily for Bush, may have felt less need to participate, given his "lock" in their states' electoral college votes. The anticipated lopsided results there also mean that many evangelicals were exempt from the massive media coverage and get-out-the-vote operations that characterized the campaign in more competitive areas. Perhaps, then, evangelical voter turnout was even higher in states closely contested between Bush and Kerry. Table 2.3 reports the proportion of the evangelical community living in the 12 closest states on Election Day and shows that evangelical turnout was 7.9 percent higher where the race was most competitive.[5]

Other religious traditions did not always exhibit a comparable increase in turnout in the most competitive states. As a result, evangelical

Table 2.2 Turnout in 2004 Presidential Election by Religious Tradition

	% *Who Voted*
Evangelical Protestants	63.2
Mainline Protestants	69.2
Black Protestants	50.4
Roman Catholics	66.9
Jews	86.5
Unaffiliated	52.4
Total amount	60.8

Source: Fourth National Survey of Religion and Politics, Bliss Institute of Applied Politics, University of Akron, November–December 2004 (*N* = 2,730).

Table 2.3   Turnout among Evangelicals in 2004 Presidential Election

	% of Evangelicals	% Who Voted
All evangelical Protestants	100.0	63.2
"Toss-up" state evangelicals	28.4	68.9
Safe state evangelicals	71.8	61.0
Marriage amendment state evangelicals	17.1	61.0
Nonmarriage amendment state evangelicals	82.9	63.6

Source: Fourth National Survey of Religion and Politics, Bliss Institute of Applied Politics, University of Akron, November–December 2004 (*N* = 2,730).

voting rates in these states actually *exceeded* that of mainline Protestants and white Catholics (data not shown). Interestingly—and contrary to much media speculation—the presence of anti–same-sex marriage ballot proposals did *not* enhance evangelical voter turnout. In fact, as table 2.3 shows, evangelical turnout was actually 2.6 percent lower on average in states that had such proposals on their ballot.[6] (Of course, most of these states were safely Republican.)

Vote Choice

As Karl Rove fervently hoped, evangelicals gave President Bush the overwhelming majority of their votes. Table 2.4 reveals that more than three-fourths of all evangelicals who cast their ballots did so for Bush and GOP congressional candidates, a proportion matched by no other tradition, although black Protestants, Jews, and the religious unaffiliated showed similarly strong support for Kerry. Mainline Protestants, Roman Catholics, and members of other religious faiths were much more evenly split between the candidates. In addition to their numbers, high turnout, and strong support for the GOP, evangelicals mattered politically because of their geographic concentration. Bush's strength among evangelicals put huge swaths of the country out of reach for Kerry. Indeed, all 14 states with the largest evangelical populations (30 percent or higher), went for Bush, giving him 123 electoral college votes.[7]

As the campaign narrowed down to the final weeks, many analysts point to 10 states as the "battleground" for the 2004 presidential election.[8] In eight of the ten toss-up states, evangelicals constituted between 22 and 28 percent of the electoral base; only Pennsylvania and New Mexico were exceptions. On the other hand, of the eight states with the fewest evangelical residents (16 percent or less), seven

Table 2.4 Two-Party Vote in 2004 Presidential Election by Religious Tradition

	Presidential (%)		Congressional (%)	
	Bush	Kerry	Republicans	Democrats
Evangelical Protestants	77.5	22.5	74.9	25.1
Mainline Protestants	50.0	50.0	53.8	46.2
Black Protestants	17.2	82.8	19.6	80.4
Roman Catholics	52.7	47.3	52.3	47.7
Jews	26.7	73.3	26.8	73.2
Unaffiliated	28.1	71.9	29.9	70.1
Entire sample	51.1	48.9	51.1	48.9

Source: Fourth National Survey of Religion and Politics, Bliss Institute of Applied Politics, University of Akron, November–December 2004 (N = 2,730).

went for Kerry (the exception was Utah with its high concentration of Mormon voters).[9] Thus, just as the significance of Jewish voters has often been magnified by their residence in states with many electoral votes, so too the geographical concentration of evangelicals enhances their influence in presidential elections.

Issues

What impact did issues have on the evangelical vote? Much of the postelection analysis in 2004 pointed to the role of "moral values" in the president's reelection victory, emphasizing the salience of social issues such as abortion and same-sex marriage. On the other hand, many more conventional analyses hold that it is still economics that drives politics, joined perhaps by foreign policy issues during wartime. According to these conventional perspectives, then, elections still ride on two simple factors—peace and prosperity.

We asked respondents a series of questions about what kinds of issues were important to their votes, seeking to tap the relative weight of economic, foreign policy, and social issues. Respondents were then asked further which of the three was *the most important* to their vote. The results appear in table 2.5.

Clearly, no subset of issues dominated in the electorate as a whole, as a plurality indicated that foreign policy issues were most important, followed closely by economic issues, and at a considerable distance by social issues, mentioned by fewer than one-quarter of the respondents.[10] The picture changes, however, when responses are broken

Table 2.5 Issue Priorities in 2004 Presidential Election by Religious Tradition

	Social (%)	Foreign Policy (%)	Economic (%)
Evangelical Protestants	37.4[a]	30.6	22.5
Mainline Protestants	18.8	37.6	33.8
Black Protestants	17.2	14.6	58.9
Roman Catholics	18.7	40.0	34.4
Jews	8.3	50.0	29.2
Unaffiliated	16.8	44.9	31.9
Entire sample	23.8	34.9	32.7

Note: [a] Percentages do not add up to 100% because some respondents either indicated "none" or chose two as equally important.

Source: Fourth National Survey of Religion and Politics, Bliss Institute of Applied Politics, University of Akron, November–December 2004 (N = 2,730).

down by religious tradition; evangelicals were far more likely to cite social issues being of primary importance. Indeed, almost three of every eight evangelical Protestants (37.4 percent) picked social issues, twice as many as in the next highest tradition (mainline Protestants at 18.8 percent). Still, evangelicals were far from monolithic; almost one-third cited foreign policy as the primary factor in their voting decision, while nearly a quarter named economic issues.

Just where do evangelicals stand on specific matters of public policy? Table 2.6 presents three major issues of the 2004 campaign—gay marriage, the war in Iraq, and major tax cuts—and analyzes stances taken by members of different religious traditions. Each question is reflective of an issue type analyzed in the previous table, that is, a social issue, a foreign policy issue, and an economic issue. And all three are issues on which President Bush campaigned in 2004. Basically, evangelicals overwhelmingly support marriage as a union of one man and one woman, are strongly convinced that the war in Iraq was justified, and clearly are in favor of large tax cuts. Moreover, compared to other major religious traditions, evangelicals exhibit the strongest cohesion on all three issues. All other traditions were more closely divided on all three issues, sometimes very closely divided indeed.

This situation represents a significant change for the evangelical community. Decades ago, evangelicals were united politically only on cultural issues—they remained divided on economic policy. Over the past several elections, however, evangelical voters have increasingly gravitated to conservative positions in all three issue domains, meaning that their stances on cultural, economic, and foreign policy issues have become more inter-correlated. As one result, Democratic

Table 2.6 Issue Positions in 2004 Presidential Election by Religious Tradition

	Evangelical Protestant (%)	Mainline Protestant (%)	Black Protestant (%)	Roman Catholics (%)	Jews (%)	Unaffiliated (%)
Law and Marriage						
Union of man and woman	77.2	45.9	72.8	47.8	21.2	27.3
Civil unions	12.5	26.5	11.4	23.4	23.1	20.3
Union of two people	10.2	26.7	15.7	28.7	55.8	51.8
War in Iraq						
Justified	77.6	58.1	38.7	60.4	46.0	42.6
Unjustified	22.4	41.9	61.3	39.6	54.0	57.4
Large tax cuts						
Support	65.5	50.0	44.1	47.5	36.0	36.5
Oppose	34.5	50.0	56.9	52.5	64.0	63.5

Source: Fourth National Survey of Religion and Politics, Bliss Institute of Applied Politics, University of Akron, March–May 2004 (N = 4,000).

candidates find it harder to appeal to evangelicals by locating economic or foreign policy "wedge" issues to counter Republican appeals to their social conservatism.

Actually, when one focuses on these "traditional" campaign subjects—economic and foreign policy issues—Senator Kerry did exceedingly well among all voters primarily concerned about such issues. Among voters who cited foreign policy or economic issues as their top issue concerns, Senator Kerry carried about 55 percent of their votes (data not shown). However, President Bush won reelection because "moral issues" were more important to almost a quarter of the electorate (see table 2.5), who gave him 70 percent of their votes (data not shown). And, as shown in table 2.5, evangelicals were the most likely to cite moral issues as the basis for their decision. Indeed, among those, 93 percent favored Bush over Kerry (data not shown).

Nevertheless, the support that evangelicals gave Bush was not simply a function of the moral issues they favored. Evangelicals voted for Bush regardless of their particular priorities—though their level of support varied with those priorities. Evangelicals who cited foreign policy as the primary basis for their decision gave Bush 79 percent of their votes, while those naming economic issues gave him only a narrow majority (53 percent).

Nor was evangelical support for Bush a function of anti-Catholicism aroused by Senator Kerry's candidacy. Although in 1960 evangelicals feared that John Kennedy would be too Catholic, in 2004 the situation was quite different. If anything, evangelicals generally expressed concern not so much that Kerry was Catholic or that he was too Catholic, but that he was not Catholic enough, as he opposed the social issues stances shared by evangelicals and the leaders of his own Catholic church.

While many argue that campaigns do matter, the proportion of Americans who change their candidate choice over the course of the campaign has declined over the past few presidential elections. In the First National Survey of Religion and Politics in 1992, for example, 72 percent of the respondents reported voting for the same presidential candidate for whom they had expressed their preference in the spring survey. In 2000, that figure had increased to 84 percent, and in our 2004 study it had increased to 89 percent—leaving fewer and fewer voters in play over the course of the election campaign. Among evangelicals only, that 2004 figure was 93 percent (data not shown).

Of course, it is possible that respondents might change their mind during the campaign, only to return to their initial preference by Election Day. However, when asked when they had arrived at their voting decision, a full 73 percent of evangelicals reported that they had made their decisions prior to the national party conventions (data not shown).

Partisanship and Bush Evaluation

As these figures suggest, evangelical voting choices are rooted in long-term political commitments. As table 2.7 reports, nearly two out of three evangelicals today identify as Republicans in partisan affiliation, while only a quarter report that they identify as Democrats.[11] In fact, no other religious tradition exhibits such strong partisan affections for the Republican Party—including mainline Protestants, long the dominant religious group in the GOP. A review of National Election Studies (NES) data since 1952 shows that Republican identification among evangelicals has reached an all-time high, while the comparable figures among mainline Protestants have fallen to its lowest point since the NES began. Clearly, by 2004, evangelicals have replaced mainliners at the center of the Republican coalition.

Evangelicals are also big fans of George W. Bush. Although many Kerry supporters may have been anti-Bush voters, such was not the case with evangelical support for Bush. Their backing for Bush was based on

Table 2.7 Proximity to Bush and Party Identification by Religious Tradition, 2004

	Evangelical Protestants (%)	Mainline Protestants (%)	Black Protestants (%)	Roman Catholics (%)	Jews (%)	Unaffiliated (%)
Proximity to Bush						
Close	57.4	36.3	15.5	39.4	21.0	17.9
Neutral	17.3	17.4	20.4	17.0	8.1	13.3
Far	25.3	46.3	64.1	43.6	71.0	68.8
Party Identification						
Republican	62.3	45.5	11.2	44.0	19.5	21.9
Independent	13.5	13.0	20.5	11.8	6.5	23.0
Democrat	24.1	41.4	68.2	44.1	74.2	55.1

Source: Fourth National Survey of Religion and Politics, Bliss Institute of Applied Politics, University of Akron, March–May 2004 (N = 4,000).

trust and affection for the president—not so much on their opposition to Kerry. As table 2.7 reveals, nearly three out of five evangelical Protestants report feeling "close to" Bush, while only a quarter feel "far from" from him. Once more, no other tradition has anywhere near this proportion of Bush admirers. (Indeed, many more mainline Protestants report feeling "far" from Bush than "near" to him).

Clearly, evangelical Protestants were strong supporters of President Bush in 2004, and the connections between Bush and many evangelicals were both deep and personal. But how can we explain this affection for Bush? Though it is not possible to draw definitive conclusions, we can delineate several possibilities.

First, the American people want presidents to have strong religious beliefs. More than two-thirds (68.5 percent) of all Americans in our preelection survey agreed that "the President should have strong religious beliefs," while nine in ten (89.8 percent) evangelicals concurred (data not shown). Bush has certainly employed religious language in his public addresses both as a candidate and a president. And while there may be considerable disagreement as to whether this use of religious language differs fundamentally from that employed by previous presidents, there is no doubt that the considerable media attention given to his religious rhetoric simply confirmed for many evangelicals that President Bush does have "strong religious beliefs."

Second, Bush's religious language probably resonates more deeply with evangelicals than with many other Americans, even those who also think that public officials should hold firm religious beliefs. The personal spiritual journey of President Bush is widely known among evangelicals, and that story conforms to the religious narrative that prevails within evangelical circles: an initial life of rebelliousness, followed by a conversion, and then a subsequent life marked by regeneration. Thus, for evangelicals, the president's well-known spiritual journey serves only to validate the public religious language he employs.

Third, Bush's religious language also reinforces the basic moral convictions of many evangelicals, for whom the root of all evil is moral relativism, the belief that there is no absolute good or evil. When in the wake of 9/11 Bush spoke of the "axis of evil," it resonated among evangelicals beyond its immediate application to matters of foreign policy. For evangelicals, moral clarity is needed not only in fighting terror, but also in fighting cultural degeneration.

Finally, many evangelicals perceive their community to be marginalized, if not held in distain, by journalists, the entertainment industry, and cultural elites. As a result, when Bush speaks of his faith or employs religious themes within the public square, he signals to those evangelicals and other Christians who feel marginalized that they too can speak of their faith in the public square and do so legitimately.

Thus, for many evangelicals, Bush is a person who is in many ways like them—at least in his spiritual journey. In this way, they sense that the president understands them—knows who they are, what they are like, and what they value. In other words, they see the president as a person they can trust and who affirms their values.

Given the strong connections of evangelicals to the GOP generally and to Bush personally, it is worth asking: what prospects do the Democrats have in wooing evangelical votes? The answer is somewhat uncertain. Perhaps, it is unlikely that any Republican presidential candidate will emerge in 2008 who resonates with evangelicals quite as well as Bush has. And should those Democratic strategists who are insistent on moving the party to the cultural center win that battle and nominate a candidate in 2008 who reflects such centrism, many evangelicals may well have less reason to reject the Democratic nominee out of hand. Thus, on both grounds, one could argue that it is unlikely that evangelicals will be so solidly Republican in 2008.

Yet, despite such considerations, there is considerable evidence to suggest that evangelicals will remain at the center of future Republican presidential coalitions. First, as table 2.4 showed, evangelicals did not confine their Republican voting to Bush in 2004. Not only did 77 percent vote by Bush, but there was virtually no fall-off in Republican voting for congressional candidates among evangelicals (74.5 percent). Clearly, whatever personal attraction evangelicals felt toward Bush appears to have been readily transferred to other Republican candidates lower on the ticket. Indeed, this pattern has been evident for at least the past two presidential elections, suggesting that more is at work than pure personal appeal of the presidential candidate.

Second, evangelicals certainly felt close to Bush, but the percentage (57.4 percent) is actually smaller than that claiming Republican identification (62.3 percent). Thus, it would appear that Republican partisanship is more widely rooted among evangelical Protestants than feelings of close proximity to President Bush, leaving limited opportunities for Democratic candidates in the next presidential election.

Nevertheless, there are two fault lines within the evangelical community that might allow a Democratic candidate—especially a cultural centrist—to reduce the Republican margin among evangelicals, at least in the right campaign environment. The first involves economic fissures within the evangelical community; the second derives from internal religious divisions.

First, economic divisions within the evangelical community offer Democrats some hope, especially if times are hard under a Republican administration. In 2004, low-income evangelicals were nearly twice as likely to vote for Kerry as were high-income evangelicals. Nearly half of all evangelicals in 2004 reported family income below $50,000 a year (49.6 percent), and nearly one-third of them voted for Kerry (30.2 percent)—nearly doubling those Kerry voters among high-income evangelicals (17.5 percent).

While economic issues are likely to be more salient for low-income than high-income evangelicals, not all low-income evangelicals report economic issues as the primary basis for their voting decision, and some high-income evangelicals do. This group of evangelicals has an even greater tendency to vote for the Democratic Party, at nearly 48 percent.

There are other internal divisions within the evangelical tradition that have largely escaped scholars and pundits alike. These divisions are religious, based on variation among evangelicals in theological orthodoxy, differences in the consistency of religious practices, as well as reported identifications with different religious movements. Table 2.8 classifies evangelicals as *traditionalist, centrist,* or *modernist,* based on survey measures of theology, religious practice, and movement identification. Briefly, traditionalists score high on theological orthodoxy, exhibit high levels of religious practice, and identify with traditionalist religious movements (e.g., the evangelical or fundamentalist movements). Modernists are more heterodox in beliefs, somewhat

Table 2.8   Evangelicals and Political Behavior: Within-Tradition Variation

	Evangelicals (%)			
	Traditionalist	Centrist	Modernist	All
Vote Turnout	68.9	53.7	66.7	63.2
Bush Vote	88.3	64.9	47.2	77.5
GOP House Vote	84.6	63.8	51.7	74.9
GOP Party Identification	73.4	51.6	37.7	62.3
Contacted by GOP	63.1	47.9	46.0	55.6
Evangelical subgroups in the columns	54.9	37.0	8.0	100

Source: Fourth National Survey of Religion and Politics, Bliss Institute of Applied Politics, University of Akron, November–December 2004 (*N* = 2,730).

less active in religious practices, and identify more with liberal religious movements (e.g., theological liberalism or ecumenism). Centrists fall between these two camps.

These evangelical subgroups exhibit different political characteristics. First, as is evident in table 2.8, the large traditionalist wing of the community is generally the most active politically. Turnout rates are highest among traditionalists, and a similar pattern holds for a whole series of political acts ranging from campaign activities to attempts to persuade others how to vote (data not shown). Second, traditionalists also provided the strongest support for President Bush and GOP House candidates. Centrists fell below the evangelical mean, while the small modernist group actually gave Kerry a slight edge. Third, traditionalists are strongly Republican in partisan identification, modernists moderately Democratic, and the centrists fall in between.

Finally, the bottom of table 2.8 shows that GOP mobilization efforts were directed more at traditionalists (or, at least, were more successful in reaching them). Almost two-thirds of the traditionalists reported at least one Republican contact, while fewer than half the centrists and modernists reported such contacts. And these contact efforts apparently made a difference. The turnout among traditionalists contacted was 20 percent higher than among those not contacted, and the Bush vote increased from 82 to 91 percent from those traditionalists reporting no contact to those reporting such a contact (data not shown). Contacting was even more effective in increasing turnout among centrists (up 27 percent) and modernists (up 42 percent) but had more mixed effects on vote choice, as contacts bolstered Bush's total from 39 to 66 percent among centrists but not at all among modernists (data not shown).

These results show at least some potential for Democratic inroads among the evangelical modernists and, to a lesser extent, among centrists. Granted, these are relatively small sectors of the evangelical community but are still large voting blocs and are somewhat more resistant to GOP appeals than their traditionalist coreligionists. They tend to see economic issues as more important and usually take much less conservative positions on the entire range of contemporary issues. In any event, these data reveal the importance of examining differences among evangelical Protestants. Although the religious divisions among evangelicals are not as large as those among mainline Protestants or Catholics, evangelical Protestants are less homogeneous than is generally assumed. Most analysts have understandably focused on the large traditionalist segment of evangelicals, but we (and perhaps the Democrats) should not lose sight of the other subgroups, particularly as they may be of greater importance in the future.

Conclusion

After a generation of intermittent involvement, evangelical Protestants have finally come into their own politically. In 2004, evangelicals played an important, though not necessarily a determinative, role in the reelection of George Bush. They were a crucial component of Bush's winning coalition due to their large numbers, their strong loyalty to the president, and their high turnout. They were, as a whole, committed to Bush from the start of the campaign to its conclusion. Such overwhelming support was based on Bush's personal appeal (his religious faith, his personality, his willingness to employ religious language in public) and the particular positions he embraced. Moreover, their support was almost equally strong for candidates down the ticket.

Several decades ago, evangelical Protestants were united politically primarily on cultural issues, but now their cultural, economic, and foreign policy stances have become more strongly inter-correlated. As a result, there are fewer wedge issues that allow Democratic candidates to play one kind of issue off against another. Evangelical Protestants entered the 2004 campaign as the foundation of the Republican Party's voter base. In the aftermath of that campaign, they have solidified their position as the bedrock of the GOP coalition; they may not dominate the party, but they are major players in it. And, in response to the fundamental question of "what does the Lord require?" related to politics, evangelicals clearly opted for public engagement.

Notes

1. It is not clear just what data served as the basis for Rove's contention. Some have argued that it was based on exit poll data showing a 4% drop between 1996 and 2000 in the percentage claiming to be members of the Christian Right. However, as discussed in the next section of the chapter, evangelical Protestants are distinct from those who claim to be part of the Christian Right. We find no evidence of a decline in evangelical turnout from 1996 to 2000 in our National Surveys on Religion and Politics.

2. The figures for mainline and black Protestants are based on the percentage claiming to be born-again in our 2004 survey. Because Roman Catholics were not asked the born-again question in 2004, their figure comes from our 2000 survey.

3. Technically speaking, Hispanic Protestants could be assigned to either the evangelical Protestant or the mainline Protestant category (as could Hispanic Roman Catholics be classified with other Roman Catholics). We have not done so here because to combine them both prevents a comparison of Hispanic Protestants and Hispanic Catholics and mutes some more notable differences between and among white religionists.

4. Based on the Third National Survey of Religion and Politics, the estimated voter turnout among evangelical Protestants in 2000 was 50%.

5. The 12 states classified as "toss-up" included those where neither major candidate received 52% or more of the ballots: New Hampshire, Pennsylvania, Florida, Ohio, Michigan, Iowa, Minnesota, Wisconsin, Colorado, Nevada, Oregon, and New Mexico.

6. The 11 states that had a proposal related to gay marriage on the ballot included Oregon, Ohio, Michigan, Montana, North Dakota, Utah, Oklahoma, Mississippi, Georgia, Arkansas, and Kentucky.

7. The 14 states with the highest evangelical concentration are Tennessee, Oklahoma, Alabama, West Virginia, Arkansas, North Carolina, Kentucky, South Carolina, Mississippi, Kansas, Georgia, Virginia, Indiana, and Montana. Evangelicals in these states reportedly constitute 30% or more of the state's population. See www.beliefnet.com/story/155/story_15570_1. html.

8. These 10 competitive states were Ohio, Michigan, Iowa, Minnesota, Wisconsin, Missouri, Pennsylvania, Florida, Oregon, and New Mexico.

9. The eight states with lowest evangelical concentration (16% or less of the population) are Vermont, California, Massachusetts, New Jersey, Utah, New York, Connecticut, and Rhode Island.

10. The percentages for the three kinds of issues do not total to 100% as some respondents indicated two such issues as equally important or could not choose a particular kind of issue as the most important in shaping their decision.

11. Those who reported that they were Independents leaning Republican were classified as identifying as Republicans, and those who reported that

they were Independents leaning Democratic were classified as identifying as Democrats.

References

Berkowitz, Laura, and John C. Green. 1997. "Charting the Coalition: The Local Chapters of the Ohio Christian Coalition." In *Sojourners in the Wilderness: The Christian Right in Comparative Perspective*, edited by Corwin E. Smidt and James Penning. Lanham, MD: Rowman and Littlefield, 57–72.

Bruce, Steve. 1988. *The Rise and Fall of the New Christian Right: Conservative Protestant Politics in America, 1978–1988*. Oxford: Oxford University Press.

Green, John C., Mark J. Rozell, and Clyde Wilcox, eds. 2003. *The Christian Right in American Politics: Marching to the Millennium*. Lanham, MD: Rowman and Littlefield.

Guth, James L. 2004. "George W. Bush and Religious Politics." In *High Risk and Big Ambition*, edited by Steven E. Schier. Pittsburgh: University of Pittsburgh Press, 117–141.

Hunter, James Davison. 1987. *American Evangelicalism: Conservative Religion and the Quandary of Modernity*. New Brunswick, NJ: Rutgers University Press.

Kellstedt, Lyman A., John C. Green, James L. Guth, and Corwin E. Smidt. 1995. "Has Godot Finally Arrived? Religion and Realignment." *Public Perspective* 6 (4): 18–22.

——— 1996. "Grasping the Essentials: The Social Embodiment of Religion and Political Behavior." In *Religion and the Culture Wars*, edited by John C. Green, James K. Guth, Corwin E. Smidt, and Lyman A. Kellstedt. Lanham, MD: Rowman and Littlefield, 174–192.

Reed, Ralph. 1996. *Active Faith*. New York: Free Press.

Rozell, Mark J., and Clyde Wilcox, eds. 1997. *God at the Grass Roots, 1996: The Christian Right in the 1996 Elections*. Landham, MD: Rowman and Littlefield.

Smidt, Corwin E. 2005. "Religion and American Attitudes toward Islam and an Invasion of Iraq." *Sociology of Religion* 66 (3): 243–262.

Smidt, Corwin E., and James K. Penning, eds. 1997. *Sojourners in the Wilderness: The Christian Right in Comparative Perspective*. Lanham, MD: Rowman and Littlefield.

Thomas, Cal, and Ed Dobson. 1999. *Blinded by Might: Can the Religious Right Save America?* Grand Rapids, MI: Zondervan.

Wilcox, Clyde. 1992. *God's Warriors: The Christian Right in Twentieth-Century America*. Baltimore: Johns Hopkins University Press.

Chapter Three

Catholics and the Politics of Change: The Presidential Campaigns of Two JFKs

John Kenneth White and William D'Antonio

When John F. Kennedy was deciding whether or not to seek the presidency in 1960, he had one particularly enthusiastic supporter: his father. Joseph P. Kennedy told his son that being a Roman Catholic would make him a powerful contender:

> Just remember, this country is not a private preserve for Protestants. There's a whole new generation out there and it's filled with the sons and daughters of immigrants from all over the world and those people are going to be mighty proud that one of their own is running for president. And that pride will be your spur, it will give your campaign an intensity we've never seen in public life. Mark my words, it's true.[1]

Hearing this, the youthful JFK had only one question left, "Well, Dad, when do we start?"[2] The elder Kennedy's analysis proved correct, and religion became the great divide in the November election. Kennedy won 78 percent of the Catholic ballots while his Republican opponent, Richard M. Nixon, won 63 percent of the votes cast by white Protestants.[3] The religion gap had become a "religion canyon."

In 1960, most Catholics were still struggling to make their way up the socioeconomic ladder, lagging behind Jews and white Protestants.[4] Franklin D. Roosevelt's New Deal saved many Catholics from complete economic ruin, as the federal government created many make-work alphabet soup agencies, including the WPA (Works Progress Administration), PWA (Public Works Administration), and the CCC (Civilian Conservation Corps). Thanks to Roosevelt, Catholics were beneficiaries of these and many other government programs—particularly, Social Security that gave many elderly and those who had lost parents or had to retire early due to poor health an economic safety net. Forty years ago, these memories were still fresh in Catholic minds.

In addition, the discrimination that Catholic immigrants suffered at the turn of the twentieth century also remained poignant recollections. "No Irish Need Apply" was not just a page in a dusty history book, but a sign whose memories still rendered a stigmata of hurt and pain. Richard Nixon wrote in *Six Crises* that during the 1960 campaign, "[I] could not dismiss from my mind the persistent thought that, in fact, Kennedy was a member of a minority religion to which the presidency had been denied throughout the history of our nation and that perhaps I, as a Protestant who had never felt the slings of discrimination, could not understand his feelings—that, in short, he had every right to speak out against even possible and potential bigotry."[5] Kennedy tacitly agreed with Nixon, telling delegates to the Democratic National Convention that his party had taken a "hazardous risk" in choosing him. He reiterated his pledge to uphold the Constitution and his oath of office, regardless of any religious pressure or obligation "that might directly or indirectly interfere with my conduct of the presidency in the national interest."[6] Later, Kennedy famously repeated his pledge not to take orders from the pope before the Greater Houston Ministerial Association:

> I am not the Catholic candidate for President. I am the Democratic Party's candidate for President who happens also to be a Catholic. I do not speak for my church on public matters—and the church does not speak for me. Whatever issue may come before me as President—on birth control, divorce, censorship, gambling, or any other subject—I will make my decision in accordance with these views, in accordance with what my conscience tells me to be the national interest, and without regard to outside religious pressures or dictates. And no power or threat of punishment could cause me to decide otherwise.[7]

Yet, even as Kennedy tried to defuse the Catholic issue, he assiduously courted their support. In addition to a strong sense of religious identity among Catholic voters, Kennedy was also aided by their agreement with him on the most profound issues of the day—especially when it came to foreign policy matters and the conduct of the cold war. For decades, Catholics had been ardent anticommunists. In 1930, the pope asked Catholic Americans to pray for the conversion of Russia— and they did. By 1949, 77 percent of all Americans saw communism and Christianity as incompatible—including 81 percent of Catholics.[8] During the 1950s, Republicans tried (with some success) to woo Catholic Democrats to their anticommunist crusade. In 1956, for example, the Republican National Committee established a Nationalities Division that distributed "I Like Ike" buttons in 10 languages, along with 500,000 pamphlets titled *The Republican Policy of Liberation.*[9] Four years later, American Nationalities for Nixon-Lodge distributed 48,000 foreign-language buttons, held freedom rallies in cities with large Polish populations (including Buffalo and Chicago), and printed thousands of postcards depicting the famous Nixon-Khrushchev "kitchen debate."[10]

But John F. Kennedy was not to be outdone in his anticommunist appeals to ethnic Catholics, especially those who had relatives behind the Iron Curtain. On the stump, he combined his anticommunist rhetoric with an appeal to old-fashioned American nationalism: "I want a world which looks to the United States for leadership, and which does not always read what Mr. Khrushchev is doing or what Mr. Castro is doing. I want to read what the president of the United States is doing."[11] Kennedy charged that the Republicans were inattentive to the communist challenge and allowed a "missile gap" to develop.

Despite John F. Kennedy's vehement anticommunism, religion remained the crucible around which the 1960 presidential contest was fought. As one elderly woman told Theodore H. White during the Democratic primary contest in Protestant-dominated West Virginia, "We've never had a Catholic president and I hope we never do. Our people built this country. If they had wanted a Catholic to be president, they would have said so in the Constitution."[12] Catholics tacitly agreed with that Protestant female that religious affiliation was *the* most important factor in their vote choice. In his 1961 book *The Religious Factor*, Gerhard Lenski noted that while many had taken note of a religious revival that had spawned the likes of Billy Graham and other evangelicals, "little attention . . . has been devoted to the . . . *consequences* of religious belief and practice in the everyday life of society."[13]

One consequence was the importance of religious self-identification and the sense of unity it created among faithful Catholics and white Protestants. In its August 1, 1960 issue, the editors of *U.S. News & World Report* stated, "There is, or can be, such a thing as a 'Catholic vote,' whereby a high proportion of Catholics of all ages, residences, occupations, and economic status vote for a well-known Catholic or a ticket with special Catholic appeal."[14] Certainly, past history proved that analysis correct. From 1948 to 1968, Catholics were reliable Democrats, giving their party's presidential candidates support in greater numbers than the rest of the country with just one exception: in 1956, Republican Dwight D. Eisenhower captured 54 percent of the Catholic vote.[15]

During the 1970s, an apocryphal tale was told among Irish Catholics of a Mrs. O'Reilly, a 70-year-old woman who was driven to the polls one election day by her son, James, aged 45. James, who enjoyed the prosperity of being a "have" member of the nation's growing middle class, often voted Democratic, but still cast the occasional Republican ballot. His mother, whose memories of FDR and JFK were still fresh, was a strong Democrat. On their way to the polls, James asked his mother how she planned to vote, receiving the predictable reply, "Straight Democratic":

> "Mom," said the frustrated son, "If Jesus Christ came back to earth and ran as a Republican, you'd vote against Him."
> "Hush!" replied Mrs. O'Reilly. "Why should He change His party after all these years?"[16]

John F. Kennedy and the Religious Divide

Twenty years ago, the late Everett Carll Ladd, Jr., wrote that social scientists were continuously searching for the right "axial principle" in order to see the nexus between social change and political conflict:

> The student of American government and politics needs to know which links between the political and social spheres have the greatest influence on politics and how changes in the larger social environment are reshaping politics, molding it, and moving it in new directions. What aspects are the most consequential? We need an "axial principle" that identifies the primary features of American society that together form the distinctive setting for political life.[17]

For much of the twentieth century, Roman Catholicism provided a kind of axial principle that helped shape voter identity and provided ample reasons for larger societal and political conflicts. According to the *New York Times* religion editor Peter Steinfels, the American Roman Catholic Church provided a sense of security to newly-arrived immigrants and, in so doing, reinforced their sense of religiosity and identification:

> Catholic fraternal societies provided insurance while preserving ethnic cultures. Catholic reading circles and Catholic summer school programs of lectures, concerts, and dramas mirrored the nineteenth century Chautauqua Movement for cultural improvement. Catholic newspapers by the hundreds were printed in a babel of languages, often for small ethnic readerships but sometimes with national impact. Catholic

publishers sprung up to serve a growing market for Bibles, prayer books, catechisms, religious novels, and pious nonfiction.[18]

Catholic religious practices also reinforced the strong ties between pew and pulpit. In 1952, 83 percent of Catholics said that religion was very important in their lives.[19] Catholics were not shy in expressing their religiosity. According to a 1952 survey, 43 percent of all Americans said that Catholics try too hard to get people to join their church; 42 percent disagreed.[20] Not surprisingly, attendance at Catholic masses was relatively high. According to a 1958 Gallup poll, 75 percent of Catholics said they went to mass every week.[21] As Bishop Kenneth Untener of Saginaw, Michigan, recalled, "When I grew up you had two choices: go to Mass . . . or go to hell. Most of us chose Mass."[22] Such religious cohesiveness had not escaped the notice of that astute observer of the American polity, Alexis de Tocqueville. In *Democracy in America*, Tocqueville wrote that the doctrines and practices of the Roman Catholic Church astonished many Americans, that "they feel a secret admiration for its discipline, and its extraordinary unity attracts them."[23]

Religious devotion combined with the nomination of only the second Catholic in history to head a major party ticket insured that there was such a thing as a Catholic vote in 1960. But even as John F. Kennedy tacitly appealed for support from his fellow Catholics on religious grounds, he called upon voters to forego the Catholic-Protestant divide and choose other conflicts upon which to base their presidential decision making:

> I hope that no American, considering the really critical issues facing this country, will waste his franchise by voting either for me or against me solely on account of my religious affiliation. It is not relevant. I want to stress, what some other political or religious leader may have said on this subject. It is not relevant what abuses may have existed in other countries or in other times. It is not relevant what pressures, if any, might conceivably be brought to bear on me. I am telling you now what you are entitled to know: that my decisions on any public policy will be my own—as an American, a Democrat, and a free man.[24]

In Kennedy's view, there were plenty of issues upon which voters could select their next president: "The spread of communist influence, until it now festers only ninety miles off the coast of Florida; the humiliating treatment of our president and vice president by those who no longer respect our power; the hungry children I saw in West Virginia; the old people who cannot pay their doctor's bills; the families forced to give up their farms; an America with too many slums, with too few schools, and too late to the moon and outer space."[25] Richard M. Nixon agreed. Appearing on the NBC television program *Meet the Press*, the Republican nominee said that the best way to avoid having religion become a campaign issue was to refrain from discussing it: "As far as I am concerned, I have issued orders to all of the people in my campaign not to discuss religion, not to raise it, not to allow anybody to participate in the campaign who does so on that ground, and as far as I am concerned, I will decline to discuss religion."[26]

But Americans stubbornly resisted the candidate's pleas to choose other conflicts. Newspaper headlines stressed Kennedy's Catholicism: "Democrats Hit Back on Religion" (*New York Times*); "Johnson Blasts 'Haters' Attacks on Catholics" (*Washington Post*); "Creed Issue Must Be Met, Bob Kennedy Says Here" (*Cincinnati Enquirer*); and "Mrs. FDR Hits Religious Bias in Talk to Negroes" (*Baltimore Sun*).[27] Meanwhile, the National Association of Evangelicals sent a distressed letter to pastors, warning, "Public opinion is changing in favor of the church of Rome. We dare not sit idly by—voiceless and voteless."[28] These headlines reflected and shaped the public's views of the candidates. The morning after the long election night, Nixon's daughter, Julie, awakened the exhausted candidate to ask, "Daddy, why did people vote against you because of religion?"[29]

An Old Fracture Loses Its Salience

Only three years after John F. Kennedy's narrow 1960 victory, there were signs that the old Catholic-Protestant divide was losing its salience. The final political meeting President Kennedy held in the White House occurred on November 13, 1963. It focused on the movement of many urban dwellers—including Catholics—to the suburbs. Richard M. Scammon, then director of the Census Bureau, told Kennedy he would be well advised to focus on the new suburbanites during the coming campaign. Kennedy was fascinated by Scammon's analysis, and he wanted to know at what point in their upward economic and social climb these former urban residents became antitax Republicans. Scammon promised to find out, but that assignment was shelved when Kennedy was assassinated just nine days later.[30]

On the eve of his dying day, John F. Kennedy understood that there was a new axial principle forming around a set of conflicts that transcended the old Catholic-Protestant divide. Kennedy was right. The Catholic vote began to divide more systemically along the socioeconomic

Table 3.1 Catholic Vote for President, 1976–2004 (%)

Party	1976	1980	1984	1988	1992	1996	2000	2004
Democratic	54	42	45	47	44	53	49	47
Republican	44	50	54	52	35	37	47	52
Independent	N/A	7	N/A	N/A	20	9	2	N/A

Note: N/A = Not available.

Source: Exit polls, 1976–2004, found in Marjorie Connelly, "How Americans Voted: A Political Portrait," *New York Times*, November 7, 2004, WK-4.

axial. According to exit poll data gathered between 1976 and 2004, only twice—in 1976 and 1996—did Democratic presidential candidates break the 50 percent barrier among Catholic voters (see table 3.1). As it happened, these elections featured appealing Democrats who were able to woo Catholics back to the fold.[31] The loss of Catholic support for the Democratic tickets was due in part to the suburban movement. When urban Catholics packed their belongings into their station wagons and headed for the suburbs, new worries associated with being "haves" in American society (especially concerns about high property tax rates) dominated their thoughts. A growing antitax movement that crested in the late 1970s—coupled with the Republican Party's vehement anticommunism and penchant for a strong national defense—helped spur Catholics into the GOP tent.

The end of a sense of close Catholic identity with the Democratic Party in the voting booth became clear when another Catholic Democrat who, like John F. Kennedy, also happened to be a U.S. senator from Massachusetts and even had the same initials, sought the presidency in 2004.

Conflict and Choice: John F. Kerry and Catholics in 2004

Election Night, 2004. Excited Republicans milled about at the Bush-Cheney headquarters during the early evening hours as election returns were just beginning to trickle in for what promised to be a close contest between George W. Bush and his Democratic challenger John F. Kerry. At the podium was Republican National Chairman Ed Gillespie who was the master of ceremonies for the evening. Trying to draw attention away from early exit polls that showed Bush losing by a substantial margin, Gillespie began introducing a series of speakers whose purpose was to inspire a dispirited crowd. Among them was "the president of my alma mater here in Washington, DC, a great institution of higher learning: The Catholic University of America." With that, the Most Reverend David M. O'Connell took to the podium and gave a benediction, saying, "We pray for our president, and for all who lead us in elected or appointed office." O'Connell also prayed for protection for those in uniform, to build a "culture of life that loves every person, born and unborn," and for "the most needy among us."[32]

As the vignette illustrates, Catholics, who once formed the backbone of the Democratic Party's New Deal coalition, were prepared, as O'Connell certainly was, to desert the party of their forebears, even when Democrats nominated only the third Roman Catholic in their history for the presidency of the United States. There were many reasons for this. One was the lessening of anti-Catholicism in the society generally and its virtual nonexistence as a political issue. Another was the fact that Catholics had become haves in American society, just as Richard Scammon had predicted, with many residing in prosperous suburbs. The lack of income differences was yet another reason. As William V. D'Antonio has reported, "Proportionately, Catholics nowadays are just as likely as Protestants to have attended and graduated from college, and even slightly more likely to enjoy above-average income. For example, Catholics represent 26 percent of the overall population, but 30 percent of those with incomes of $75,000 or more."[33] According to a December 2004 Zogby Interactive poll, only 16 percent of Catholics reported being worried that they could not find a job; among all Protestants, the figure was 14 percent.[34]

Catholic and ethnic identities—once powerful and intertwined factors in voting behavior—no longer dominated. Today, we are as far away in time from the New Deal as the New Deal was from the Civil War. Thus, political conflicts that once seemed especially salient no longer matter quite as much. In particular, preexisting prejudices about Catholic or Protestant candidates for high office no longer carry the same weight. For example, in 1980, the most heavily Catholic state in the nation, Rhode Island, was represented in the U.S. Senate by two old-stock white Protestant Yankees: Democrat Claiborne Pell and Republican John Chafee. According to Pell, if religious or ethnic considerations had been important to voters, "I wouldn't be here."[35] The end of the old Catholic-Protestant divide as an axial principle in determining voting patterns and social conflict was also in evidence in 1982, when the New York State Democrats selected Mario Cuomo, an Italian Catholic, as their candidate for governor. The Empire State had been a cauldron of religious and ethnic strife for most of the twentieth century, as upstate Protestants battled New York City Catholics (and Jews). But in 1982, that old rivalry came to a close when only 45 percent of the state's Catholics sided with fellow Catholic Cuomo (who barely won the governorship with 50 percent of the statewide vote).[36] Social issues, especially Cuomo's opposition to the death penalty, cost him valuable support among his fellow Catholics. In a state that was once the epitome of the Protestant-Catholic divide, an old fracture had lost its salience.

Another factor contributing to the loss of intense Catholic voter identification was that American Catholics no longer saw themselves as objects of discrimination. This was vividly demonstrated when George W. Bush visited South Carolina's Bob Jones University during the 2000 campaign. The university had a long history of anti-Catholicism. Its founder, Bob Jones, once likened the pope to the biblical anti-Christ. On its Web site, the university characterized Roman Catholicism as follows: "Any religion, including Catholicism, which teaches that salvation is by religious works or church dogma is false. Religion that makes the words of its leader, be he Pope or other, equal with the Word of God is false."[37] Not surprisingly, at the self-described "World's Most Unusual University," Catholic materials were found in the campus bookstore under the heading "Cults."[38] William Donohue, head of the Catholic League, denounced Bush's choice of a locale for his speechmaking, saying, "He just doesn't get it." Yet Donohue, a Bush supporter, quickly added, "But I don't think he's a bigot."[39]

The fact that so few Catholics were outraged that George W. Bush used an anti-Catholic venue to rally support from Southern white Protestants demonstrated just how dramatically times had changed. In November 2000, only 50 percent of all Catholics voted for Democrat Al Gore, while 47 percent backed Republican Bush.[40] In fact, among regular Churchgoing Catholics, Bush's support stood at 57 percent, while 59 percent of less observant Catholics supported Gore.[41] As these results clearly demonstrate, a new axial principle has evolved. Today, Americans increasingly see values and lifestyle issues as crucial to making their voting choices. During the 1992 campaign, pollsters began asking whether a particular presidential candidate (Bill Clinton, George H. W. Bush, or Ross Perot) "shares your values." It became understood that values—not economics alone—were instrumental in determining election outcomes. After all, if the 2000 election had been decided on the economy, Al Gore would have won 51–60 percent of the popular vote based upon several mathematical models developed by political scientists. These formulas relied heavily on the public's perceptions about the economy as well as an incumbent president's job approval scores.[42]

In the emerging culture wars, religion became a crucial factor. But instead of the old Catholic-Protestant split, church attendance (whatever the voter's denominational preference) became the new axial principle of political conflict. On one side were those who liked their Morality-Writ-in-Absolutes—the idea that right and wrong have been handed down by a transcendent God and are not subject to change. On the other side, were those who liked their Morality-Writ-in-Reason-and-Context—the idea that human beings must think for themselves in their struggle for truth and a moral order to live by. Church attendees tended to side with the Morality-Writ-in-Absolutes crowd; those who saw life in more complex terms liked their Morality-Writ-in-Reason-and-Context. Thus, frequent churchgoers understood and applauded George W. Bush's response to the question "who is your favorite philosopher?"; his answer was "Christ, because he changed my heart."[43]

This new divide has turned the Protestant-Catholic split on its head. In 1960, Americans wondered whether a Catholic could become president. For Protestants, the answer was a clear and loud—"NO!" Reverend Billy Graham's magazine *Christianity Today* declared in a 1960 editorial that the Vatican "does all in its power to control the governments of nations."[44] But in 2004, many Protestants and some Catholics wondered whether John F. Kerry was Catholic enough to serve as president. *Christianity Today*, a staunch opponent of John F. Kennedy's 1960 candidacy, completely reversed its position. In a June 2004 editorial, the magazine writers declared it is "certainly appropriate" for bishops to expect a Catholic president to submit to Vatican authority on value matters, especially abortion.[45] Gary Bauer, a former Republican presidential contender and head of a conservative group called American Values, observed, "When John F. Kennedy made his famous speech that the Vatican would not tell him what to do, evangelicals and Southern Baptists breathed a sigh of relief. But today, evangelicals and Southern Baptists are hoping that the Vatican *will* tell Catholic politicians what to do."[46]

John F. Kerry sought to allay the worries of the religiously observant that he was inattentive to their values concerns. In fact, Kerry had long grounded his religiosity to his public service. For example, at a February 4, 1993 National Prayer breakfast, Kerry declared,

> Jesus tells us that the real spiritual renewal that we need requires a faith that goes beyond even accepting the truth of His message. It requires literally a movement toward the person of Jesus, an attachment that requires us to live our lives in a manner that reflects the fullness of our

faith and that allows Jesus to become for us truly a life-saving force, so that ultimately it may even be said of us that he who does what is true comes to the light, that it may be clearly seen that his deeds have been wrought in God.[47]

A decade later, Kerry described himself in an autobiography titled *A Call to Service* as "a believing, practicing Catholic, married to another believing, practicing Catholic."[48] But during his long political career, Kerry had been reluctant to provide a strong public voice to his religious beliefs, perhaps believing as many New Englanders do that religion should be a private matter. Thus, Kerry's 1993 National Prayer Breakfast speech was unearthed by NPR reporter Barbara Bradley Hagerty and was excerpted on the NPR network during Kerry's 2004 presidential campaign. In the absence of any religious dialogue coming from Kerry, Churchgoing Catholics focused on Kerry's public record, including his strong support for abortion rights and so-called partial-birth abortions. Kerry's stances caused considerable friction between himself and the Catholic hierarchy, and they alienated many others, especially voters who described themselves as having a "born-again" experience. (Kerry won just 21 percent of white evangelicals who claimed to have had a born-again experience.[49]) Catholic prelates in Camden, New Jersey; St. Louis, Missouri; Lincoln, Nebraska; Denver, Colorado; and Colorado Springs, Colorado issued statements forbidding Kerry from receiving Holy Communion should he attend mass in their dioceses. The Colorado Springs Bishop Michael Sheridan went further, noting that Catholics who supported Kerry were jeopardizing their salvation by supporting any candidate who backed abortion rights;[50] the Denver Bishop Charles Chaput described Catholic voters for Kerry as "cooperating in evil."[51]

When the 2004 election results are examined according to the old Catholic-Protestant divide, it is clear that John F. Kerry's support among all Catholics was far less impressive than John F. Kennedy's. In fact, Kerry *lost* the Catholic vote. Nationally, Kerry received just 47 percent of the Catholic vote, while Methodist George W. Bush got 52 percent. Among white Catholics, Kerry's performance was an even more dismal—43 percent to Bush's 56 percent. And in the all-important state of Ohio, Bush won 55 percent of the Catholic vote (compared to 50 percent in 2000). This represented a shift of 172,000 votes into the Republican column and gave George W. Bush the necessary electoral votes to win another term.

Yet equally noteworthy were the votes among all Catholic faithful who regularly attended weekly mass: in 2004, Bush received 56 percent of their votes to Kerry's 43 percent. National Public Radio reporter Barbara Bradley Hagerty interviewed several massgoers following one 8 a.m. daily mass at St. Matthew's Cathedral in Washington, DC. Most supported Bush and derided Kerry for what they saw as his unfaithfulness to Catholic principles. Among the anti-Kerry comments were these:

- It's really character, personal integrity. And a man who does not seem committed to his faith, I don't see why he would be committed to his ideas or, necessarily, even his country.
- It seems that he does not take his faith seriously, and that he's using that as a political card rather than something that he deeply believes in and is committed to.
- I would work very hard against Senator Kerry. Because I believe he is actually from start to finish a four-star phony.[52]

Yet, among Catholics who attended mass less often, Kerry beat Bush 50 percent to 49 percent. And in another sign of the times, those Catholics who went to mass less frequently outnumbered those who said they attended weekly (14 percent to 11 percent).[53]

Back in 1960, Kennedy told the Southern Baptists that he dreamed of a country "where there is no Catholic vote."[54] Forty-four years later—in 2004—Kennedy's wish came true in the sense that there is not a Catholic vote per se. Pollster John Zogby notes that in 2004 Catholic voters went "to the polls as something else: veterans, union members, residents of the northeast, young, old." "Being Catholic," says Zogby, "was not the major identifier."[55] *Washington Post* columnist E. J. Dionne agreed: "The differences among us are rooted in ideas and impulses only marginally connected to the fact that we are Catholic. For this reason, one cannot talk about a Catholic vote. One can talk, at most, about a Catholic tendency."[56]

But the lack of a Catholic vote in 2004 did not signify an absence of conflict. As political scientist E. E. Schattschneider once wrote, "*The substitution of conflicts is the most devastating kind of political strategy.*"[57] In this case, the Catholic-Protestant conflict gave way to a conflict over the internalization and exposition of religious values. Those who attend church gave 61 percent of their votes to Bush in 2004; those who never attended a church gave Kerry 62 percent.[58] The Bush campaign understood the new political realities and sought to mobilize churchgoers. In Pennsylvania, for example, the Bush-Cheney team sent an e-mail seeking to identify 1,600 "friendly congregations" where voters who supported George W. Bush "might gather on a regular basis."[59] According to the 2004 exit polls, moral values outranked all other issues: 22 percent cited moral values as the top concern, followed by the economy and jobs (20 percent), terrorism (19 percent), and Iraq (15 percent). Moreover, of those who mentioned moral values, 80 percent voted for George W. Bush.[60] In short, a new form of religious conflict—and with it a new axial principle—has emerged. While George W. Bush stressed his religiosity during the campaign, John Kerry did not. Like the other JFK, Kerry seemed committed to the notion that the religious beliefs and practices of candidates for public office should not be an issue in a political campaign. The irony was that Kerry was an active Catholic churchgoer. Although he had been married twice, he received an annulment from his first marriage by Catholic authorities. Moreover, Kerry often reflected upon the relationship between his religious beliefs and his stands on social justice issues. Only his positions on abortion, stem-cell research, and homosexual rights deviated from Catholic Church teachings, but such aberrations were exceptions, not the rule. Like many New Englanders, including Kennedy and George H. W. Bush, religion was not a subject for popular discourse. Only rarely did Kerry explicitly discuss religion in public. Once at a candidate debate sponsored by CBS News, Kerry elaborated on his religious views: "I believe in God. And I believe in the power of redemption and the capacity of human beings to make a difference because as President Kennedy said, 'Here on earth, God's work must truly be our own.'" [61] This represented one of the few times that Kerry interweaved God into his public discourse. But it was too little, too late.

While Kerry and the Democratic Party leadership were struggling to balance the religious with the strongly secular elements within the party, faithful Catholic Democrats sought a more aggressive voice within the Kerry campaign. Thus, there came into being "Catholics for Kerry" and the "People of Faith for Kerry" coalitions during the spring of 2004.[62] The movement grew from small numbers to more than 30,000 by the end of the campaign. The Democratic National Committee hired a director of Religious Outreach, an unpaid deputy director, and several staff leaders and volunteers who directed their efforts into 21 states. As their numbers grew, the targets they met were impressive: 335,000 Catholic households were contacted via direct mail in Michigan, Wisconsin, and Iowa; 4,500 undecided Catholics were directly spoken to by their fellow Catholics for Kerry in Iowa and Michigan; 80,000 brochures were distributed in 10 battleground states, while flyers were distributed outside hundreds of churches on the Sunday prior to election day; People of Faith volunteers canvassed in targeted precincts in Missouri, Pennsylvania, Minnesota, Michigan, and Ohio.

In some states these efforts paid rich dividends. For example, in Michigan a full-time Religious Outreach staff worked with the support of Kerry's State Director Donnie Fowler. More than 130,000 Catholic households were sent direct mail advocating Kerry's election, including an oped written by Detroit Bishop Tom Gumbleton. Nuns phoned more than 3,000 undecided Catholic voters; pro-Kerry flyers were distributed outside churches statewide; and new and more nuanced language on abortion issues were provided to all phone banks. Dozens of letters to the editor and television and print coverage of Catholic outreach efforts were made. The result: Kerry won the Michigan Catholic vote and the state. Likewise, in Iowa, Kerry won the Catholic vote in Dubuque County where Catholics for Kerry used phone banks, direct mailings, and purchased radio time targeting Catholic voters.

But in other places there were few direct appeals made to Catholics. In Ohio, the state Religious Outreach staff focused only on African American clergy and not Catholics and evangelicals. Direct mail and targeted phone banking directed at Catholics were not approved by the state staff. No surrogates were sent to large interfaith gatherings, and there was minimal canvassing of Catholic-targeted precincts. Media efforts were limited, and no major opeds appeared either from Catholics for Kerry or any other faith-based group.

It is impossible to reconstruct the John F. Kennedy 1960 Catholic coalition, as John F. Kerry so amply demonstrated in 2004. While Kennedy and Kerry shared the same initials, home state, and party, the *context* in which each man sought the presidency had changed dramatically. While Kerry could have hardly appealed to the strong sense of Catholic self-identification that existed in 1960, he could have fought Bush much more aggressively for votes among religiously-minded Americans from all persuasions. Because he did not, Kerry unwittingly amplified and widened a religious divide that has become the axial principle of twenty-first century presidential politics.

Notes

1. Quoted in Michael Barone, *Our Country: The Shaping of America from Roosevelt to Reagan* (New York: Free Press, 1990), 310.
2. Ibid.
3. Ibid., xii.
4. See Gerhard Lenski, *The Religious Factor* (New York: Doubleday, 1961). Lenski reported that Catholics in the Detroit area were more likely to be found in the working and lower middle classes, and Jews and white Protestants in the middle and upper middle classes. Further, these differences

were reflected in their religious beliefs and practices, and in such areas as family size and the values they emphasized in preparing their children for life. Thus, Catholics were more likely than white Protestants and Jews to value obedience over personal autonomy. While Lenski's survey was limited to the Detroit area, it gained widespread acceptance because of the care used in drawing the sample and the mix of racial, ethnic, and religious groups in the Detroit area that closely mirrored the American population as a whole.

5. Richard M. Nixon, *Six Crises* (New York: Warner Books, 1979 edition), 436.
6. John F. Kennedy, Acceptance Speech, Democratic National Convention, Los Angeles, CA, July 15, 1960.
7. John F. Kennedy, Speech before the Greater Houston Ministerial Association, Houston, TX, September 12, 1960.
8. Gallup poll, July 22–28, 1949.
9. See Robert A. Divine, *Foreign Policy and U.S. Presidential Elections, 1952–1960* (New York: New Viewpoints, 1974), 114.
10. Ibid., 275–277.
11. Quoted in Theodore C. Sorensen, *Kennedy* (New York: Bantam Books, 1966), 207.
12. Quoted in Theodore H. White, *The Making of the President, 1960* (New York: New American Library, 1961), 125.
13. Lenski, *The Religious Factor*, vii.
14. Quoted in Nixon, *Six Crises*, 364.
15. See Monika L. McDermott, "Can Kerry Carry the Catholic Vote?" KCBS, May 24, 2004.
16. The story is told in E. J. Dionne, Jr., "Catholics and the Democrats: Estrangement but not Desertion," in *Party Coalitions in the 1980s*, ed. Seymour Martin Lipset (San Francisco, CA: Institute for Contemporary Studies, 1981), 308.
17. Everett Carll Ladd, Jr., "Foreword," in John Kenneth White, *The Fractured Electorate: Political Parties and Social Change in Southern New England* (Hanover, NH: University Press of New England, 1983), ix–x.
18. Peter Steinfels, *A People Adrift: The Crisis of the Roman Catholic Church in America* (New York: Simon and Schuster, 2003), 104.
19. See Samuel P. Huntington, *Who Are We?: American National Identity and the Challenges It Faces* (New York: Simon and Schuster, 2004), 101–102.
20. Ben Gaffin and Associates poll, June–July 1952.
21. See William V. D'Antonio, James D. Davidson, Dean R. Hoge, and Ruth A. Wallace, *American Catholic Laity in a Changing Church* (Kansas City, MO: Sheed and Ward, 1989), 44.
22. Steinfels, *A People Adrift*, 172.
23. Alexis de Tocqueville, *Democracy in America*, ed. J. P. Mayer (New York: Harper and Row, 1966), 450.

24. Kennedy, Acceptance Speech, July 15, 1960.
25. John F. Kennedy, "Address to Southern Baptist Leaders," *New York Times*, September 13, 1960.
26. Quoted in Nixon, *Six Crises*, 389.
27. Ibid., 433–434.
28. Quoted in Laurie Goodstein, "How the Evangelicals and Catholics Joined Forces," *New York Times*, May 30, 2004, WK-4.
29. Nixon, *Six Crises*, 465.
30. See Robert Dallek, *An Unfinished Life: John F. Kennedy, 1917–1963* (Boston, MA: Little, Brown, 2003), 691.
31. See John Kenneth White and William V. D'Antonio, "Catholics Return to the Fold: The Catholic Vote in 1996," *Public Perspective*, June/July 1997, pp. 45–48.
32. Phil Essington, "O'Connell Spoke at Bush Event on Election Night," *Tower*, November 12, 2004, 1.
33. *Emerging Trends* (Princeton Religious Research Center, 1993) "Catholics Are Becoming the New Middle Class," Vol. 15 (March): 5, cited in William V. D'Antonio, James D. Davidson, Dean R. Hoge, and Ruth A. Wallace, *Laity American and Catholic: Transforming the Church* (Kansas City, MO: Sheed and Ward, 1996).
34. Zogby Interactive poll, December 1–3, 2004. Text of the question was as follows: "In today's complex world, there are lots of pressures, problems and issues that cause fear and anxiety. Please tell me which of the following causes you significant fear and anxiety. Significant meaning you spend a lot of time thinking about the impact, consequences and negative effects of this issue on your life." The result was as follows: cannot find a job, 18%; Catholics, 16%; Protestants, 14%; Jewish, 22%.
35. John Kenneth White, interview with Claiborne Pell, Washington, DC, October 19, 1979.
36. See John Kenneth White and Dwight Morris, "Is New York's New Deal No More?" *Public Opinion*, June/July 1983, 46.
37. "Bob Jones University Responds," http://www.sullivan-county.com/news/bob_jones/bju.htm (last accessed January 2005).
38. See David van Biema, "Catholic Bashing?" CNN.com/ALL POLITICS, February 28, 2000, http://www.cnn.com/AllPOLITICS/time/2000/02/28/catholic.html (last accessed January 2005).
39. Ibid.
40. Voter News Service exit poll, November 7, 2000, http://www.cnn.com/ELECTION/2000/results.index.epoll.html.
41. See John C. Green, James L. Guth, Lyman A. Kellstedt, and Corwin B. Smidt, "How the Faithful Voted: Religion and the 2000 Presidential Election," press release, November 2000.
42. See Dan Merkle, "Gore's Sunny Forecast," ABC News.com, August 28, 2000, http://abcnews.go.com/US/story?id=96000page=1; and Adam Clymer, "And the Winner Is Gore, if They Got the Math Right," *New York Times*, September 4, 2000, A-15.

43. Cited in Rich Lowry, "It's Not, Mr. Bush," *Washington Post*, July 1, 2001, p. B-1.
44. Goodstein, "How the Evangelicals and Catholics Joined Forces."
45. Ibid.
46. Susan Page, "Churchgoing Closely Tied to Voting Patterns," *USA Today*, June 3, 2004, A-1 (italics is in the original).
47. John Kerry, Speech at the National Prayer Breakfast, February 4, 1993.
48. Quoted in Karen Tumulty and Perry Bacon, Jr., "A Test of Kerry's Faith," *Time*, April 5, 2004, 42.
49. National Election Pool, exit poll, November 2, 2004.
50. Daniel J. Wakin, "A Divisive Issue for Catholics: Bishops, Politicians, and Communion," *New York Times*, May 31, 2004, A-12.
51. See Maureen Dowd, "Vote and Be Damned," *New York Times*, October 17, 2004, WK-11.
52. Barbara Bradley Hagerty, "Kerry and the Catholic Vote," National Public Radio, *Morning Edition*, April 30, 2004.
53. National Election Pool, exit poll, November 2, 2004.
54. Kennedy, "Address to Southern Baptist Leaders."
55. Matt Malone, "Catholics and Candidates," *America*, May 17, 2004, 8.
56. Ibid.
57. E. E. Schattschneider, *The SemiSovereign People: A Realist's View of Democracy in America* (Hindale, IL: the Dryden Press. 1975. 71) (italics is in the original).
58. National Election Pool, exit poll, November 2, 2004.
59. See David D. Kirkpatrick, "Bush Campaign Seeks Help from Congregations," *New York Times*, June 3, 2004, A-1.
60. National Election Pool, exit poll, November 2, 2004.
61. Quoted in Hagerty, "Kerry and the Catholic Vote."
62. See William V. D'Antonio, "Voter Mobilization in the 2004 Election." Unpublished paper presented at the *37th World Congress of the International Institute of Sociology*, Stockholm, Sweden, July 8, 2005.

Chapter Four

The Mainline Protestant Vote

Laura R. Olson and Adam L. Warber

Since the founding of the United States, religion has played a significant role in shaping both presidential elections and fundamental debates about public policy (Fowler et al. 2004; Wald 2003). For over two centuries, mainline Protestants have been one of the more visible and influential religious voices in American politics. Accordingly, they have had their political preferences taken seriously by elected officials throughout American history. During the twentieth century, Mainline Protestants traditionally favored the economic conservatism of presidents Dwight D. Eisenhower and Richard M. Nixon while also eschewing the strict moral conservatism of presidents Ronald Reagan and George W. Bush. Mainline Protestants' ties to the Republican Party were solid and strong until the 1980s (Layman 2001; Manza and Brooks 1999, 2002), when the Republicans began emphasizing a policy agenda of moral conservatism alongside economic conservatism, much to the dismay of some mainline Protestants. By 2004, a drift among mainline Protestant laity toward the Democratic Party had become evident (Kohut et al. 2000; Leege et al. 2002). This partisan shift most likely has occurred as a reaction against the recent alliance between the Republican Party and evangelical Protestants.

Mainline Protestants now represent a much overlooked swing constituency in American politics. Their emerging status as a swing constituency was especially evident during the 2004 presidential election, when they split their votes between George W. Bush and John F. Kerry (Green et al. 2004). Although they may not receive the same amount of media attention accorded to evangelical Protestants and Catholics, mainline Protestants account for nearly the same proportion of the American electorate (22 percent) as either of these other two politically prominent religious traditions (Kohut et al. 2000). Some observers argue that "oldline" Protestant voting behavior is losing its relevance as mainline denominations lose members (see Hertzke 1991). However, we argue that despite some decline in formal church membership rolls, mainline Protestant voters retain great electoral significance because of their high socioeconomic status and strong commitment to civic participation—two factors that combine to make them likely voters. This chapter examines the political orientations of mainline Protestants during the 2004 presidential election year.

Mainline Protestantism: Cornerstone of American History

Mainline Protestantism is a religious tradition that is distinctive for its strong adherence to hierarchical denominationalism. Historically mainline denominations have maintained clear lines of organizational authority, whereas many evangelical and African American Protestants favor the more autonomous congregational model of religious organization. As such, mainline Protestant denominations often provide clear guidance to their congregations on a variety of matters including worship practices, religious education, and social and political issues. The typical mainline Protestant congregation has less organizational autonomy than the average evangelical or African American congregation. Nevertheless, many mainline Protestant laity and clergy do not abide by all of the teachings and dictates of their denominational leaders, in large part because mainline Protestantism also tolerates (and in fact encourages) a great deal of diversity in doctrinal interpretation. Despite mainline Protestantism's clear lines of organizational hierarchy, it is not always clear what it means, politically or otherwise, to be a mainline Protestant in the United States today.

The major denominations that comprise mainline Protestantism include the American Baptist Churches (USA), the Christian Church (Disciples of Christ), the Episcopal Church, the Evangelical Lutheran Church in America (ELCA), the Presbyterian Church (USA), the Reformed Church in America, the United Church of Christ, and the United Methodist Church. American Baptists are historically connected to American frontier revivalism, much like their Southern Baptist cousins, but because of disputes over slavery and theological interpretation, they diverged from Southern Baptists during the Civil War. Although the Disciples of Christ share the same revivalist roots as American Baptists, they are more theologically and politically liberal than the Baptists and have a more centralized organizational structure. The Episcopal Church, which has its greatest strength in numbers in the Northeast, is the American branch of the Anglican Church. Episcopalians, who cherish high-church religious rituals, traditionally

have long been more socioeconomically advantaged than other mainline denominations. The Evangelical Lutheran Church in America
(ELCA) was the result of a 1987 merger of three smaller Lutheran
bodies (the American Lutheran Church, the Association of Evangelical
Lutheran Churches, and the Lutheran Church in America) that originally served immigrants affiliated with Scandinavian state churches.
Today the ELCA is a politically moderate-to-liberal denomination whose
numeric strength lies in the Midwest. The Presbyterian Church (USA),
with its roots in the theological teachings of John Calvin, is the most
liberal of America's Presbyterian denominations today. Also steeped in
Calvinism is the politically moderate Reformed Church in America,
whose early adherents were immigrants from the Reformed Church in
the Netherlands. Many of its current members still retain Dutch ances-
tral ties. The most liberal mainline Protestant denomination is the
United Church of Christ, which was the result of a merger of five
different denominational traditions in 1957, including the historic
Congregational Church (founded by the Puritans) and several off-
shoots of Reformed and Lutheran Church families. Finally, the largest
and most diverse denomination within mainline Protestantism is the
United Methodist Church, which began as a revival movement in
the Episcopal Church in the eighteenth century (Guth et al. 1997;
Smidt 2004).

The history of mainline Protestantism in the United States has been
one of great advantage, access, and privilege. Mainline Protestants
enjoyed a large measure of hegemony in American society over many
generations, and historically many of America's socioeconomic elites
have been mainline Protestants (Roof and McKinney 1987; Wuthnow
1988). Mainline Protestants today remain better educated than the
American population at large, and they tend to occupy higher-paying,
higher-status jobs than the average American worker (Park and
Reimer 2002; Smith and Faris 2005; Wuthnow and Evans 2002).
Moreover, mainline Protestant churches are typically among the oldest
and most socially prestigious congregations in every American city
(see Wellman 1999). These socioeconomic advantages have brought
mainline Protestants ample access to the channels of political power in
the United States. Indeed, members of this religious tradition often
occupy many of those channels of power.

In recent decades, however, mainline Protestantism's position as a
cornerstone of American society has been challenged. The flowering of
evangelical Protestantism has stolen some of mainline Protestantism's
share of the American religious marketplace (Finke and Stark 1992;
Hammond 1992; Iannaccone 1994; Kelley 1977; Wuthnow 1996). At

the same time, increasing numbers of Americans are becoming secular or embracing non-Western religious traditions and new religious movements (Bellah et al. 1985; Fowler et al. 2004; Gallagher 2004; Roof 1999). It is an undeniable fact that mainline Protestant denominations have experienced some membership losses. Between 1965 and 1990, the Episcopal Church, the Presbyterian Church (USA), and the United Church of Christ each lost roughly 25 percent of their members (Wuthnow and Evans 2002).

Nevertheless, mainline Protestantism has not disappeared from the American landscape. Today there are an estimated 21.7 million mainline Protestants in the United States, which accounts for roughly 22 percent of the U.S. population (Kohut et al. 2000; Wuthnow and Evans 2002). According to Robert Wuthnow, a majority of these mainline Protestants perceive neither a widespread numeric decline nor a decrease in their religious tradition's public influence (Wuthnow 2000; Wuthnow and Evans 2002). Wuthnow further characterizes mainline Protestantism as having a "quiet" influence on American society and politics (Wuthnow 2000; Wuthnow and Evans 2002). Mainline denominations and congregations serve the spiritual and social needs of millions of American families each week. They also fight outside the physical walls of their churches for social justice at both the national and grassroots levels, and although their work is done primarily out of the limelight, it is unfair to say that they are no longer an important political force (Wuthnow and Evans 2002).

Politically speaking, American Protestantism reached a crossroads in the 1920s when industrialism and modernization brought challenges to traditional religious modes of understanding. Protestants disagreed intensely about the extent to which religious beliefs ought to be reconciled with expanding scientific knowledge and with modernity in general. Most of the mainline Protestant establishment adapted quickly and accepted the modernization of secular society. This adaptation required the abandonment of some traditional religious perspectives, including literal scriptural interpretation, which drove away members who wished to preserve more traditional worldviews (Marty 1970; Thuesen 2002). The accommodation to modernity also gave rise to the Social Gospel movement within mainline Protestantism, which emphasized the need for congregations and their members to become more active in "this world" by serving the less fortunate (Niebuhr 1951; Thuesen 2002; Wuthnow 1988).

Mainline Protestants today are still experiencing the residual effects of this 1920s-era bifurcation within Protestantism. They retain their open and tolerant approach to scriptural interpretation. Clergy are not seen as the authoritative and final arbiters on most issues, whether theological, social, or political. This outlook is exemplified quite clearly by television advertisements run by the United Methodist Church since 2003 in which it advertises itself as a denomination of "open hearts, open minds, [and] open doors." Mainline Protestants also retain a strong emphasis on working to achieve justice for the disadvantaged, and their denominations often espouse broad liberal political agendas.

Mainline Protestants in American Politics

Mainline Protestantism is best characterized by its long-standing emphasis on social justice, especially among clergy and denominational leaders, and its equally long history of Republican voting preferences and party identification on the part of those in the pews. For the most part, mainline Protestants refused to join President Franklin D. Roosevelt's New Deal coalition, in part because the coalition included Catholics. Many mainline Protestant leaders of the early twentieth century espoused staunchly anti-Catholic views rooted in xenophobia (Kohut et al. 2000; Wuthnow 1988). As anti-Catholic sentiment fell away by mid-century, however, mainline leaders came to embrace equality and tolerance as central political ideals. The politics of mainline leaders grew increasingly liberal as the twentieth century progressed, in conjunction with the liberalization of mainline Protestant seminaries (Carroll et al. 1997; Wuthnow 1988). Scholars soon began identifying and evaluating a "new breed" of leftist mainline clergy (Hadden 1969; Guth et al. 1997; Quinley 1974). Yet for the most part, mainline laity remained solidly in the Republican camp well into the later years of the twentieth century, in large part because they were socioeconomic elites who wanted to protect their financial interests (Layman 2001; Manza and Brooks 1999, 2002).

The roots of mainline Protestantism's leftward political turn lie in the 1920s, when it embraced the Social Gospel movement (Guth et al. 1997; Marty 1970; Wuthnow 1988), a theological and political perspective that emphasized the need to work for social transformation rather than focusing strictly on spiritual conversion and personal sanctification. Many of the modernist faithful rallied to the cause of social reform, emphasizing the need to bring the kingdom of God to earth by helping the poor and disadvantaged in this world (Marty 1970; Niebuhr 1951; Thuesen 2002; Wuthnow 1988).

This imperative to reform society by correcting its injustices was reinvigorated in the 1950s and 1960s when thousands of mainline Protestants, particularly from the North, linked arms with African Americans in their struggle for civil rights in the South (Campbell and Pettigrew 1959; Findlay 1993; Friedland 1998). Guiding this activism was a widely accepted image of Jesus Christ as a champion for the poor and disadvantaged. When Northern mainline Protestants, many of whom were lifelong Republicans, went South to aid the Civil Rights Movement, they naturally found themselves clashing with the white Southern power structures. Because the Southern polity was run uniformly by the Democratic Party, many mainline activists were able to retain their ties to the Republican Party while still fighting for what some perceived to be a "liberal" cause. The Democratic Party, of course, was by no means a liberal entity in the South in the civil rights era (Black and Black 2002).

Mainline Protestantism's involvement in civil rights activism gave rise to subsequent efforts to transform society. Many mainline clergy engaged in protests against the war in Vietnam (Hall 1992; Quinley 1974), which then led to organized activism against the policies of President Ronald Reagan during the 1980s. Despite the fact that many mainline laity remained staunch Republicans, hundreds of mainline Protestant clergy and denominational leaders resisted the Reagan administration through their participation in the nuclear freeze movement and the Sanctuary Movement, which was designed to give shelter to refugees of war-torn Latin America, where the Central Intelligence Agency was working to overthrow various socialist governments (Hertzke 1988; Smith 1996).

Since the 1980s, mainline Protestants have been less visible on the national political stage than they were a generation ago, but this does not mean that they no longer have an active hand in politics (Wuthnow 2000; Wuthnow and Evans 2002). All of the mainline Protestant denominations retain lobbying offices in Washington, DC (Hertzke 1988; Hofrenning 1995; Olson 2002), and their political and social outreach increasingly has focused on addressing injustice at the local level, especially regarding the causes and consequences of poverty (Ammerman 2005; Chaves 2004; Cnaan 1999, 2002; Djupe and Gilbert 2003; Olson, Crawford, and Deckman 2005; Steensland 2002; Warren 2001; Wellman 1999). In part, this shift in emphasis has been a result of the federal government's devolution of policy authority to the states as well as recent enthusiasm for the work that faith-based organizations undertake to address social problems at the local level (Black, Koopman, and Ryden 2004; Cnaan 1999, 2002). Other factors contributing to this turn toward antipoverty work at the grassroots level have included the decay of cities that resulted from the drift of the middle class to the suburbs and the increase in poverty and homelessness that began in the 1980s.

A political gap began to divide liberal mainline clergy from their conservative laity during the second half of the twentieth century, which frustrated many politically oriented ministers who found their rank-and-file congregation members unwilling to mobilize for social-justice-oriented causes (Adams 1970; Hertzke 1988; Jelen 1993; Koller and Retzer 1980). Despite ideological disagreements, however, generations of mainline Protestants have agreed about the value of civic engagement (Chaves, Giesel, and Tsitsos 2002; Guth et al. 1997; Quinley 1974; Wuthnow 1988). Working on behalf of the less fortunate, staying abreast of political issues and debates, and voting are all highly valued by mainline Protestants.

One of the most significant political trends that we have observed among mainline Protestants lately is the fact that the twenty-first century is pushing them ever further toward the Democratic Party (Green 2004; Green et al. 2004; Kohut et al. 2000; Leege et al. 2002; Manza and Brooks 2002). This shift in partisanship most likely has been a reaction against the strong alliance between the Republican Party and evangelical Protestants in recent decades. Mainline Protestants appear to be reevaluating their ties to the Republican Party as the Republicans increasingly emphasize moral conservatism in their rhetoric and policy initiatives. It is now fair to say that mainline Protestants make up an important swing constituency, even though they are not collectively mobilized on the basis of their religious affiliation. Many of President Bill Clinton's 1996 "soccer moms," for example, were undoubtedly mainline Protestants.

Mainline Protestantism and George W. Bush

A question worth exploring is whether the George W. Bush administration pushed mainline Protestants even further away from the Republican Party. Bush appears to be a leader who relies heavily on his religious convictions (Aikman 2004; Caldwell 2004; Cooperman 2004; Kengor 2004). Yet, some scholars claim that Bush's personal faith has no bearing on how he governs from the Oval Office. Instead, religion serves as a source of personal strength for Bush as he copes with the stress of serving as president (Renshon 2004). Regardless of the specific role of religion in Bush's presidency, it is clear that he has been a polarizing figure within the Washington community and among the American public at large, at least in part because he has made his spirituality and religious commitment so public. Mainline Protestants tend to be rather private about open expressions of faith, which may have made Bush somewhat less attractive to them as a candidate and as a president.

Nonetheless, George W. Bush maintains strong ties to mainline Protestantism. Bush was raised Episcopalian, but he is now a committed United Methodist. He maintains especially close ties with Reverend Mark Craig, pastor of Highland Park United Methodist Church in Dallas (Aikman 2004). Bush also named many mainline Protestants to positions of prominence during his presidency (Kengor 2004; Mansfield 2003), such as Vice President Dick Cheney (a lifelong United Methodist), National Security Advisor and later Secretary of State Condoleezza Rice (whose father was a Presbyterian minister), former Chief of Staff Andrew Card (whose wife is a United Methodist minister), and former counselor to the president Karen Hughes (who has served as an elder in her Presbyterian congregation).

When Bush was a young man, personal faith and religiosity partially served as the moral ties that bound the George H. W. Bush family together. George W. Bush's parents immersed their children in the values, beliefs, and philosophies of mainline Protestantism, particularly in their own Episcopalian faith. As privileged, educated, wealthy northeasterners, the Bush family was well acquainted with the mainline Protestant virtue of noblesse oblige. This value was exemplified by George H. W. Bush's emphasis on volunteerism when he asked Americans to volunteer their time to help others and thus comprise "a thousand points of light." However, George W. Bush's personal faith throughout his life has not been rooted in one particular religious tradition, but instead has been formed from a diversified experience with many manifestations of Protestantism. Bush attended worship services at the First Presbyterian Church as a child while growing up in Midland, Texas, and once his family moved to Houston in 1959, he attended St. Martin's Episcopal Church (Aikman 2004; Bush 1999). Eventually, Bush followed his wife Laura's Methodist faith by becoming a member of the First United Methodist Church of Midland (Mansfield 2003).

Today, Bush remains a United Methodist, but when he speaks of his personal faith, he uses the terminology and rhetorical styling of evangelical Protestantism rather than that of mainline Protestantism. Just as Bill Clinton did not resemble evangelical Protestants in many ways despite being a lifelong Southern Baptist, George W. Bush is also not an exemplar of mainline Protestantism. Furthermore, mainline Protestant support has not always been a guarantee for President Bush. In fact, the United Methodist Church ran television advertisements before the beginning of the war in Iraq in which it specifically stated its opposition to Bush's foreign policy.

In addition, Bush's domestic policy has not won him widespread support from mainline Protestants. During the 2000 presidential election campaign, candidate Bush frequently told voters that if elected he would incorporate his ideals of "compassionate conservatism," which were formulated by Marvin Olasky, Bush's supporter and a journalism professor at the University of Texas. One of the pillars of Bush's compassionate conservatism was the contention that the contemporary social welfare state, first enacted during the Franklin Roosevelt administration and later developed during President Lyndon Johnson's War on Poverty, could no longer meet the demands placed on government in the twenty-first century. According to this philosophy, welfare payments create financial dependency on government among welfare recipients. Instead, Bush viewed Christian, Jewish, and Muslim religious organizations as outlets that could assist government in dispensing social welfare programs more effectively and efficiently. These organizations also serve as core repositories for "spiritual and intellectual empowerment" that could break a recipient's reliance on welfare in the long term (Hilliard, Lansford, and Watson 2004; Kengor 2004; Kessler 2004; Minutaglio 1999; Olasky 2000). While compassionate conservatism may resonate with the virtue of noblesse oblige, it is inconsistent with mainline Protestantism's more recent view that government should take direct responsibility for the poor and dispossessed (Steensland 2002). Based on this notion, Bush's connection of religion to politics is not reflective of contemporary mainline Protestant social and political thought.

Mainline Protestants and the 2004 Presidential Election

We now present a portrait of mainline Protestants' political orientations based on an analysis of the National Election Studies (NES) data for the 2004 presidential election year.[1] In our analysis, we classify mainline Protestants as respondents who self-identified themselves as members of one of the following eight mainline Protestant denominations: American Baptist Churches (USA), Disciples of Christ, Episcopal Church, Evangelical Lutheran Church in America, Presbyterian Church (USA), Reformed Church in America, United Church of Christ, and

Table 4.1   Religion and Ideology, 2004

	Liberal (%)	Moderate (%)	Conservative (%)
Mainline Protestants	20.0	31.4	48.6
Evangelical Protestants	14.8	28.0	57.2
African American Protestants	22.0	47.5	30.5
Catholic	29.4	35.1	35.5
Jewish	51.5	18.2	30.3
Other	33.3	33.3	33.3
None	41.0	28.8	30.2

Note: $N = 1,049$, where N stands for sample size. Percentages are based on a standard ideology measure that asks respondents to self-identify themselves as liberal, moderate, or conservative.

Source: National Election Studies (NES) 2004.

the United Methodist Church.[2] Mainline Protestants accounted for 15.0 percent of the 2004 NES sample.

We begin by assessing mainline Protestants' general orientations toward politics as they compare with other major American religious groups. As we might expect, mainline Protestants on the whole are a rather diverse group in terms of ideology and issue positions on public policy. Table 4.1 shows that 20.0 percent of mainline Protestants in the 2004 NES sample classified their political ideology as liberal, whereas nearly half (48.6 percent) reported that they were conservative. Evangelical Protestants were more likely than their mainline counterparts to classify themselves as conservative (57.2 percent), but notice that only 30.5 percent of African American Protestants and 35.5 percent of Catholics claimed they were conservative.

In order to move beyond basic self-reported ideology, we are also interested in determining the extent to which mainline Protestants identify themselves with two general sets of political values: egalitarianism and moral traditionalism. The long-standing emphasis on equality and social justice within mainline Protestantism leads us to expect that mainline Protestants value the general notion of egalitarianism rather highly. On the other hand, we also expect mainline Protestants to be somewhat less committed to moral traditionalism because of their churches' emphasis on diversity and social tolerance. To test these hypotheses, we constructed an additive "egalitarianism" index based on six statements included in the 2004 NES survey. The survey asked respondents to report their level of agreement with each item:

1. "Our society should do whatever is necessary to make sure that everyone has an equal opportunity to succeed" (greater agreement indicates greater egalitarianism).

2. "We have gone too far in pushing equal rights in this country" (greater disagreement indicates greater egalitarianism).
3. "One of the big problems in this country is that we don't give everyone an equal chance" (greater agreement indicates greater egalitarianism).
4. "This country would be better off if we worried less about how equal people are" (greater disagreement indicates greater egalitarianism).
5. "It is not really that big a problem if some people have more of a chance in life than others" (greater disagreement indicates greater egalitarianism).
6. "If people were treated more equally in this country we would have many fewer problems" (greater agreement indicates greater egalitarianism).

Respondents recorded their level of agreement with each statement using a five-point response set (agree strongly, agree somewhat, neither agree nor disagree, disagree somewhat, disagree strongly). We coded responses so that respondents received higher scores for more egalitarian opinions. The minimum score on the egalitarianism index is 6, while the maximum is 30. As table 4.2 shows, mainline Protestants' average score (20.6) was slightly lower than the average for the entire sample (21.1), which is somewhat surprising, but they were also far more egalitarian than evangelicals (19.9). In addition, the level of egalitarianism expressed by mainline Protestants is very similar to the level for that of Catholics.

We also constructed an additive "moral traditionalism" index based on four NES items. The 2004 NES survey asked respondents to report their level of agreement with each item:

1. "The world is always changing and we should adjust our view of moral behavior to those changes" (greater disagreement indicates greater moral traditionalism).
2. "The newer lifestyles are contributing to the breakdown of our society" (greater agreement indicates greater moral traditionalism).
3. "We should be more tolerant of people who choose to live according to their own moral standards, even if they are very different from our own" (greater disagreement indicates greater moral traditionalism).
4. "This country would have many fewer problems if there were more emphasis on traditional family ties" (greater agreement indicates greater moral traditionalism).

Table 4.2   Religion and Level of Egalitarianism, 2004

	Average Score
Mainline Protestants	20.6
Evangelical Protestants	19.9
African American Protestants	24.2
Catholic	20.8
Jewish	22.4
Other	22.0
None	21.5
Overall sample	21.1

Note: $F = 14.4$; $p < 0.001$; $N = 1,046$. The F statistic is a statistical measure of the size of the differences among the average scores; p is the probability that the F statistic would be as large as it is if there were no significant differences among the averages in the table. Because p is less than 0.05, we can assume that the differences among these averages is statistically significant. N is the total sample size. Scores are based on an additive index of six survey items that assess the extent to which respondents express egalitarian attitudes. Possible index scores range from 6 to 30, with higher scores representing greater egalitarianism.

Source: National Election Studies (NES) 2004.

As with the egalitarianism index, respondents recorded their level of agreement with each of these four statements using a five-point response set (agree strongly, agree somewhat, neither agree nor disagree, disagree somewhat, disagree strongly). We coded responses so that respondents received higher scores for more morally traditionalist opinions. The minimum score on the moral traditionalism index is 4, while the maximum is 20. Table 4.3 reveals that mainline Protestants were just slightly more traditionalist (13.7) than the sample at large (13.0), but also much less traditionalist than evangelical Protestants (14.4). What this analysis shows us is that mainline Protestants should by no means be viewed as either a conservative or a liberal monolith. While they are, on the whole, less conservative than evangelicals, they are also quite a bit more conservative than some of the other major American religious groups. What is perhaps most striking is how close mainline Protestants' mean scores on both scales are to the overall sample means, which provides tentative evidence of their status as a moderate swing constituency.

The 2004 NES also asked respondents their opinions about a range of hot-button policy issues, including same-sex marriage, abortion, and proposals that called for the privatization of Social Security. Same-sex

Table 4.3 Religion and Level of Moral Traditionalism, 2004

	Average Score
Mainline Protestants	13.7
Evangelical Protestants	14.4
African American Protestants	13.0
Catholic	12.9
Jewish	9.9
Other	13.0
None	10.6
Overall sample	13.0

Note: $F = 26.3$; $p < 0.001$; $N = 1,047$. The F statistic is a statistical measure of the size of the differences among the average scores; p is the probability that the F statistic would be as large as it is if there were no significant differences among the averages in the table. Because p is less than 0.05, we can assume that the differences among these averages is statistically significant. N is the total sample size. Scores are based on an additive index of four survey items that assess the extent to which respondents express morally traditionalist attitudes. Possible index scores range from 4 to 20, with higher scores representing greater moral traditionalism.

Source: National Election Studies (NES) 2004.

marriage was the leading social issue of the 2004 election cycle, with voters in 11 states deciding whether to allow same-sex unions in their states (all 11 referenda failed). Although mainline Protestants are deeply divided on the subject of homosexuality, all of the mainline denominations have engaged in recent debates about the place of gays and lesbians in their churches. As a result, this issue is well defined and personalized for many mainline Protestants (Cadge 2002). Support for same-sex marriage, of course, should be expected to propel mainline Protestants toward the Democratic Party.

Table 4.4 displays the relationship between religious background and opinions about same-sex marriage. Again we find that mainline Protestants are politically moderate on this heated social issue. They are substantially more tolerant on the issue than their morally traditionalist evangelical and African American Protestant counterparts, but they are also more conservative than members of non-Protestant religious traditions, including Catholics, whose religious leaders have officially denounced homosexuality as immoral. It is noteworthy that a rather large number of mainline Protestants (8.0 percent) firmly favor civil unions but not actual same-sex

Table 4.4   Religion and Opinions about Same-Sex Marriage, 2004

	Oppose (%)	Favor Civil Unions (%)	Favor (%)
Mainline Protestants	60.5	8.0	31.5
Evangelical Protestants	79.7	2.7	17.1
African American Protestants	75.0	1.5	23.5
Catholic	57.8	3.4	38.8
Jewish	20.0	8.6	71.4
Other	52.7	3.6	43.6
None	38.2	2.2	59.6

Note: N = 1,134. N is the total sample size. Percentages are based on responses to the question "Should same-sex couples be allowed to marry, or do you think they should not be allowed to marry?"

Source: National Election Studies (NES) 2004.

marriage when answering this survey question, which represents a moderate, compromising position on this issue.

Abortion never disappears from the political agenda, particularly in an election year. The debate over late-term or partial-birth abortion was fresh in voters' minds in 2004. Mainline Protestant leaders typically do not teach the "abortion is murder" message that is frequently offered in evangelical and Catholic circles. Therefore, we might expect mainline Protestants to be more polarized around the issue than members of other religious traditions. Finally, one's opinion about privatizing Social Security might be viewed as a referendum on the Bush presidency, as President Bush made his privatization proposal a centerpiece of his reelection campaign, as well as a general statement of one's general economic conservatism. We would expect mainline Protestants to favor privatizing Social Security due to their historic embrace of fiscal conservatism.

The results regarding abortion as shown in table 4.5 reveal an even greater leap toward liberalism on the part of mainline Protestants. Only 7.1 percent say that they oppose abortion in all instances, whereas 39.0 percent favor it in all instances. Only Jews (88.5 percent) and seculars (58.1 percent) report more consistently pro-choice attitudes toward abortion. Abortion would therefore appear to be one of the issues most responsible for the political cleavage between mainline Protestants and members of other American religious traditions, especially evangelical Protestants.

Table 4.6 illustrates the relationship between religious tradition and level of support for privatizing Social Security. One finding that stands out in this table is the relatively small number of mainline Protestants

Table 4.5 Religion and Opinions about Abortion, 2004

	Always Oppose (%)	Favor in Cases of Rape or Incest (%)	Favor in Cases Where There Is Any Established Need (%)	Always Favor (%)
Mainline Protestants	7.1	32.5	21.4	39.0
Evangelical Protestants	23.3	36.4	16.7	23.6
African American Protestants	14.8	36.1	16.4	32.8
Catholic	14.0	33.5	17.9	34.6
Jewish	0.0	7.7	3.8	88.5
Other	10.6	36.2	17.0	36.2
None	13.2	31.9	17.8	58.1

Note: $N = 1,036$. N is the total sample size. Percentages are based on responses to the question "There has been some discussion about abortion during recent years. Which one of the opinions on this page best agrees with your view?"

Source: National Election Studies (NES), 2004.

Table 4.6 Religion and Opinions about Privatizing Social Security, 2004

	Favor (%)	No Opinion (%)	Oppose (%)
Mainline Protestants	45.9	28.0	26.1
Evangelical Protestants	48.4	33.9	17.7
African American Protestants	33.1	41.3	25.6
Catholic	48.1	24.6	27.3
Jewish	29.6	22.2	48.1
Other	28.0	44.0	28.0
None	38.5	29.5	32.1

Note: $N = 1,048$. N refers to the total sample size. Percentages are based on responses to the question "A proposal has been made that would allow people to put a portion of their Social Security payroll taxes into personal retirement accounts that would be invested in private stocks and bonds. Do you favor this idea, oppose it, or neither favor nor oppose it?"

Source: National Election Studies (NES) 2004.

(28.0 percent) who have no opinion on this matter. This may reflect mainline Protestants' generally high levels of educational attainment and their facility with political information. We see that mainline Protestants were almost twice as likely to favor privatizing Social Security as they were to oppose it, which again might reflect their long-standing economic conservatism. Inconsistent with their moderate-to-liberal attitudes on social issues such as abortion and (to a lesser extent) same-sex marriage, we see that mainline Protestants tend to exhibit more conservative views regarding economic policy.

How did mainline Protestants feel about the first term of the George W. Bush presidency? In particular, how did they feel about the way President Bush handled high-profile public policy issues? The NES included items measuring respondents' attitudes regarding Bush's handling of the economy, foreign relations, the federal budget deficit, the War on Terror, and the Iraq War. Table 4.7 provides the percentages of each major American religious group that disapproved of Bush's handling of these five issues. Mainline and evangelical Protestants nearly mirror one another regarding their views about Bush's handling of economic issues. In fact, no religious group was more approving of Bush's handling of the economy in general than mainline Protestants. When it comes to foreign policy, however, mainline Protestants were substantially more critical of Bush than were their evangelical counterparts. This divergence is particularly clear regarding the war in Iraq. Half of all mainline Protestants, but only 39.9 percent of evangelicals, disapproved of Bush's handling of the war.

We now assess how mainline Protestants' evident move away from conservatism on a variety of public policy issues translates into partisan politics. Table 4.8 reveals that mainline Protestants were much more likely than evangelicals to identify themselves as Democrats (28.3 percent compared to 17.4 percent). Although a

Table 4.7　Religion and Disapproval of President George W. Bush's Handling of Public Policy Issues, 2004

	The Economy (%)	Budget Deficit (%)	Foreign Relations (%)	War on Terror (%)	War in Iraq (%)
Mainline Protestants	45.7	58.8	49.1	35.8	50.8
Evangelical Protestants	47.0	53.2	35.6	27.5	39.9
African American Protestants	89.4	89.4	88.5	78.7	89.5
Catholic	60.2	68.3	57.4	43.7	57.9
Jewish	78.8	90.0	65.7	57.2	71.7
Other	66.7	79.1	71.2	64.7	72.3
None	67.0	71.3	65.9	55.4	64.1
N	1,157	1,061	1,158	1,164	1,177

Note: N is the total sample size. Percentages are based on a series of questions asking respondents to assess the extent to which they "approve or disapprove of the way George W. Bush is handling" a series of public policy issues. Percentages do not sum to 100 because they reflect the proportion of each religious group that disapproved of Bush's handling of each issue.

Source: National Election Studies (NES) 2004.

Table 4.8 Religion and Partisanship, 2004

	Democrat (%)	Independent (%)	Republican (%)
Mainline Protestants	28.3	34.4	37.2
Evangelical Protestants	17.4	37.2	45.4
African American Protestants	67.6	32.4	0.0
Catholic	32.2	38.1	29.8
Jewish	60.0	22.9	17.1
Other	25.5	52.7	21.8
None	29.5	49.4	21.0

Note: N = 1,057. N is the total sample size. Percentages are based on standard partisanship measures that ask respondents to self-identify themselves as Democrats, Independents, or Republicans.

Source: National Election Studies (NES) 2004.

Table 4.9 Religion and Presidential Vote, 2004

	George W. Bush (%)	John F. Kerry (%)
Mainline Protestants	59.0	41.0
Evangelical Protestants	72.1	26.5
African American Protestants	6.3	92.6
Catholic	48.0	50.0
Jewish	24.0	76.0
Other	42.9	54.3
None	47.1	50.4

Note: N = 444. N is the total sample size. Percentages indicate respondents' self-reported voting behavior in the 2004 presidential election. Percentages do not sum to 100 because candidates other than Bush and Kerry are not included in this table.

Source: National Election Studies (NES) 2004.

sizable number of mainline Protestants do appear to have an affinity for both conservatism and the Republican Party, they are strikingly more moderate on both counts than evangelicals. Fifty years ago, mainline Protestants would have appeared to be far more conservative than virtually every other American religious group (Layman 2001). Today, however, they display a good deal of diversity in their political orientations.

How did mainline Protestants vote on Election Day in 2004? As table 4.9 shows, John F. Kerry received 41.0 percent of the mainline Protestant vote but only 26.5 percent of the evangelical Protestant vote. According to the NES, George W. Bush received a majority of mainline Protestant votes (59.0 percent), but the contest between the two candidates was much closer among mainline Protestants than it was among evangelicals (72.1 percent of whom voted for Bush). Another study, however, concludes that the mainline Protestant vote was split evenly between the two presidential candidates, and that Kerry enjoyed the overwhelming support of "modernist" (those least adherent to tradition) mainline Protestants (Green et al. 2004). The 2004 NES data also show that mainline Protestants who hold the least orthodox views about scripture were far more likely to vote for Kerry (55.6 percent) than theologically traditionalist mainline Protestants (35.9 percent). These "modernists" were also far more likely to claim both a liberal ideology and a Democratic Party affiliation, although these results should be interpreted with caution because of small sample-size concerns (data not shown).

Since mainline Protestant voters clearly were not well mobilized for either candidate in 2004, we must ask whether it would be valuable for either party to court them aggressively in future elections. The key to answering this question lies in knowing whether mainline Protestants are likely to participate heavily in politics compared to other religious groups—and we know that one of the historic corner-stones of mainline Protestantism has been its long-standing commitment to civic engagement. In many congregations, social—and even political—action is not just tolerated; it is often de rigueur (Djupe and Gilbert 2003; Jelen 1993; Olson 2000; Wuthnow and Evans 2002). Indeed, we find that mainline Protestants were more likely than any other major American religious group aside from Jews to say that they were "very much interested" in the 2004 elections, and they were substantially more interested in the campaign season than evangelical Protestants (56.3 percent compared to 48.6 percent, data not shown). We also constructed an additive political participation index that consists of seven items: trying to influence the vote choice of other individuals; attending campaign meetings, rallies, or speeches; display-ing a campaign button, sticker, or sign; campaigning for a political party or candidate; contributing money to a candidate; contributing money to a political party; and contributing money to any other political group, such as a political action committee.

Respondents received one point for each activity they reported under-taking; the maximum score on the participation index is therefore 7. The higher a respondent's score on this index, the more he or she participated in politics during the 2004 campaign season.

Mainline Protestants outrank every other religious group on the par-ticipation index except for Jews and members of religious traditions

Table 4.10 Religion and Political Participation Beyond Voting, 2004

	Average Score
Mainline Protestants	1.11
Evangelical Protestants	1.02
African American Protestants	0.80
Catholic	1.04
Jewish	2.00
Other	1.14
None	1.11
Overall sample	1.06

Note: $F = 3.56$; $p < 0.01$; $N = 1,052$. The F statistic is a statistical measure of the size of the differences among the average scores; p is the probability that the F statistic would be as large as it is if there were no significant differences among the averages in the table. Because p is less than 0.05, we can assume that the differences among these averages is statistically significant. N is the total sample size. Scores are based on an additive index of seven survey items that assess the extent to which respondents participated in politics beyond voting in the 2004 presidential election. Respondents received one point for each of seven forms of political participation in which they reported engaging. The maximum score on the index is therefore 7.

Source: National Election Studies (NES) 2004.

outside of Christianity and Judaism, as table 4.10 shows. As such, it is fair to conclude that mainline Protestants ought not to be ignored as a constituency in American politics. They might not make up as large a proportion of the electorate as they did a generation or two ago, but they vote and increasingly have become a swing constituency in the American electorate, which means that either party would benefit from attempting to appeal to them.

Conclusion

Our analysis indicates that mainline voters were both moderate (especially on social issues) and politically active during the 2004 presidential election year. Although our sample was too small to allow us to subdivide mainline Protestants into specific denominations, a growing body of literature (see Green et al. 2004) shows that the most modernist mainline Protestants are moving most rapidly into the Democratic Party. This partisan shift is significant in light of the long-standing

Republicanism of the mainline community, but it is indicative of two important trends in American politics.

The first of these trends is that denominationalism on its own does not predict either partisanship or political behavior to the extent that it did through the first half of the twentieth century (Green 2004; Green et al. 2004; Kohut et al. 2000; Layman 2001; Leege et al. 2002; Wuthnow 1988). Until the post–World War II era, it was reasonably safe to assume that all white Protestants would vote for Republican candidates, whereas Catholics, Jews, and African American Protestants would vote for Democrats (Herberg 1955). In more recent decades, however, the cultural ties holding some American religious groups together have diminished. This loss of collective identity has left such groups (especially mainline Protestants and Catholics) open to mobilization by either party (Leege et al. 2002).

The second emerging trend is that liberal mainline Protestants may be ripe for mobilization by Democratic candidates who can connect their policy goals with the mainline emphasis on fighting for social justice. Our analysis shows that there are at least some mainline Protestants who are disenchanted with George W. Bush, the Republican Party, and its emphasis on morality politics. These individuals could become an important constituency for the Democratic Party if Democratic candidates can reach them through their political rhetoric. However, at this point, it is not clear whether the Democratic Party fully realizes that mainline Protestants are becoming a religious swing constituency. Both John Kerry and John Edwards spoke briefly of the immorality of poverty on the campaign trail in 2004, but religion was not a major campaign theme for the Democrats. This lack of attention may have been an electoral mistake, at least in terms of attracting the votes of liberal mainline Protestants.

Notes

1. The National Election Studies (NES), Center for Political Studies, University of Michigan. Electronic resources from the NES Web site, http://www.umich.edu/~nes, University of Michigan, Center for Political Studies (producer and distributor), Ann Arbor, MI, 1995–2004. These materials are based on work supported by the National Science Foundation under grant numbers SBR-9707741, SBR-9317631, SES-9209410, SES-9009379, SES-8808361, SES-8341310, SES-8207580, and SOC77–08885. Any opinions, findings, conclusions, or recommendations expressed in these materials are those of the authors and do not necessarily reflect those of the National Science Foundation.

2. For a useful discussion of how to classify survey respondents according to their religious affiliation, see Steensland et al. (2000).

References

Adams, James L. 1970. *The Growing Church Lobby in Washington.* Grand Rapids, MI: Eerdmans.

Aikman, David. 2004. *A Man of Faith: An Inside Look at the Faith of the President and Its Impact on the World.* Nashville, TN: Thomas Nelson.

Ammerman, Nancy T. 2005. *Pillars of Faith: American Congregations and Their Partners.* Berkeley, CA: University of California Press.

Bellah, Robert N., Richard Madsen, William M. Sullivan, Ann Swidler, and Steven M. Tipton. 1985. *Habits of the Heart: Individualism and Commitment in American Life.* San Francisco, CA: Harper and Row.

Black, Amy E., Douglas L. Koopman, and David K. Ryden. 2004. *Of Little Faith: The Politics of George W. Bush's Faith-Based Initiatives.* Washington, DC: Georgetown University Press.

Black, Earl, and Merle Black. 2002. *The Rise of Southern Republicans.* Cambridge, MA: Belknap Press of Harvard University Press.

Bush, George W. 1999. *A Charge to Keep.* New York: William Morrow.

Cadge, Wendy. 2002. "Vital Conflicts: The Mainline Protestant Denominations Debate Homosexuality." In *The Quiet Hand of God: Faith-Based Activism and the Public Role of Mainline Protestantism,* edited by Robert Wuthnow and John H. Evans. Berkeley, CA: University of California Press.

Caldwell, Deborah. 2004. "An Evolving Faith." Beliefnet.com, October 30. http://www.beliefnet.com/story/121/story_12112_1.html (last accessed July 15, 2006).

Campbell, Ernest Q., and Thomas F. Pettigrew. 1959. *Christians in Racial Crisis: A Study of Little Rock's Ministry.* Washington, DC: Public Affairs.

Carroll, Jackson W., Barbara G. Wheeler, Daniel O. Aleshire, and Penny Long Marler. 1997. *Being There: Culture and Formation in Two Theological Schools.* New York: Oxford University Press.

Chaves, Mark. 2004. *Congregations in America.* Cambridge, MA: Harvard University Press.

Chaves, Mark, Helen M. Giesel, and William Tsitsos. 2002. "Religious Variations in Public Presence: Evidence from the National Congregations Study." In *The Quiet Hand of God: Faith-Based Activism and the Public Role of Mainline Protestantism,* edited by Robert Wuthnow and John H. Evans. Berkeley, CA: University of California Press.

Cnaan, Ram A. 1999. *The Newer Deal: Social Work and Religion in Partnership.* New York: Columbia University Press.

——— 2002. *The Invisible Caring Hand: American Congregations and the Provision of Welfare.* New York: New York University Press.

Cooperman, Alan. 2004. "Openly Religious, To a Point." *Washington Post*, September16, A1.

Djupe, Paul A., and Christopher P. Gilbert. 2003. *The Prophetic Pulpit: Clergy, Churches, and Communities in American Politics*. Lanham, MD: Rowman and Littlefield.

Findlay, James F., Jr. 1993. *Church People in the Struggle: The National Council of Churches and the Black Freedom Movement, 1950–1970*. New York: Oxford University Press.

Finke, Roger, and Rodney Stark. 1992. *The Churching of America, 1776–1990: Winners and Losers in Our Religious Economy*. New Brunswick, NJ: Rutgers University Press.

Fowler, Robert Booth, Allen D. Hertzke, Laura R. Olson, and Kevin R. den Dulk. 2004. *Religion and Politics in America: Faith, Culture, and Strategic Choices*. 3rd ed. Boulder, CO: Westview.

Friedland, Michael B. 1998. *Lift Up Your Voice Like a Trumpet: White Clergy and the Civil Rights and Antiwar Movements, 1954–1973*. Chapel Hill, NC: University of North Carolina Press.

Gallagher, Eugene V. 2004. *The New Religious Movements Experience in America*. Westport, CT: Greenwood.

Green, John C. 2004. "The American Religious Landscape and Political Attitudes: A Baseline for 2004." http://www.uakron.edu/bliss/research.php (last accessed February 27, 2007).

Green, John C., Corwin E. Smidt, James L. Guth, and Lyman A. Kellstedt. 2004. "The American Religious Landscape and the 2004 Presidential Vote." http://www.uakron.edu/bliss/research.php (last accessed February 27, 2007).

Guth, James L., John C. Green, Corwin E. Smidt, Lyman A. Kellstedt, and Margaret M. Poloma. 1997. *The Bully Pulpit: The Politics of Protestant Clergy*. Lawrence, KS: University Press of Kansas.

Hadden, Jeffrey K. 1969. *The Gathering Storm in the Churches*. Garden City, NY: Doubleday.

Hall, Mitchell. 1992. "CALCAV and Religious Opposition to the Vietnam War." In *Give Peace a Chance: Exploring the Vietnam Antiwar Movement*, edited by Melvin Small and William D. Hoover. Syracuse, NY: Syracuse University Press.

Hammond, Phillip. 1992. *The Protestant Presence in Twentieth-Century America: Religion and Political Culture*. Albany, NY: State University of New York Press.

Herberg, Will. 1955. *Protestant-Catholic-Jew*. Garden City, NY: Doubleday.

Hertzke, Allen D. 1988. *Representing God in Washington: The Role of Religious Lobbies in the American Polity*. Knoxville, TN: University of Tennessee Press.

——— 1991. "An Assessment of the Mainline Churches Since 1945." In *The Role of Religion in the Making of Public Policy*, ed. James E. Wood, Jr., and Derek Davis. Waco, TX: J. M. Dawson Institute.

Hilliard, Bryan, Tom Lansford, and Robert P. Watson. 2004. *George W. Bush: Evaluating the President at Midterm*. Albany, NY: State University of New York Press.

Hofrenning, Daniel J. B. 1995. *In Washington but Not of It*. Philadelphia, PA: Temple University Press.

Iannaccone, Laurence R. 1994. "Why Strict Churches Are Strong." *American Journal of Sociology* 99: 1180–1211.

Jelen, Ted G. 1993. *The Political World of the Clergy*. Westport, CT: Praeger.

Kelley, Dean M. 1977. *Why Conservative Churches Are Growing: A Study in Sociology of Religion*. San Francisco, CA: Harper and Row.

Kengor, Paul. 2004. *God and George W. Bush: A Spiritual Life*. New York: HarperCollins.

Kessler, Ronald. 2004. *A Matter of Character: Inside the White House of George W. Bush*. New York: Sentinel.

Kohut, Andrew, John C. Green, Scott Keeter, and Robert C. Toth. 2000. *The Diminishing Divide: Religion's Changing Role in American Politics*. Washington, DC: Brookings Institution.

Koller, Norman B., and Joseph D. Retzer. 1980. "The Sounds of Silence Revisited." *Sociological Analysis* 41: 155–161.

Layman, Geoffrey. 2001. *The Great Divide: Religious and Cultural Conflict in American Party Politics*. New York: Columbia University Press.

Leege, David C., Kenneth D. Wald, Brian S. Krueger, and Paul D. Mueller. 2002. *The Politics of Cultural Differences: Social Change and Voter Mobilization in the Post-New Deal Period*. Princeton, NJ: Princeton University Press.

Mansfield, Stephen. 2003. *The Faith of George W. Bush*. New York: Penguin.

Manza, Jeff, and Clem Brooks. 1999. *Social Cleavages and Political Change: Voter Alignments and U.S. Party Coalitions*. New York: Oxford University Press.

———— 2002. "The Changing Political Fortunes of Mainline Protestants." In *The Quiet Hand of God: Faith-Based Activism and the Public Role of Mainline Protestantism*, edited by Robert Wuthnow and John H. Evans. Berkeley, CA: University of California Press.

Marty, Martin E. 1970. *Righteous Empire: The Protestant Experience in America*. New York: Dial.

Minutaglio, Bill. 1999. *First Son: George W. Bush and the Bush Family Dynasty*. New York: Times Books.

Niebuhr, H. Richard. 1951. *Christ and Culture*. New York: Harper and Row.

Olasky, Marvin. 2000. *Compassionate Conservatism: What It Is, What It Does, and How It Can Transform America*. New York: Free Press.

Olson, Laura R. 2000. *Filled with Spirit and Power: Protestant Clergy in Politics*. Albany, NY: State University of New York Press.

———— 2002. "Mainline Protestant Washington Offices and the Political Lives of Clergy." In *The Quiet Hand of God: Faith-Based Activism and the Public Role of Mainline Protestantism*, edited by Robert Wuthnow and John H. Evans. Berkeley, CA: University of California Press.

Olson, Laura R., Sue E. S. Crawford, and Melissa M. Deckman. 2005. *Women with a Mission: Religion, Gender, and the Politics of Women Clergy.* Tuscaloosa, AL: University of Alabama Press.

Park, Jerry, and Samuel Reimer. 2002. "Revisiting the Social Sources of American Christianity, 1972–1998." *Journal for the Scientific Study of Religion* 41: 735–748.

Quinley, Harold E. 1974. *The Prophetic Clergy: Social Activism among Protestant Ministers.* New York: Wiley.

Renshon, Stanley A. 2004. *In His Father's Shadow: The Transformations of George W. Bush.* New York: Palgrave Macmillan.

Roof, Wade Clark. 1999. *Spiritual Marketplace: Baby Boomers and the Remaking of American Religion.* Princeton, NJ: Princeton University Press.

Roof, Wade Clark, and William McKinney. 1987. *American Mainline Religion: Its Changing Shape and Future.* New Brunswick, NJ: Rutgers University Press.

Smidt, Corwin E., ed. 2004. *Pulpit and Politics: Clergy in American Politics at the Advent of the Millennium.* Waco, TX: Baylor University Press.

Smith, Christian. 1996. *Resisting Reagan: The U.S. Central America Peace Movement.* Chicago, IL: University of Chicago Press.

Smith, Christian, and Robert Faris. 2005. "Socioeconomic Inequality in the American Religious System: An Update and Assessment." *Journal for the Scientific Study of Religion* 44: 95–104.

Steensland, Brian. 2002. "The Hydra and the Swords: Social Welfare and Mainline Advocacy, 1964–2000." In *The Quiet Hand of God: Faith-Based Activism and the Public Role of Mainline Protestantism*, edited by Robert Wuthnow and John H. Evans. Berkeley, CA: University of California Press.

Steensland, Brian, Jerry Z. Park, Mark D. Regnerus, Lynn D. Robinson, W. Bradford Wilcox, and Robert D. Woodberry. 2000. "The Measure of American Religion: Toward Improving the State of the Art." *Social Forces* 79: 291–318.

Thuesen, Peter J. 2002. "The Logic of Mainline Churchliness: Historical Background since the Reformation." In *The Quiet Hand of God: Faith-Based Activism and the Public Role of Mainline Protestantism*, edited by Robert Wuthnow and John H. Evans. Berkeley, CA: University of California Press.

Wald, Kenneth D. 2003. *Religion and Politics in the United States.* 4th ed. Lanham, MD: Rowman and Littlefield.

Warren, Mark R. 2001. *Dry Bones Rattling: Community Building to Revitalize American Democracy.* Princeton, NJ: Princeton University Press.

Wellman, James K., Jr. 1999. *The Gold Coast Church and the Ghetto: Christ and Culture in Mainline Protestantism.* Urbana, IL: University of Illinois Press.

Wilcox, Clyde. 1992. *God's Warriors: The Christian Right in Twentieth-Century America.* Baltimore, MD: Johns Hopkins University Press.

Wuthnow, Robert. 1988. *The Restructuring of American Religion: Society and Faith since World War II.* Princeton, NJ: Princeton University Press.

———— 1996. *The Crisis in the Churches*. New York: Oxford University Press.

———— 2000. "The Moral Minority." *American Prospect* 11 (May 22): 31–33.

Wuthnow, Robert, and John H. Evans, eds. 2002. *The Quiet Hand of God: Faith-Based Activism and the Public Role of Mainline Protestantism*. Berkeley, CA: University of California Press.

Chapter Five

The Politics of the Religious Minorities Vote in the 2004 Elections

*Paul A. Djupe, Eric McDaniel, and
Jacob R. Neiheisel*

Introduction

In the months leading up to the 2004 presidential election the airwaves were saturated with commentators predicting that the contest would be decided by so-called values voters, many of whom were expected to turn out in droves to cast their ballots for George W. Bush. To most, values voters implied evangelical Christians, but much was also made of the prospect of conservative adherents of other faiths departing from their traditional partisan appointments because of their support for the traditional values that had come to be identified with the Republican Party. In the aftermath of the election it seemed as though such predictions concerning the role of religiously minded voters had come to fruition, as exit polls showed that moral values was at the top of the list of factors that influenced voters' decisions in casting their ballots (Seelye 2004, P4).

Conservative Christians certainly seemed to command much of the media attention surrounding the findings of such polls, but any account of the involvement of religious interests in the 2004 elections would not be complete nor accurate without taking into consideration the various religious minorities that were active participants and per-haps "in play" in the election. Even though talk of the polarization between the different religious traditions resurfaced once again in the 2004 elections, there seems to be at least some evidence that points toward a partisan realignment within certain religious groups that have long been thought to be bastions of support for one party, the Democrats. It would not be fair to say that the 2004 election chal-lenged conventional wisdom concerning the partisan identifications of the different religious traditions, but there was enough change to allow us to comment on the role of religion in the political presence of religious minorities.

In this chapter we explore the politics of "religious minorities," specifically of American blacks, Jews, and Muslims, in the 2004 election. These groups became enmeshed in the politics of Bush's first election and first term and some represent bell weathers evaluating that first term as well as the issues of the 2004 campaign. Muslims, in particular, show how the commitments of voters can shift drastically from election to election.

The 2004 election was a referendum on the administration's policies and performance of the previous four years, but it also turned on the politics generated by the election campaign, including almost a dozen high-profile ballot measures coordinated to advance an antigay rights agenda. On that basis and considering the issues generated by the Bush campaign, a debate has ensued about whether the election was primarily about values, which is code for culture war debates. There is strong evidence that most voters are not participants in the culture war (e.g., Williams 1997; Fiorina 2005), and the politics of religious minorities provide us with a convincing perspective why.

At the same time that we describe the politics of these groups, we confront a theoretical question. That is, this chapter begs an essential question: to what extent did these groups function as groups in politics and why? Should we consider these black, Jewish, and Muslim voters as members of a *religious group* in an election campaign? The campaign not only represents a dialogue between representations of society (campaigns) and groups but also can expose fault lines within those groups. That is, we can assess how groups view the actions of the administration and evaluate their place in society, but we can also appraise the extent to which the groups are groups and the role of religion in fostering and sustaining group solidarity.

Religion is not just about values or a value system, though of course these are important key elements of what religion is about. Religion can also be understood as a group of people, often assembled in a house of worship (which may be virtual in the case of televangelists), pursuing a variety of ends, which may or may not primarily include the exploration of the spiritual. As Kellstedt and Green (1993, 53) note, "[I]t has never been clear whether [denominational] measures refer to ethnic histories, doctrinal beliefs, social status, or social group attachments."

In fact, it is even less clear in the case of the groups under study here. African Americans would be classified primarily as evangelical Protestants were it not for their race (though a significant minority is

Catholic, Muslim, or not affiliated). And, of course, there is considerable variation in the religious beliefs and practices among black Protestants (e.g., Lincoln and Mamiya 1990). Jews and Muslims are defined according to their religion, though "Jewish" is defined not through attendance at a synagogue but through personal identification and/or the religious identification of parents, mostly the mother. Most Muslims, by scholarly account, do not practice and attend a mosque—perhaps as low as 10–20 percent (Haddad and Lummis 1987, as cited in Leonard 2003), though that figure is controversial. And there are significant religious and cultural differences among the Jewish movements (e.g., Djupe and Sokhey 2003a). Many, especially among Muslims, are first generation immigrants, and the community is divided largely along ethnic and denominational lines (e.g., Leonard 2003; Smith 1999). Jews and Muslims have a religious homeland as well as, most likely, a different ethnic homeland. Among both the Jewish and Muslim populations, not all are practicing their faith though would still identify themselves as members of a religious group.

These various factors describing the contours of each group—religion, ethnicity/race, status, and so on—help to define their politics and also can serve as fault lines on which the group may one day founder. In 2004, the politics of these groups can be primarily described as cohesive, though the reasons for cohesion in each group differ. The role religion plays in these stories is varied and functions differently for the three groups depending on how religion is integrated into the groups' communities.

Religion, Groups, and Political Life

In their attempt to provide a comprehensive theory of the presence of religion in public life, Wald, Silverman, and Fridy (2005, 124) suggest that the engagement of religious groups in politics can be best understood by using elements of social movement theory, particularly by investigating their motives, means, and opportunities to participate. Motives, sometimes better known as grievances, flow from the clash of society and cultural identities, which establish groups and group norms (see also Wildavsky 1987). Means constitute the "organizational capacity" to bring grievances into the political sphere and are generally thought to include the intensity of grievances, leadership, money and materiel, networks, and physical meeting space (Wald, Silverman, and Fridy 2005, 131; Zald and McCarthy 1987). Groups operate within a political system that provides many points of access that are inviting or discouraging to a group's claims at different times (McAdam 1982; Wald, Silverman, and Fridy 2005). This framework is particularly relevant in election campaigns. In electoral "rituals," candidates and other elites attempt a rather ordinary and important dialogue, by which "1) it defines and regulates social relationships; 2) it provides a social message through dominant cultural values; 3) it conforms to known realities; and 4) it reduces uncertainty by conveying the actor's intentions" (Leege et al. 2002, 58). The implications of this understanding of a campaign are important for our purpose here.

In part, the campaign defines social relationships in the sense that certain groups are valued over others, sometimes not only insofar as the group is electorally valuable but also insofar as the validation that the group's claims have merit. African Americans and women provide the most extreme example of groups denied that validation, though all groups vacillate in and out of favor over time. Muslims were heavily courted by the Bush campaign in 2000, with some success, though events changed that potential by 2004. The Reverend Al Sharpton's campaign for the Democratic nomination for president might be seen as a new bid for validation, both for himself and for the African American community.

The struggle to define the relevant issues is the dominant battle among campaigns, as elites attempt to use favorable frames to mobilize select groups and perhaps demobilize others, carving up the electorate in a strategy to capture a majority of those participating. Though, theoretically, the size of a party's constituency is not capped, there are practical and traditional forces that may impose limits. Traditional party identification, which is embedded in the social relations of the group and ingrained in the minds of its members, would certainly be one, though Muslims provide a counterpoint on that score. The issue space in which campaigns troll for voters may circumscribe a campaign's efforts when pushing an issue drives out another part of the target constituency. Touting Bush's leadership during wartime may solidify the Republican base but do little to keep many Muslims who favored Republican small government themes.

In the next sections, we explore the politics of Jewish, black, and Muslim Americans in the 2004 presidential election.

The Politics of Jewish Americans

While certainly not the only religious minority to illustrate the kind of changes that seemed to punctuate the 2004 election, some Jewish

Americans, in spite of their lengthy record of unified support for the Democratic Party as members of Roosevelt's New Deal coalition, exhibited tentative signs of partisan fragmentation (Fowler et al. 2004). To some observers, the migration of some of the more religiously orthodox Jewish Americans toward the Republican Party has been a long time in the making, as Jews have long presented something of a paradox in American electoral politics. The Jewish proportion of the population, though it constitutes less than 2 percent of the United States, is highly educated, relatively affluent, and politically engaged—characteristics that might indicate high levels of identification with the Republican Party (Fowler et al. 2004). On many of the issues that divide the parties, though, the beliefs of most Jews lie squarely within the Democratic camp. To this effect, Jewish lobbies in Washington, DC, and Jewish voters have supported a woman's right to an abortion, stood in opposition to school prayer and school vouchers, advocated the strict separation of church and state, and backed gender equality. The support of Jewish lobbies for such contentious viewpoints has often thrust them into political conflict with evangelical Protestants (Fowler et al. 2004), except on U.S. foreign policy on Israel (Guth et al. 1996).

Indeed, the vast majority of Jews in the United States are liberals who have embraced the Democratic Party in spite of racial tensions, including crude remarks by Reverend Jesse Jackson on the campaign trail in 1984, the Crown Heights riots in 1991, and Democratic Party support for affirmative action (Wald 1997; Greenberg and Wald 2000). A large percentage of the Jewish vote has gone to and remained in the Democratic Party since the solidification of Jewish loyalty to the Democrats during the New Deal (Fowler et al. 2004; Wald 1997). Jews generally harbor the belief that society should tolerate minorities and aid the disadvantaged; in addition, Jews often lend their support to civil rights issues, progressive taxation, and other causes often championed by the political left in the United States (Cohen 1989; Fowler et al. 2004).

There are several theories advanced to explain the liberal tendencies of the Jewish community that belie the economic standing of the group (see Cohen and Liebman 1997; Djupe 2006; Levey 1996; Wald 1997). One popular theory as to why Jewish voters support liberal policies even when it would seem to contradict their interests is that liberalism is somehow implicit in Jewish theology. This theory, however, has been undercut by the finding that Jews exhibiting the highest levels of religiosity are also those who most closely identify with conservative political ideals. Rather, it would seem that the Jewish community's sense of itself as vulnerable to persecution and anti-Semitism has led them to identify with the left because of the sympathetic stance that those on the left have historically taken toward minorities (Wald 1997). Perhaps the most visible manifestation of this is the strong support for groups protecting the civil liberties of minority groups, such as the American Civil Liberties Union and the Anti-Defamation League (Chanes 2001), bolstered by Jewish public opinion (Cohen 1989; Djupe 2006; Levey 1996; Lipset and Raab 1995; Svonkin 1997).

The historical connection between Jews and liberalism in the United States certainly has not prevented the Republican Party from attempting to drive a wedge in this lasting partisan coalition over the years, particularly over the contentious issue of support for Israel. In the 2004 election, though, both President Bush and Democratic challenger Senator John Kerry campaigned on a pro-Israel platform and traded barbs on the campaign trail over who would be the better friend to Israel in the White House (Weisman 2004, 15). Both sides attempted to court the Jewish vote, as Jews concerned with global terrorism and the future of Israel threatened to leave the Democratic fold in key states such as Florida, Ohio, and Pennsylvania (Baxter 2004, 7A; Hotakainen 2004, 15A; Thomas 2004). GOP leaders in particular have been looking to attract Jewish voters and have found that their efforts had not gone completely without result, as preelection polls showed an increase in the number of Jews who identified themselves as Republicans, from 9 percent in 2000 to 16 percent in 2004 (Zoll 2004). Like many elections in the past, GOP strategists predicted that Jewish voters would move away from the Democratic Party in 2004, because of the War on Terrorism and George W. Bush's reputation for being pro-Israel (Horowitz 2004; Lakely 2003, A03), a switch from 2000 (see the section titled "The Politics of Muslim Americans" below).

Other factors seemed to indicate GOP gains among Jewish voters in 2004 as well, as an increasing number of socially conservative Jews had been getting behind Bush's policies concerning abortion and gay marriage (Sarna 2004). Orthodox Jews have been becoming increasingly more likely to vote Republican than their Reform or Conservative Jewish counterparts (among rabbis, see Djupe and Sokhey 2003a). Jews hailing from the former Soviet Union, many of whom cast their first votes for Ronald Reagan over 30 years ago, also support the conservative values that have come to be associated with the GOP (Sarna 2004, D12). Bush's strategists took note of this basic rift between conservative Jews and most mainstream Democrats and sought to bring more Jews into the coalition of religious voters that Bush had been hoping to amass (Goodstein and Yardley 2004, 22).

Fiscally, conservative Jews also seemed to be moving toward the Republican camp, and a growing number of younger Jews were voting with their economic peers in the Republican Party (Sarna 2004, D12). According to political strategist Hank Sheinkopf, the steady movement of Jews into the economic classes normally associated with higher levels of identification with the Republican Party has caused many Jews to break ranks with the Democrats (Tigay 2003, 28). That seems more wishful thinking than reality since 20 years ago Milton Himmelfarb, an astute observer of Jewish politics, quipped that Jews earn like Episcopalians and vote like Puerto Ricans. Urban Jews too appeared to be becoming moderate Republicans, as "Coleman Republicans," that is, Jewish candidates running for office who have modeled themselves after Minnesota Senator Norm Coleman, were beginning to run on a platform of tort reform, tax relief, and, of course, issues such as Israel that are of particular concern to most Jews (Kessler 2003).

Aside from predictions of mass defections from the Jewish community toward the GOP, a fair amount of media attention was generated surrounding the Jewish groups that were active throughout the campaign. Although Jewish Americans have always voted in higher proportions than most Americans (U.S. Newswire 2004a; Wald 1997, 310), the 2004 election saw a combined get-out-the-vote effort by several Jewish groups. Produced jointly by a consortium of Jewish groups, the *Get Out the Vote* 2004 voter guide provided information about those issues most important to Jewish Americans (UPI 2004; U.S. Newswire 2004a).

When all was said and done with the election it seemed as though Jewish voters had given careful reflection to those issues that were important to them and cast their vote in a manner that belied GOP predictions of massive Jewish migrations toward the political right. Nationwide, Jews voted for John Kerry over George W. Bush by a 78 percent to 22 percent margin (U.S. Newswire 2004b). In New York, California, and Florida—the states with the largest Jewish populations—American Jews gave Kerry an even higher percentage of their vote (U.S. Newswire 2004b).

The average percentage of the Jewish vote that Republican presidential candidates have received since exit polls that first began to be conducted in 1972 has been 27.4 percent (U.S. Newswire 2004b). In the end, Bush's poor showing among Jewish voters appears to have reaffirmed the strong ties that Jews hold with the Democratic Party (U.S. Newswire 2004b), though 22 percent is right in line with another estimate of Jewish voting from 1992 to 2000 using General Social

Survey data (Djupe 2006). The 2004 election did not radically depart from previous elections—it highlighted the relative cohesion of the Jewish vote.

The American Jewish Committee (AJC) survey also found that most Jews still identified with the Democratic Party, even though an increasing number were beginning to rally to the GOP banner. The percentage of Jews who identified themselves as Democrats in 2004— 51 percent—was significantly lower than the percentage in the 1960s and 1970s (a figure that would not include Independents who lean toward a party). Republicans appeared to have made inroads in this once solidly Democratic constituency, as the AJC survey found that 18 percent of the Jews sampled identified with the GOP. A number of Jews, roughly 31 percent, consider themselves to be Independents. Perhaps one of the reasons for this shift is regional socialization working on sunbelt migration—Wald and Jelen (2004) found that Southern Jews outside of Florida are more likely to identify as conservatives (see also Djupe 2006, who found a different but related pattern). Using a different scale (and the GSS data), however, Djupe (2006) finds a relative constancy in Jewish party identification, hovering around 70 percent with the Democrats (including leaners) since the 1970s, and declining GOP identification since the mid-1980s from about 30 percent to below 20 percent.

Not surprisingly, 44 percent of Jews identified themselves as liberal, 27 percent as conservative, and the remaining third identified themselves as moderate, according to the AJC surveys. Jewish conservatives such as Norm Coleman may have received a great deal of media attention, but the AJC survey found that the majority of Jewish Americans identify themselves as liberal. Those surveyed were strongly opposed (73 percent) to faith-based initiatives and were worried about what they perceived as the anti-Semitic undertones of the Religious Right— 40 percent of respondents to the AJC survey believed that "most" members of the Religious Right were anti-Semites (Besser 2004). Others have claimed that the rise of religious conservatives in the Republican Party in the mid-1980s reversed growing Jewish Republican tendencies, and it seems that the continued clout of Christian conservatives in the Republican Party continues to repel many Jewish voters (Greenberg and Wald 2001; Levey 1996).

An analysis of the Jewish vote conducted after the 2004 election under the auspices of the Solomon Project revealed similar findings concerning the way in which Jews voted in 2004, but contradicted other findings of the AJC survey, particularly with regard to the number of Jews who identified themselves with the Democratic Party.

The roughly 24 percent of the Jewish vote that the AJC survey predicted that President Bush would receive was higher than any of the other preelection surveys, whereas the best estimate of the actual percentage of Jewish Americans who gave their vote to George W. Bush was closer to 22 percent. The Solomon Project Study found that the Democratic two-party Jewish vote has been remarkably stable over the last few election cycles, in agreement with Djupe's (2006) analysis, when compared with the voting patterns of the general public. The vast majority of Jewish voters remained Democratic and liberal in 2004, with 55 percent of those surveyed in a study conducted by the Mellman Group self-identifying as Democrats (Mellman et al. 2005).

According to the AJC preelection survey, American Jews, in spite of their generally pessimistic beliefs with regard to the intentions of Arabs, a majority—54 percent—indicated that they would support the creation of a Palestinian state, and 69 percent said that Israel should be willing to pull out of the West Bank (Besser 2004). Such findings ran counter to the predictions of many GOP strategists, many of whom fully expected to see Jews flock to the pro-Israel policies forwarded by the Bush administration. Other assertions of conventional wisdom surrounding the voting patterns of Jewish Americans were dispelled too as the 2003 American Jewish Committee (AJC) survey of Jewish public opinion showed that Jews were not the enthusiastic backers of the Iraq War that many had suspected. The majority of U.S. Jews—54 percent—disapproved of the way in which the president was dealing with the war, which grew to 66 percent in the 2004 AJC survey (Besser 2004).

There was some evidence of a shift toward the GOP among young Jews, Orthodox Jews, and Russian Jews, but the sample sizes of both Orthodox Jews and Russian Jews were not large enough to accurately gauge their vote. The Solomon Project analysis of the Jewish vote in 2004 did find that Jews who attended synagogue frequently were more likely to vote Republican—a finding that reinforced some political strategists' preelection hopes (Mellman et al. 2005). Djupe (2006) finds, however, that greater religious attendance drives a more conservative ideology but not partisanship over a 32-year span of the GSS, suggesting that some other factor has limited the conversion of ideology to partisan affiliation.

Conventional wisdom would hold that polarization between different religious traditions is the norm when it comes to the electoral politics of religious groups, but the polarization within religions between those who are most dedicated to their faith and those who are more secular in their leanings is a more appropriate understanding

(Wuthnow 1988; Harper 2005). Though it may seem paradoxical, there is a fairly united Jewish community outside of Orthodox Jews. The historic liberal and Democratic attachments of Jews, based on commitments to social welfare, nondiscrimination, and civil rights and liberties, were intact in 2004. Socially conservative and staunchly pro-Israel Orthodox Jews, who are also the least connected to secular Jewish political groups, are starting to forge tentative links to the Republican Party that are likely to grow over time (Djupe and Sokhey 2003b). In all, with the gradual disappearance of discrimination from society, the Jewish community is generating new and distinct interests along its fault lines of religion, social context, and status. The 2004 campaign, however, was not strong enough tremor to generate significant new cracks.

The Politics of African Americans

The 2004 election presented a great deal of opportunities for the Black Church to play a significant role. With the reemergence of a black clergy member as a presidential candidate and the Republican Party's continued courting of black clergy, the Black Church appeared to be a central institution in another close election. We focus on Reverend Al Sharpton's presidential bid, the Republican Party's attempt to recruit blacks, and how the same-sex marriage debate affected blacks' electoral considerations. While press reports may have presented a fractured black religious community, a systematic analysis of the data does not support that claim. Instead, the black community, especially the religious component, demonstrated remarkable continuity.

Sharpton's Presidential Bid

The most literal representation of the Black Church in the 2004 presidential election was the Reverend Al Sharpton's bid for the Democratic nomination for president. In many ways Sharpton's campaign for the presidency could be seen as a renewal of Reverend Jesse Jackson's campaigns in 1984 and 1988. Sharpton, like Jackson, had made a name for himself protesting what he saw as injustices against the black community. The commonalities were extended to the context of the election as well: there was a Republican president seeking reelection, and African Americans seemed angry with the sitting president. Much of the same rhetoric that Jackson used in 1984 and 1988 reappeared in Sharpton's campaign. Sharpton, like Jackson, accessed the network of black churches to attempt to gain support for his campaign. His campaign seemed imminent as he and Jesse Jackson launched a "Shadow" inauguration during President Bush's actual inauguration in 2001. During this demonstration, which protested the Florida recount and subsequent election of George W. Bush, Sharpton argued that the nation was in the middle of a battle between "the Christian Right and right Christians" (Harris 2001). Because of the circumstances of the 2000 election and the war in Iraq, there appeared to be a highly agitated black community from which Al Sharpton could draw support, similar to the circumstances in 1988 that underlay Jackson's populist bid (Hertzke 1993).

However, Sharpton was unable to gain the support and fanfare that Jackson captured 20 years ago. From the beginning, Sharpton's campaign seemed doomed to fail as many saw him trying to push Jesse Jackson aside in order for him to become the new national spokesman for black America (Nagourney 2001). This issue was further exacerbated by Jackson's neutrality toward Sharpton and Jesse Jackson, Jr.'s support for Vermont Governor Howard Dean. What appeared to hurt Sharpton the most was the belief by many blacks that voting for Sharpton was not a good use of their vote. Many African Americans who voted in the Democratic Party's primaries may have supported Sharpton's positions, but they did not feel he could defeat President Bush. Voting for Sharpton did not seem practical in the eyes of many African Americans. Republican James E. Clyburn of South Carolina (D-SC6) suggested a sophisticated electorate in an era of tough political choices for liberal Democrats: "Black people aren't crazy. They're looking for somebody they think can win in November" (Balz 2004).

Courting of the Black Vote

President Bush has been vilified by the African American community from the beginning in 2000, when 90 percent of the African American community voted against him and when many were outraged about the treatment of black voters in Florida.[1] In what appeared to be an attempt to make amends with the black community, Bush appointed Condoleezza Rice as his national security advisor and Colin Powell as secretary of state. However, these high-profile figures only appeared to improve white opinions about the Republican Party on race issues (Philpot 2004).

Another way to reduce this animus of blacks toward the Bush administration was through faith-based initiatives. President Bush consistently brought black clergy into the discussion of faith-based initiatives and appeared publicly with them. It appeared that he was winning over black clergy (Oppel and Niebuhr 2000), who seemed to approve of increased funding for social services in poor communities, and several of whom came out in support of President Bush and much of his agenda (Kirkpatrick 2004). However, these clergy have faced a great deal of criticism from others in the black community. The National Association for the Advancement of Colored People (NAACP), for one, has spoken out against many of the policies of the Bush administration, including faith-based initiatives (Miller 2001).

During the 2004 election, George W. Bush became even more aggressive in courting the black vote by arguing that the Democratic Party did not truly support the interests of blacks (Stevenson 2004). While he made this claim, again perhaps to soften the views of white voters, he was criticized for not attending the NAACP's meeting, which he had done in the previous election. On the Democratic Party's side, the Kerry campaign appeared to keep the black community at arm's length. While many African Americans held a strong animus toward the Bush administration, his approval dropping to 2 percent among blacks in one poll a year after the election (Froomkin 2005), Kerry was not an enticing alternative, especially in comparison to Bill Clinton's comfort with and embrace of the black community (Dwyer and Wilgoren 2004). However, others, mainly African American elites, criticized Kerry for not attempting to mobilize African Americans (Fears 2004). Not until late in the campaign did he make concerted appeals to black voters to energize them for the upcoming election.

The Effect of the Gay Marriage Debate

While the activities of the candidates provided a sense of the importance of the Black Church in 2004, the issue of same-sex marriage placed the institution in an interesting situation. Gay marriage presented a problem for the Black Church in many ways. First, the Black Church has been soundly criticized for ignoring issues of homosexuality. Cathy Cohen (1999) and other scholars, for instance, have argued the growth of the AIDS/HIV epidemic stemmed from the Black Church's reluctance to address the issue homosexuality. Second, the African American community has had a hard time seeing the plight of homosexuals as similar to theirs. In response to homosexual groups comparing their quest for equal rights to the African American Civil Rights Movement, Jesse Jackson referred to it as a "stretch," though Lewis (2003) has suggested that blacks may disapprove of homosexuality, but are, in fact, more supportive of gay civil rights. On the heels of heavy mobilization efforts from interests pushing antigay rights initiatives in the states (e.g., Djupe, Neiheisel, and Sokhey 2005), many black clergy came out in support of a constitutional ban on same-sex marriage and argued that this was one of the main reasons why they would vote for Bush in the upcoming election. One clergy member went as far as stating, "If the K.K.K. opposes gay marriage, I would ride with them" (Clemetson 2004). Not all black clergy took this stance, and there was a small but significant number of clergy who argued that banning homosexuals from the institution of marriage was discrimination. As one clergy member put it, "oppression is oppression is oppression" (Banerjee 2005).

Analysis of the Black Church in the 2004 Election

The above review of activities during the 2004 campaign provide an idea of the various ways in which blacks and the Black Church engaged the electoral process, but we do not yet understand how religion affects how African Americans viewed the issues central to the election. Did the events of the campaign matter? Past research would suggest that the issues of this election would not be salient enough to drastically change black voting behavior (Calhoun-Brown 1998). While the beliefs and practices of its leaders and members reflect an evangelical Protestant leaning, it is also the center of the African American community, which is almost unanimously Democratic (Leege and Kellstedt 1993). Because of this central connection to the African American community, many believe that when the threats of racism expire the social conservatism of the institution will become prominent (Cohen 1999). But, with the issues of morality and welcoming words from George W. Bush, maybe this time religiously conservative blacks could be moved.

To assess how religion affects how blacks reacted to campaign issues and candidates, we turned to the 2004 National Election Studies (NES). The 2004 NES, with its national sample of 1,212 adults, just under 10 percent of which is black (184), includes a wealth of questions about political attitudes, political behavior, and religiosity.

Though the 2004 NES does not have a large sample of African American respondents, it certainly has enough to provide a satisfactory comparison with whites.

We compare the effect of religious beliefs, specifically biblical literalism, on blacks' and whites' affect toward the presidential candidates, gay marriage attitudes, and presidential vote choice. The degree to which an individual views the Bible as the literal word of God has been shown to provide a great deal of leverage in explaining differences in Christian attitudes toward candidates and policies (Boone 1989; Leege and Kellstedt 1993). We interact literalism with race, expecting that religious beliefs may work differently for blacks and whites. Literalism is not simply a proxy for religiosity since we control for religious commitment (church attendance) and Protestant/Catholic differences. From the results of a multivariate analysis[2] (not shown), we calculate predicted probabilities and values to better examine to what extent literalism's effect on blacks and whites differs in the context of the 2004 election.[3] The results are presented in table 5.1.

Feeling thermometers are used to examine general attitudes toward the candidates. As table 5.1 shows, the movement of whites from believing that the Bible is a book of legends to the literal word of God leads to warmer feelings toward Bush and cooler feelings toward Kerry. For blacks it is the exact opposite. A white nonliteralist gives Bush a 50.4 on the feeling thermometer and Kerry a 54.1. A white literalist gives Bush a 62.6 and Kerry a 48.3. A black nonliteralist gives Bush a 56.0 and Kerry a 49.5. A black literalist gives Bush a 50.1 and Kerry a 58.9.[4]

Literalism decreases support for gay marriage among blacks (see table 5.1), but does so more strongly for whites. This can be attributed to the fact that there is more cohesion on gay marriage in the black community—black nonliteralists are strongly opposed to this policy (19.8 percent chance of support) compared to their white counterparts (51.7 percent support). In this case literalism's effect on blacks can and does have a limited (and insignificant) effect on support for gay marriage, cutting support in half.

An examination of voters' presidential choice shows that literalism has a clear effect to augment white's likelihood of choosing George W. Bush, but does not do the same for blacks. For whites, movement from nonliteralist to literalist increases the probability of voting for Bush by 23.9 percentage points (and an insignificant 1.1 percentage points for blacks). Literalism appears to increase the probability that blacks will vote for Kerry (26.9 percentage point change), while decreasing the probability that whites will (−13.5 percentage point change). But,

Table 5.1 The Estimated Effects of Biblical Literalism for Whites and Blacks on Candidate Affect, Support for Gay Marriage, and Presidential Vote (Cell Entries Are Predicted Values or Probabilities)

	Whites			Blacks		
	Bible Is a Book of Legends	Bible Is the Literal Word of God	Difference	Bible Is a Book of Legends	Bible Is the Literal Word of God	Difference
Bush thermometer	50.4	62.6	12.2	56.0	50.1	−5.8
Kerry thermometer	54.1	48.3	−5.8	49.5	58.9	9.4
Support for gay marriage	0.52	0.13	−0.39	0.20	0.12	−0.08
Vote for Bush in 2004	0.42	0.66	0.24	0.13	0.14	0.01
Vote for Kerry in 2004	0.46	0.33	−0.13	0.58	0.85	0.27

Note: Cell entries are the predicted values (in the case of the feeling thermometers) and probabilities (for the other two) calculated from estimation results not presented here.

Source: National Election Study (NES) 2004.

again, literalism's effect is not significant for blacks. If literalism did have a significant effect, it would push blacks and whites in opposite directions.

This analysis indicates that blacks' religious beliefs did not factor into the election as many would have thought. Only in the case of gay marriage did literalism move blacks and whites in the same direction, though there is already unity in the black community on this issue. In the case of candidate affect and vote choice, ties to the black religious community in the form of religious beliefs cemented ties to the Democratic candidate. While there may be some evidence of gains in the black vote for Bush in 2004 compared to the 2000 election, these gains were small—the 2000 NES reports that slightly over 7 percent of blacks voted for Bush; in 2004, the NES reports that Bush gained slightly over 12 percent of the black vote share (a difference easily inside the margin of error). Even if there were gains they would soon evaporate after the Bush administration's handling of the aftermath of hurricane Katrina.

Blacks clearly exist outside of any culture war in the larger society. As a group, blacks are religiously fervent and socially conservative but end up on the opposite side of the fervent religious and socially conservative whites. In fact, ties to the Black Church only serve to maintain traditional ties to the Democratic Party and any slim gains for Bush seem to have come from *outside* of the black religious establishment. This should not be surprising as black religious institutions have repeatedly been found to reinforce a connection to the group and its political agenda (Allen, Dawson, and Brown 1989; Calhoun-Brown 1996; Dawson 1994; Ellison 1991; Harris 1999; McClerking 2001). Future examinations of the role of the black churches role in politics should pay close attention to this factor as scholars attempt to determine the various ways in which the religion of African Americans shapes African American politics.

The Politics of Muslim Americans

The Council on American-Islamic Relations (CAIR) Executive Director Nihad Awad announced after the 2000 elections, "Muslims based their vote on the best choice. . . . It happened to be George Bush, but in four years it may be different" (quoted in Rose 2001). Was it ever. Unlike both Jewish and African American voters, Muslim Americans showed a marked departure from the partisan proclivities they had displayed in 2000. The aftermath of the September 11, 2001 attacks inside the United States brought the Muslim community together around shared experiences—wholesale intolerance and prejudice in society, weakened liberties from government intrusion, and a foreign policy that seemingly targeted Middle Eastern Muslims. In some contrast to the other minority groups covered in this chapter, we spend more time here looking at opinion data of Muslims since so little is known about their politics. That discussion will set the stage for the dramatic shifts in Muslim voting from 2000 to 2004.

The Muslim Community

We need to begin with what the Muslim community in the United States comprises. As a relatively new community (of considerable size, anyway) with diverse elements, it may come as no surprise that there is a great deal of dispute about the constitution of the Muslim community in the United States, starting with its size (see Ba-Yunus and Kone 2004 for a comprehensive review). While some Muslim interest groups place the Muslim population in the 7–8 million range, scholars estimate a group size of about a quarter of that figure—about 1.4 million (Smith 2001). As Djupe and Green (2006) observe, this estimate of the Muslim population suggests it is about one-quarter of the American Jewish population, though the Muslim population is quickly growing.

Perhaps until recently, Muslims in America were highly fractured along lines of race, national origin, and religious observance, mirroring the Catholic experience in America (see Leonard 2003). Leonard begins her review of research on American Muslims exploring "the ways in which national origin, language, sectarian affiliation, race, class, and gender have structured Muslim communities" (2003, ix–x). Though the classification schemes vary (e.g., see Smith 1999), the Muslim community is composed of largely African Americans, South Asians (such as Pakistanis and Indians), Africans, Arabs (such as Saudi Arabians), among other smaller groups including European Muslims and converts. The true distribution of these groups in the Muslim population borders on unknown, though the Muslims in American Public Square (MAPS) survey data collection efforts in 2001 and 2004 provide us with at least an estimate.[5] With a quota sample of African Americans pegged at 20 percent of the overall population (a dubious decision), one-third are South Asian, one-quarter Arabs, one-twelfth Africans, and one-sixth Other Muslims. Of course there are many denominational variants that can cut across these ethnic/national origin groups, including Sunnis, Shi'a, and other smaller branches;

unfortunately the MAPS surveys did not include a "denominational" question.

The Political Commitments of American Muslims

Inside the United States, there is yet more diversity to consider, especially in socioeconomic status, but also regional settlement patterns, profession, and religious commitment (see Djupe and Green 2006 for a more in-depth overview). By far, African Americans are the most religiously devout, while Arab and Other Muslims are the least; Arab and South Asian Muslims are the most well-off and most highly educated, while African Americans and Africans are the least.

Because the Muslim community is so diverse, it is difficult to present a united front in politics, despite the intonations of the interest groups. Status alone does a good job differentiating groups into political camps in 2000. As we would predict, African American (60 percent), Other (49 percent), and African (46 percent) Muslims are the most Democratic, while Arabs (32 percent) and South Asians (38 percent) are the least Democratic and have the highest status. The remainder were not Republican; however, Arabs (32 percent), South Asians (29 percent), and Africans (29 percent) were the most Republican, while African Americans were the only group to dip below 20 percent Republican.

Again like many Catholics, Muslims are ideologically split across the two major parties. This may surprise many, since information about Muslim public opinion is not widely disseminated and stereotypes are common. Table 5.2 provides us a comprehensive view of the domestic politics of American Muslims.[6] The first column presents stances on cultural, or what is commonly called moral, issues. On balance, it is fair to call Muslims socially conservative. Eighty-five percent oppose same-sex marriage; three-quarters oppose the sale of pornography; seven-tenths favor faith-based initiatives, oppose cloning research, and oppose doctor-assisted suicide; and two-thirds favor vouchers to attend private schools. Beyond those issues, there is far less cohesion. Slightly above a majority favor limiting abortion, and just under a majority favor school prayer. If there is a pattern, it suggests that Muslims have a strict sense of personal morality that they feel the government should enforce, but are somewhat uncomfortable or at least split on whether government should intervene on behalf of religious practice.

Table 5.2 American Muslims and Social Issues, 2004

Cultural/Moral Issues	Favor (%)	Social Welfare Issues	Favor (%)
Favor banning sale of pornography	75.8	Favor universal health care	96.3
Favor faith-based initiative	69.9	Favor eliminating racial discrimination	94.7
Favor school vouchers	65.6	Favor stricter environment law	94.0
Favor death penalty	60.8	Favor more aid to poor	92.4
Favor research on stem cells	59.9	Favor increased foreign aid	88.4
Favor limiting abortions	55.0	Favor debt relief for poorer countries	88.2
Favor Ten Commandments in public	51.1	Favor limits on buying guns	81.1
Favor school prayer	47.9	Favor stronger laws to fight terrorism	68.9
Favor doctor-assisted suicide	31.4	Favor more income tax cuts	65.0
Favor research on cloning	28.2	Favor requiring fluency in English	52.3
Favor same-sex marriage	15.0	Favor eliminating affirmative action	37.1

Note: The percentages combine strongly favor and somewhat favor; the other two categories for each include somewhat oppose and strongly oppose—there is no middle option.

Source: MAPS 2004.

In the second column is displayed Muslim support of a number of social welfare issue positions. In contrast to the first column, there is strong to near universal support for activist, liberal government, both at home and in foreign policy. Perhaps most striking is the almost unanimous support for universal health coverage, stricter environmental laws, and aid to the poor. Muslims also would like debt relief for poor nations. They are more ambivalent on the War on Terrorism, certainly tempered by personal experience, as well as income tax cuts and ending affirmative action. In summary, Muslims wish to see their religious values represented in their government, reflecting Islam's focus on strict personal morality and generous support of those less fortunate (*zakat* or almsgiving, which is one of the Five Pillars—Smith 1999, 13).

While Rose (2001, 27) suggests that leaders of Muslim political interest groups keep their members independent for strategic reasons, their ability to do so is doubtful, and there are certainly good reasons for Muslims to be ambivalent about their candidate choices in American politics. It is manifestly true that the agenda of the Muslim public is not represented faithfully by either party, though the greater cohesion seen among Muslims on social welfare issues suggests more of an affinity for the Democratic Party. The key, of course, is placement of these issues on Muslims' agendas, which we can only infer.

Thus far, we have reviewed the status and ideological bases for Muslim politics, which are standard sources of explanation for any voter. Religious minorities are distinctive not only because of their minority status and how that is acknowledged but also because of their ties to ethnic and religious homelands. That is, perhaps more important to American Muslims is how they are treated in the United States and how the wars in Afghanistan and Iraq are going.

Table 5.3 addresses both of these matters, showcasing how Muslims feel about American foreign policy and their reports of discrimination since September 11, 2001. The first column, on foreign policy, shows that American Muslims provide tepid support for the war in Afghanistan (40 percent) but did not buy the administration's justifications about invading Iraq. About one-sixth think that invading Iraq was worth it, and fewer support the effort or want to send more

Table 5.3 A More Personal Agenda: American Muslim Foreign Affairs Opinions and Reports of Discrimination

Foreign Policy Issues	Support/ Agree (%)	Discrimination Reports	Agree (%)
Support Afghanistan war	39.7	I have experienced discrimination since 9/11	40.1
Support Iraq War	13.9	Others have experienced discrimination since 9/11	58.5
Iraq War was worth it	16.0	Verbal abuse, 2001	25.3
More troops to Iraq	10.7	Verbal abuse, 2004	43.7
Iraq War could mean more terrorism in the United States	86.7	Physical abuse, 2001	6.2
Iraq War could destabilize the Middle East	87.6	Physical abuse, 2004	11.9
Iraq War will bring democracy to Middle East	30.7	Racial profiling, 2001	8.3
Terrorism is best combated by reducing inequalities in the world	92.7	Racial profiling, 2004	24.0
United States should reduce financial support of Israel	89.6	Denied employment, 2001	2.8
United States should support a Palestinian state	94.3	Denied employment, 2004	18.0

Source: MAPS 2001, 2004. All results are from 2004 unless indicated.

troops there. Instead, Muslims feel that the Iraq War could destabilize the region and invite more terrorism in the United States. Consistent with their support for expanded government social welfare support, Muslims feel that terrorism can be undermined by reducing inequality, a point the recent film *Syriana* attempted to drive home. On other issues, Muslims, not surprisingly, support the creation of a Palestinian state and reductions in U.S. support for Israel. Overall, there is very little disagreement among Muslims on these issues.

To discuss the amount of discrimination experienced by Muslims, here we include data from the 2001 survey for comparison, which highlights that time does not heal all wounds, but merely allows them to accumulate. And the wounds are astounding. Fully two-fifths of Muslims report intolerant acts targeted at them, and three-fifths know that others have been victims. All forms of abuse have at least doubled since 2001. Of course the most common is verbal abuse, which jumped from 25 percent having experienced it in 2001 to 43 percent in 2004. Just over a tenth suffered physical abuse, up from 6 percent in 2001, while racial profiling tripled to 24 percent in 2004, and 18 percent perceived they were denied employment in 2004 up from 3 percent in 2001. While we do not have measures assessing their treatment by government, perhaps the extent of discrimination experienced and the strong majority (65 percent) dissatisfaction with "things in U.S. society today" is a sufficient commentary.

Muslims in Elections 2000 and 2004

Though the Muslim community seems to lean Democratic, in the 2000 election a plurality of Muslim voters (48 percent) chose Bush; 36 percent voted for Gore according to the MAPS data. Other reports brought down support for both candidates—the Associated Press (2004) suggested Bush received 42 percent of the Muslim vote, as compared to the 31 percent garnered by Al Gore. Some suggested an affinity with Bush because Muslims are conservative on social issues such as abortion, women's rights, and sexual behavior (Iqbal 2004). The fact that several prominent Muslim groups endorsed George W. Bush for the presidency might also suggest a natural alignment. Rose (2001), for one, debunks both notions, suggesting that these groups are not representative of the Muslim community, since they are largely "Islamists", which would be somewhat akin to saying that the Christian Right speaks for all Christians. He also argues that several short-term factors pushed Muslims toward Bush, including an assumption that Bush would limit government intrusiveness and was less enthusiastically supportive of Israel than Gore.

The Bush administration's response to the terrorist attacks on the World Trade Center and the Pentagon appeared to shatter any hopes of a Muslim pairing with the Republican Party, as Muslims and Arab Americans were forced to endure the brunt of what many saw as the Bush administration's assault on civil liberties and particularly the liberties of Arab Muslims in America (e.g., Ghazali 2004; Iqbal 2004; Turner 2002). To combat such transgressions, the Muslim community showed signs of even greater political activity than they had demonstrated in the past. Even though Muslims traditionally vote in great numbers, with an estimated 79 percent registered to vote, and 85 percent of those registered saying that they vote, the events of September 11 have encouraged Muslims to be even more active politically (Ghazali 2004), a media assertion more or less confirmed with opinion data (Djupe and Green 2006).

In addition to shaking the Muslim community at its foundations, many Muslim organizations were also spurred into action in the aftermath of the attacks. Muslim groups such as the Muslim Public Affairs Council (MPAC), the Council on American-Islamic Relations (CAIR), and the Free Muslim Coalition Against Terrorism began a public relations campaign to raise awareness of the widespread condemnation of terrorism among U.S. Muslims (Cooperman and Murphy 2004). Muslim organizations also launched voter registration campaigns in an effort to register a full 85 percent of the estimated 2 million Muslims estimated to be living in the United States (Iqbal 2004). Additionally, and as a direct result of the crackdown on Islamic charities since September 11, 2001. Muslims began to donate more money, not to overseas charities as they had been but to Muslim civil rights advocacy groups such as CAIR (Goodstein 2004, 1). Indeed, civil rights seemed to be the main issue confronting most Muslims, and many Muslim organizations stressed the importance of active political participation to defend against the erosion of civil liberties (U.S. Newswire 2004c).

In the 2004 election, the defining events of Bush's first term defined the election for American Muslims to produce a radically different outcome (Ghazali 2004; Iqbal 2004). According to the MAPS data, 7 percent of Muslims voted for Bush, 82 percent voted for Kerry, and 10 percent voted for Nader, who is Lebanese. Many Muslims turned against Bush citing civil rights concerns and Bush's avoidance of clear advice from the Muslim community on the Iraq War (Associated Press 2004), for which there is essentially no support in the American Muslim community.

Table 5.4   Vote Switching from 2000 to 2004 among American Muslims

2000 Vote	2004 Vote				
	Kerry (%)	Bush (%)	Other (%)	Did Not Vote (%)	Total (%)
Gore	91.3	3.3	4.2	1.3	40.0
Bush	72.9	14.5	12.7	0.0	28.0
Nader	65.8	0.7	30.3	3.3	11.0
Other	79.2	4.2	16.7	0.0	1.7
Did not vote	80.1	6.4	9.4	4.1	19.3
Total	80.9	6.6	10.8	1.7	~100

Source: MAPS 2004.

The full scope of the transformation is displayed in table 5.4, which shows vote switching from 2000 to 2004 using the self-reports of respondents in 2004. The first thing to note is that many fewer respondents were willing to admit in 2004 that they voted for Bush in 2000—only 35 percent of respondents admitted voting for Bush in 2000 compared to 50 percent for Gore (excluding the self-described non-voters), a 20-point swing. All told, Kerry hung on to the Gore vote and swept every other category, picking up over 70 percent of former Bush voters. Bush was able to maintain about 15 percent of his 2000 voters and picked up a few random voters from other candidates.

The explanations are straightforward (see Djupe and Green 2006 for a complete analysis). For instance, some voters turned because of the discrimination they experienced—Bush kept 22 percent of his 2000 electorate that did not experience discrimination, but only 9.3 percent of his 2000 electorate that did experience discrimination. Bush kept 30 percent of those believing the United States was waging a War on Terrorism versus only 3 percent of those who saw it as a war on Islam. Strikingly, Bush kept 65 percent of those Muslims who got their international news from Fox News versus 12 percent of those who watched other networks.[7]

Until Muslims are better integrated into society and until hot political issues dissipate, the community is unlikely to have strong partisan moorings. For now, it seems unlikely that Muslims will back a Republican candidate, especially one with ties to Bush and strong support for the recent wars as Bush has pursued them. In the long run, Muslims will probably return to a state of fragmentation, largely along class lines, but profoundly shaped by the values that Muslims hold as they try on baggy fit party platforms.

Conclusion

The story emerging from the experience of these three groups in the 2004 election is difficult to summarize. One thing that is definitively not true is that these groups were participants in a culture war and, with the potential exception of Orthodox Jews, do not conform to the idea of a secular-orthodox electoral divide. Instead, to talk about the role of religion, we might conclude that religion is a comprehensive institution that can work in a variety of ways depending on circumstance—adapting to what confronts it and how believers use it.

In the not too distant future, it may become inappropriate to speak of a singular Jewish political community, as the Orthodox slowly distance themselves politically from others who identify as Jews. That is, in the Jewish community religion is a divisive force in the absence of social prejudice that would isolate the community and impose unity. Essentially, the diversity of interests in the Jewish community is starting to exert its natural effect, which is to diversify political commitments, though recently at a glacial pace. In 2004, however, Jews reprised 2000 with their overwhelming opposition to George W. Bush serving another term.

For blacks, religion, by and large, unites and maintains black politics as we have known them, which it has done since the scattered founding of the Black Church (e.g., Lincoln and Mamiya 1990). While there is a small minority of black clergy that has broken off to support Republicans, black political attachment to the Democratic Party is energized by involvement in the Black Church, which is still a center-piece of the black community. Though blacks are socially conservative, Republican attempts to drive a wedge into black support for Democrats has failed without picking up the rest of the agenda. Blacks, it seems, demand representation instead of token support and are unwilling to risk a new party on that gamble.

Political movement within the Muslim community, if such a thing could be said to exist in the United States, appears to have little to do with common commitments to Islam. Whether committed or not, both switched en masse to vote against George W. Bush in 2004. In 2000, religiosity had little to do with vote choice, as social status seemed to win the day. On the other hand, there are few issues on which Muslims are divided, as shown in tables 5.2–5.3, which would lend support to the potency of a common element, such as being Muslim. But the political pattern in 2000 and 2004 implies that the Muslim community does not have a common agenda except for the top priority of maintaining the existence of Muslims—it was only the threat from society and government that united the community. Outside of that common threat, however, there is not yet a set of institutions that can knit together believers, clergy, community organizations, interest groups, and political candidates. Though certainly such a movement may develop in the future, it seems unlikely given the extreme and consequential diversity among Muslims. If Iraq and the Middle East continue to dominate American politics paired with continued domestic intolerance, these issues could supply the community a reason to organize further, as it did historically for Jewish Americans.

The interests of the three groups, described with the best available opinion data, do not comport well with the dominant culture wars politics. The opinions and values of the groups cut across the major axes of conflict—in two cases, blacks and Muslims, in line with Republicans on moral issues and with Democrats on social welfare. For Jews, the community is starting to rend, though still maintaining the elemental incongruity that Jewish vote tendencies do not match the average socioeconomic status of the community. In any event, the movement from one partisan home to another will not be a smooth one, interrupted by traditional momentum and short-term issues and events.

These three stories suggest why culture wars politics does not fit these groups. In part because of their experiences with American government and society, they place a primacy on group interests, which, of course, may include their values. As Sharpton's bid suggests, no group feels the major parties are perfect representatives of their interests. Because of this, it is difficult for these groups to identify with an organized attempt to remake society in either a Christian or secular image since they share much with neither camp. Furthermore, the issues of this particular election, dominated by wars and domestic turmoil over civil rights and liberties and federal programs, did not lend themselves to serious consideration of moral values for these groups. Perhaps once the basic interests of these three groups are secure, which is more the case for Jews than blacks or Muslims, will they open themselves to the pleas of new partisan suitors.

Notes

1. For example, 56.8% of blacks in the 2000 NES thought the presidential election was unfair compared to 34.8% of nonblacks. By the 2004 NES, 83.7% of blacks remembered the 2000 election as unfair compared to

42.4% of nonblacks, which belies, partly, polarization between the parties.

2. The multivariate models also control for socioeconomic status, region, group affiliation, ideology, partisanship, and other standard demographics.

3. The predicted probabilities were calculated with the categorical variables set at their mode, while all other variables were set at their mean.

4. While these effects are drastically different, it is important to note that the literalism effect was significant for whites but not for blacks, mostly due to the small black sample size.

5. The authors wish to thank John Green of the University of Akron for generously sharing these data with us and John Zogby and Zogby International for making the data available to Green. The authors wish to thank John Green for sharing the MAPS data.

6. There are differences between ethnic groups, though surprisingly few differences on social welfare issues. See Djupe and Green (2006) for a full presentation and discussion of these data.

7. Caution must be applied here since only 20 respondents voted for Bush in 2000 and suggested they turned to Fox for "information about international affairs." Only 3.8% turned to Fox in the sample (70 respondents), while the plurality turned to CNN (38.2%). The difference can also be due, in part, to a self-selection effect, as Fox News watchers are more Republican than others, though Bush did only keep about one-sixth of his 2000 electorate.

References

Allen, Richard L., Michael C. Dawson, and Ronald E. Brown. 1989. "A Schema-Based Approach to Modeling an African-American Racial Belief System." *American Political Science Review* 83 (2): 421–441.

American Jewish Committee. 2003. "2003 Annual Survey of American Jewish Opinion." http://www.ajc.org/site/apps/nl/content2.asp?c=ijITI2 PHKoG&b=838459&ct=1051549 (accessed December 15).

——— 2004. "2004 Annual Survey of American Jewish Opinion." http://www.ajc.org/site/apps/nl/content2.asp?c=ijITI2PHKoG&b=838459& ct=1051473 (accessed December 15, 2006).

Associated Press. 2004. "Elections Hold Critical Importance for Religious Voters." October 9.

Balz, Dan. 2004. "Black Voters in S.C. Look to Electability; Sharpton's Message Has Played Better on the Stump Than in the Polls." *Washington Post*, February 3, A9.

Banerjee, Neela. 2005. "Black Churches Struggle Over Their Role in Politics." *New York Times*, March 6.

Baxter, Tom. 2004. "Election 2004: GOP Tries to Pull Jewish Voters to Bush; Kerry Hopes Traditional Patterns Hold." *Atlanta Journal-Constitution*, September 12, 7A.

Ba-Yunus, Ilyas, and Kassim Kone. 2004. "Muslim Americans: A Demographic Report." In *Muslims' Place in the American Public Square: Hopes, Fears, and Aspirations*, edited by Zahid H. Bukhari, Sulayman S. Nyang, Mumtaz Ahmad, and John L. Esposito. New York: Alta Mira.

Besser, James D. 2004. "AJC Poll Punctures Political Wisdom." *Jewish Journal of Greater Los Angeles*, January 16.

Boone, Kathleen. 1989. *The Bible Tells Them So: The Discourse of Protestant Fundamentalism*. Albany, NY: State University of New York Press.

Calhoun-Brown, Allison. 1996. "African American Churches and Political Mobilization: The Psychological Impact of Organizational Resources." *Journal of Politics* 58: 935–953.

——— 1998. "The Politics of Black Evangelicals: What Hinders Diversity in the Christian Right?" *American Politics Quarterly* 26 (1): 81–109.

Chanes, Jerome A. 2001. "Who Does What? Jewish Advocacy and the Jewish Interest." In *Jews in American Politics*, edited by L. Sandy Maisel, Ira N. Forman, Donald Altschiller, and Charles W. Bassett. Lanham, MD: Rowman and Littlefield.

Clemetson, Lynette. 2004. "Both Sides Court Black Churches in the Debate Over Gay Marriage." *New York Times*, March 1: A1.

Cohen, Cathy J. 1999. *The Boundaries of Blackness: AIDS and the Breakdown of Black Politics*. Chicago, IL: University of Chicago Press.

Cohen, Steven M. 1989. *The Dimensions of American Jewish Liberalism*. New York: American Jewish Committee.

Cohen, Steven M., and Charles S. Liebman. 1997. "American Jewish Liberalism: Unraveling the Strands." *Public Opinion Quarterly* 61 (3): 405–430.

Cooperman, Alan, and Carlye Murphy. 2004. "Muslims in U.S. Begin PR Campaign Denouncing Terrorism." *Washington Post*, May 28, A10.

Dawson, Michael C. 1994. *Behind the Mule: Race and Class in African American Politics*. Princeton, NJ: Princeton University Press.

Djupe, Paul A. 2006. "The Evolution of Jewish Pluralism: Public Opinion of American Jews." In *From Pews to Polling Places: Political Mobilization in the American Religious Mosaic*, edited by J. Matthew Wilson. Washington, DC: Georgetown University Press.

Djupe, Paul A., and John C. Green. 2006. "The Politics of American Muslims." In *From Pews to Polling Places: Political Mobilization in the American Religious Mosaic*, edited by J. Matthew Wilson. Washington, DC: Georgetown University Press.

Djupe, Paul A., Jacob R. Neiheisel, and Anand E. Sokhey. 2005. "Clergy and Controversy: A Study of Clergy and Gay Rights in Columbus, Ohio." Paper presented to the annual meeting of the Midwest Political Science Association, Chicago, IL.

Djupe, Paul A., and Anand E. Sokhey. 2003a. "American Rabbis in the 2000 Elections." *Journal for the Scientific Study of Religion* 42 (4): 563–576.

——— 2003b. "The Mobilization of Elite Opinion: Rabbi Perceptions of and Responses to Anti-Semitism." *Journal for the Scientific Study of Religion* 42 (3): 443–454.

Dwyer, Jim, and Jodi Wilgoren. 2004. "Gore and Kerry Unite in Search for Black Votes." *New York Times*, October 25, 1.

Ellison, Christopher G. 1991. "Identification and Separatism: Religious Involvement and Racial Orientations among Black Americans." *Sociological Quarterly* 32 (3): 477–494.

Fears, Darryl. 2004. "Kerry Urged to Do More to Get Black Votes; Lack of Diversity among Top Campaign Officials, Absence in Community Are Concerns." *Washington Post*, June 29, A04.

Fiorina, Morris P. (with Samuel J Abrams and Jeremy C. Pope). 2005. *Culture War? The Myth of a Polarized America*. 2nd ed. New York: Pearson-Longman.

Fowler, Robert Booth, Allen D. Hertzke, Laura R. Olson, and Kevin R. Den Dulk. 2004. *Religion and Politics in America: Faith, Culture, and Strategic Choices*. Boulder, CO: Westview Press.

Froomkin, Dan. 2005. "A Polling Free Fall among Blacks." Washingtonpost. com, October 13. www.washingtonpost.com/wp-dyn/content/blog/2005/10/13/BL2005101300885.html (accessed December 22, 2005).

Ghazali, Abdus Sattar. 2004. "Outside View: Muslims and the '04 Election." *United Press International*, December 6, http://www.upi.com/InternationalIntelligence/Outside_View_Muslims_and_the_04_election/20041203–112431–8425r/ (accessed November 21, 2005).

Goodstein, Laurie. 2004. "Since 9/11, Muslims Look Closer to Home." *New York Times*, November 15, 1.

Goodstein, Laurie, and William Yardley. 2004. "President Benefits from Efforts to Build a Coalition of Religious Voters." *New York Times*, November 5, 22.

Greenberg, Anna, and Kenneth D. Wald. 2000. "Still Liberal after all These Years? The Contemporary Political Behavior of American Jews." In *Jews in American Politics*, edited by L. Sandy Maisel and Ira Forman. Lanham, MD: Rowman and Littlefield.

Guth, James L., Cleveland R. Fraser, John C. Green, Lyman A. Kellstedt, and Corwin E. Smidt. 1996. "Religion and Foreign Policy Attitudes: The Case of Christian Zionism." In *Religion and the Culture Wars: Dispatches from the Front*, edited by John C. Green, James L. Guth, Corwin E. Smidt, and Lyman A. Kellstedt. Lanham, MD: Rowman and Littlefield.

Haddad, Yvonne Yazbeck, and Adair T. Lummis. 1987. *Islamic Values in the United States: A Comparative Study*. New York: Oxford University Press.

Harper, Jennifer. 2005. "Americans Used Faith Factor in Choosing Their President." *Washington Times*, February 4, A07.

Harris, Fredrick C. 1999. *Something Within: Religion in African-American Political Activism*. New York: Oxford University Press.

Harris, Hamil R. 2001. "Blacks Reach Out to Bush." *Washington Post*, January 27, B8.

Hertzke, Allen D. 1993. Echoes of Discontent: Jesse Jackson, Pat Robertson, and the Resurgence of Populism. Washington, DC: CQ Press.

Horowitz, Ami. 2004. "Oy Vey!; Could the Jewish Vote Help George W. Bush Recapture the White House?" *Daily Standard*, March 17. http://www. weeklystandard.com/Content/Public/Articles/000/000/003/866iduji.asp (accessed November 21, 2005).

Hotakainen, Rob. 2004. "Florida: A Battleground State; Jewish Republicans Making Inroads." *Star Tribune*, October 27, 15A.

Iqbal, Anwar. 2004. "Muslims Seek a Role in 2004 Election." United Press International, March 8.

Kellstedt, Lyman A., and John C. Green. 1993. "Knowing God's Many People: Denominational Preference and Political Behavior." In *Rediscovering the Religious Factor in American Politics*, edited by David C. Leege and Lyman A. Kellstedt. Armonk, NY: M. E. Sharpe.

Kessler, E. J. 2003. "Trend: Urban Jews Becoming Moderate Republicans." http://portland.indymedia.org/en/2003/10/274075.shtml (accessed October 11, 2005).

Kirkpatrick, David D. 2004. "Black Pastors Backing Bush Are Rarities, but Not Alone." *New York Times*, October 5, 15.

Lakely, James G. 2003. "Strategists See Jewish Turn to GOP; Cite War on Terror, Israel Support." *Washington Times*, December 28, A03.

Leege, David C., and Lyman A. Kellstedt, eds. 1993. *Rediscovering the Religious Factor in American Politics*. New York: M. E. Sharpe.

Leege, David C., Kenneth D. Wald, Brian S. Krueger, and Paul D. Mueller. 2002. *The Politics of Cultural Differences: Social Change and Voter Mobilization Strategies in the Post-New Deal Period*. Princeton, NJ: Princeton University Press.

Leonard, Karen Isaksen. 2003. *Muslims in the United States: The State of Research*. New York: Russell Sage Foundation.

Levey, Geoffrey Brahm. 1996. "The Liberalism of American Jews—Has It Been Explained?" *British Journal of Political Science* 26 (3): 369–401.

Lewis, Gregory B. 2003. "Black-White Differences in Attitudes toward Homosexuality and Gay Rights." *Public Opinion Quarterly* 67 (1): 59–78.

Lincoln, C. Eric, and Lawrence H. Mamiya. 1990. *The Black Church in African-American Experience*. Durham, NC: Duke University Press.

Lipset, Seymour Martin, and Earl Raab. 1995. *Jews and the New American Scene*. Cambridge, MA: Harvard University Press.

McAdam, Doug. 1982. *Political Process and the Development of Black Insurgency, 1930–1970*. Chicago, IL: University of Chicago Press.

McClerking, Harwood K. 2001. "We Are in This Together: The Origins and Maintenance of Black Common Fate Perceptions." PhD dissertation, Department of Political Science, University of Michigan, Ann Arbor, MI.

Mellman, Mark, Aaron Strauss, Anna Greenberg, Patrick McCreesh, and Kenneth D. Wald. 2005. "The Jewish Vote in 2004: An Analysis." *Solomon Project*, April 12. www.thesolomonproject.org (accessed December 15, 2006).

Miller, Steve. 2001. "NAACP Votes to Fight Bush on His Faith-Based Initiative." *Washington Times*, July 11, A6.

Muslims in American Public Square (MAPS). 2001. "American Muslim Poll, 2001." Zogby International.

—— 2004. "Muslims in the American Public Square: Shifting Political Winds & Fallout from 9/11, Afghanistan and Iraq." Zogby International.

Nagourney, Adam. 2001. "The Post-Sharpton Sharpton." *New York Times*, March 18, 42.

National Election Study (NES), 2004. [machine-readable data file] / Center for Political Studies. University of Michigan [principal investigator(s)] / Ann Arbor, MI: University of Michigan. Center for Political Studies [distributor].

Oppel, Richard A., and Gustav Niebuhr. 2000. "Bush Meeting Focuses on Role of Religion." *New York Times*, December 21, 37.

Philpot, Tasha S. 2004. "A Party of a Different Color? Race, Campaign Communication, and Party Politics." *Political Behavior* 26 (3): 249–270.

Rose, Alexander. 2001. "How Did Muslims Vote in 2000?" *Middle East Quarterly* 8 (3): 13–27.

Sarna, Jonathan D. 2004. "The Battle for the Jewish Vote a Constituency Up for Grabs." *Boston Globe*, October 10, D12.

Seelye, Katharine Q. 2004. "Moral Values Cited as a Defining Issue of the Election." *New York Times*, November 4, P4.

Smith, Jane L. 1999. *Islam in America*. New York: Columbia University Press.

Smith, Tom W. 2001. *Estimating the Muslim Population in the United States*. New York: American Jewish Committee.

Stevenson, Richard A. 2004. "Bush Urges Blacks to Reconsider Allegiance to Democratic Party." *New York Times*, July 24, 1.

Svonkin, Stuart. 1997. *Jews against Prejudice: American Jews and the Fight for Civil Liberties*. New York: Columbia University Press.

Thomas, Ken. 2004. "Jewish Voters Hotly Contested in Florida." Associated Press, October 13.

Tigay, Chanan. 2003. "Will Bush Win Over the Jews?" *Jerusalem Report*, December 1, 28.

Turner, Allan. 2002. "MPAC Houston: 9/11 and the Muslim Community." *Houston Chronicle*, September 8.

UPI (United Press International). 2004. "Jewish Groups Issue Election Guidelines." June 28.http://www.upi.com/NewsTrack/Top_News/Jewish_groups_issue_election_guidelines/20040628–022343–5678r/ (accessed November 21, 2005).

U.S. Newswire. 2004a. "Major U.S. Jewish Groups Release 'Get Out the Vote '04' Guides; To Help Jewish Community Organizations Register, Educate Voters." June 28.

—— 2004b. "Exit Polls: Bush Fails to Attract Jewish Vote; Jewish Vote For Kerry Far Exceeds Recent Averages, Says NJDC." November 3.

—— 2004c. "U.S. Muslims Form Election Task Force." February 17.

Wald, Kenneth D. 1997. *Religion and Politics in the United States*. Washington, DC: CQ Press.

Wald, Kenneth D., and Ted G. Jelen. 2004. "Religion and Political Socialization in Context: A Regional Comparison of the Political Attitudes of American Jews." *American Review of Politics* 25 (Spring–Summer): 99–116.

Wald, Kenneth D., Adam L. Silverman, and Kevin S. Fridy. 2005. "Making Sense of Religion in Political Life." *Annual Review of Political Science* 8: 121–143.

Weisman, Steven R. 2004. "Kerry and Bush Compete for the Role of Israel's Best Friend." *New York Times*, October 31, 15.

Wildavsky, Aaron. 1987. "Choosing Preferences by Constructing Institutions: A Cultural Theory of Preference Formation." *American Political Science Review* 81: 3–21.

Williams, Rhys H., ed. 1997. *Culture Wars in American Politics: Critical Reviews of a Popular Myth*. New York: Aldine de Gruyter.

Wuthnow, Robert. 1988. *The Restructuring of American Religion*. Princeton, NJ: Princeton University Press.

Zald, Mayer N., and John D. McCarthy. 1987. "Religious Groups as Crucibles of Social Movements." In *Social Movements in an Organizational Society*, edited by Mayer N. Zald and John D. McCarthy. New Brunswick, NJ: Transaction.

Zoll, Rachel. 2004. "Polls Show Jews Identify with Dem Values, Hopefuls." Associated Press, January 12.

Part II

Religion and the Policies of the Bush Administration

Chapter Six

Keeping the Charge: George W. Bush, the Christian Right, and the New Vital Center of American Politics

John W. Wells and David B. Cohen

"A Charge to Keep Have I"

George W. Bush is not the first president to reveal at least a portion of his ideology via the artwork in his office, but few have found so obvious a connection to a single painting. The image in question depicts a Methodist circuit rider on horseback, struggling to move up a steep grade. The wind and elements are in his face and yet he trudges on as he moves from town to town, spreading the gospel. This dramatic painting, a visual representation of Charles Wesley's hymn, "A Charge to Keep Have I," hung in the Texas governor's mansion when George W. Bush was serving in Austin. By Bush's own explanation, the W. H. D. Koerner painting provides a stark reminder of the role of chief executive. He serves not simply as the servant of the people but as the servant of God as well. Such is the ascribed meaning of the painting, a symbol of one of the most openly religious modern presidents (Bush 1995; see also Slater 2003/2004).

There is no denying the fact that George W. Bush is a deeply religious man, but so too were other recent presidents such as Jimmy Carter, Ronald Reagan, and Bill Clinton. Despite obvious similarities to some of his predecessors, Bush has become a symbol in America's culture war. Critics see in his religious references a pious confession that seeks to undermine the separation of church and state. Defenders, on the other hand, see a man who is attempting to reconnect an artificially secular public realm to its more religious historical roots.

Much of the current discussion regarding George W. Bush and his relationship to the Christian Right focuses on the unusually close alliance forged between the Bush administration and the leadership of many socially conservative Christian groups. In light of this, the charge that the president is using his faith as a means of sharply dividing the electorate along the lines of culture is widespread in popular anti-Bush literature (e.g., see Corn 2003; Martos 2004; Miller 2004). The contention of this chapter, however, is that whereas the Christian Right forms a key element in the pro-Bush coalition, the administration is by no means a parrot for these same groups. In fact, far from attempting to use religion as a means of isolating the Left culturally and solidifying his claim to right-leaning voters, Bush has skillfully used religion and issues of importance to conservative people of faith as a means of creating a new vital center in American politics. This strategy, while having important differences, is reminiscent of Bill Clinton's famous *triangulation* approach of the mid-1990s. President Clinton was able to resurrect his moribund presidency by placing himself between the conservatives of the 104th Congress and his liberal base. While defending the goals of traditional liberal constituencies, Clinton was able, at the same time, to distance himself from the more ideological elements of his coalition and fashion a center-left position in American politics. In one domestic issue area after another, the Bush White House has sought to carve out a unique center-right solution that appeals to social conservatives without alienating his more secular constituency. This new "vital center" situates the Bush administration's agenda in such a way that it avoids the ideological excesses of his base while at the same time shifts the national conversation in a direction that is more favorable to social conservatives.

Although church attendance emerged as one of the key predictors of vote choice in the 2000 and 2004 elections, Bush's coalition included many voters who considered themselves moderate and even secular. It may very well be the case that the nation's political fault lines, once defined by class, are increasingly being renegotiated along the lines of culture, but that process is far from complete. Democrats are still capable of appealing to the religiously minded and not all evangelicals embrace President Bush or the agenda of the Christian Right. Such realities do not fit easily into the widespread perception of an American culture war of stark polarization. In fact, it is apparent that the political strategists in the Bush White House have not succumbed to the popular descriptions of complete division and still regard elections as being won nearer the center of the electorate.

Bush and the Christian Right:
Origins and Evolution

George W. Bush's relationship to the Christian Right has its origins in his father's successful 1988 campaign. By all accounts, while the elder Bush's relationship with leaders in the Christian Right movement was strained, the younger Bush established a warm rapport. Interestingly, George W. Bush was not the original choice of the Christian Right's rank and file in 2000 as many favored Senator John Ashcroft (R-MO), a devout Pentecostal, who was a standard bearer for social conservatives during the Clinton impeachment effort (Sawyer 1999a, 1999b). After Ashcroft dropped out of the race in 1999, much of that support went to Bush (Schleifer 2000). A key event allowing Bush to gain the support of the evangelical community involved his proclamation during a December 1999 Republican presidential candidate debate that Jesus was his favorite philosopher. According to John Green, Bush's declaration had "a very important political effect. Evangelical Christians and other conservative Protestants immediately understood what he was talking about, and they began to identify with President Bush. . . . By using that personal reference and that personal rhetoric, Bush in effect undercut the campaigns of his rivals, and brought many millions of conservative Christians into his camp" (Green 2003).

Bush steadily gained the support and trust of religious conservatives during the 2000 campaign and added to it four years later. This support has not been offered without some expectations, as many evangelical leaders insisted from the very beginning of the first term that the White House reciprocate in key areas of social policy (e.g., see Gilgoff and Schulte 2005). These demands were made in light of what some Christian Right leaders described as their decisive role in securing the good fortunes experienced by Bush and his party at the ballot box. As evidence, they point to the fact that the Republican Party gained seats in the 2002 congressional elections—a rare occurrence for the incumbent president's party at midterm. In Minnesota, Missouri, and Georgia, where seemingly Democratic-tilting seats all slipped into the Republican column, many Christian Right leaders pointed to the mobilization of evangelical voters as the crucial difference (Hutchinson 2004).

Frustrated commentators on the Left have accused the Bush administration of using religious rhetoric to distract otherwise class-conscious voters from pocketbook issues—issues that might otherwise have led those same people to vote Democratic. Whether or not accurate, it is undeniable that the Christian Right is having a decisive electoral impact throughout the more conservative and rural parts of the country. A good example was the defeat of Brad Carson, the popular former congressman from Oklahoma and failed 2004 Democratic Senate nominee. In a postmortem article on the election, he painted a bleak picture for his party. Carson recounted his experience of attending a church in Tulsa where the minister, who had invited both of the major candidates to appear at a forum on morality and politics, opened the meeting with the question of "who would Jesus vote for?" The minister concluded that Jesus could not support the social libertarianism of the Democratic Party. According to Brad Carson, for a significant portion of the Oklahoma electorate, few other issues mattered (Carson 2004). Such scenes demonstrate the potent position of the Christian Right in the Republican coalition.

It is not always easy to explain the influence of the Christian Right, but one central reality may be that the movement is no longer defined by a single issue. To be sure, abortion remains central, but it is a part of a wider constellation of issues that, while not uniformly endorsed by evangelicals, still constitute a loosely shared socially conservative worldview. In light of this system of beliefs, George W. Bush spent his first term attempting to formulate policy initiatives to shore up his support among groups in the Christian Right community while simultaneously holding on to more secular elements within the GOP.

The GOP coalition is not monolithic, however. Balance is necessary in order to secure a majority of the electorate. Such careful balancing of secular and religious considerations is often overlooked by those who view Bush as simply endorsing the agenda of the Christian Right (Lind 2003). He has in fact often gone to great lengths to reassure secular voters that his is a more balanced approach. At a 2004 town hall meeting in Oregon, for example, Bush was asked by a member of the audience to lead the gathering in prayer for the non-churchgoing majority in the state. Bush declined and then provided an impromptu lecture on the benefits of the separation of church and state. Such episodes demonstrate the extent to which the president attempts to remain balanced. In light of his moderation, what explanations can be offered as to why the Christian Right so enthusiastically supports the Bush administration?

First and foremost, George W. Bush's personal religious narrative fits the familiar pattern of evangelicals. His is a story of early rebellion and mistakes made, followed by later regret. He differs from his father, President George H. W. Bush, a New England Episcopalian, who seemed less interested in reaching out to social conservatives. While the elder Bush's positions on issues such as abortion were considered

tepid, the younger Bush's record is far more conservative. L
father, therefore, George W. Bush was in no need of a politic
sion. Despite an early endorsement from Jerry Falwell at the
the 1988 race for the Republican nomination, George H. W. Bush
never achieved the level of comfort with and support of the leadership
of the Christian Right that his son has enjoyed.

A second factor is the emergence of evangelicals into the cultural
mainstream. The year of Bush's reelection campaign was marked by the
release of the Mel Gibson film *The Passion of the Christ*, which grossed
$360 million in just the first 10 weeks of its release. The Left Behind
Series, a fictionalized treatment of the eschaton by Tim LeHaye, has sold
over 40 million copies and numerous new Christian pop groups have
witnessed their sales levels reaching points normally achieved by their
more secular counterparts (Sheler, Hsu, and Marek 2004). Statistics such
as these provide evidence of the growing strength of evangelicals as a specific subculture. Thus, there is a shrinking gap between evangelicals and
the broader culture, and the increasingly mainstreamed evangelical
movement is more willing than ever to build coalitions with groups less
insistent on doctrinal conformity. The Bush administration's efforts to
incorporate the policy preferences of his Christian Right constituency
may now reflect the religious sensibilities of as much as 25 percent of the
American people (Sheler, Hsu, and Marek 2004).

Domestic Policy and the Christian Right in Bush's First Term

Among the policy areas that Bush addressed in his first term were
abortion, stem-cell research, same-sex marriage, and his much
vaunted faith-based initiative. In the area of abortion, Bush was successful in refashioning the debate by elevating the matter of late-term
abortions over the more general issue of the legality of the practice
overall. In the stem-cell research debate, which garnered a great deal
of attention in the early months of his first term, Bush decided on a
middle course of using existing stem-cell lines for research. Although a
supporter of a constitutional amendment to ban same-sex marriages,
Bush made a late campaign announcement in support of civil unions.
Finally, regarding the faith-based initiative, a core feature of the
"compassionate conservative" agenda, Bush pursued a policy with the
potential of reshaping the nation's political landscape while reforming
the welfare state. In each of these areas, Bush utilized the approach of
finding the pragmatic center-right.

Late-Term Abortion

There is no issue that is more readily identified with the culture war in America than abortion. For 30 years the debate has raged as to whether a woman should have the legal right to choose abortion as a means of contraception. In recent years, the debate has shifted away from earlier controversial flashpoints such as public funding, parental consent, and spousal notification, to newer concerns such as "partial-birth" abortion. The issue of abortion, while clearly a winner for the Republican Party in socially conservative areas of the country such as the rural South and West, is an issue that is nevertheless fraught with political danger. Areas of the electoral map that once offered strong support to national Republicans such as Ronald Reagan have been made at least more competitive for Democrats because of a perceived inflexibility on the part of social conservatives in the Republican Party. Such areas would include the suburbs of many cities in the Northeast and upper Midwest (Judis and Teixeira 2002).

Nevertheless, because the issue is so central to the concerns of such a significant part of the Republican base, it could not be ignored in the first term. The key strategy of focusing on partial-birth abortion shifted the focus of the debate away from the issue of choice, a rhetorical framing device that clearly benefits Democrats, to stressing the graphic details of late-term abortion procedures. The stress on late-term abortions clearly changed the nature of the conversation as evidenced by the testimony of Congressional Democrats in the Red States who found themselves decidedly on the defensive during much of Bush's first term. Congressman Mike Ross (D-AR), for example, found it necessary in his 2002 campaign to stress his opposition to the national Democratic Party's resistance to the Bush administration's late-term abortion legislation (see Carson 2004; Edsall 2000). He was not alone. Democrats throughout the most conservative parts of the country felt compelled to go to great lengths to distance themselves from the national party's perennial support for abortion rights. Jerry Taylor, the mayor of a small Mississippi Delta town articulated a typical refrain when he related his pastor's declaration that it was unchristian to vote for anyone who favored partial-birth abortions (Edsall 2000).

While public opinion continues to show the American electorate at least ambivalent, if not slightly in favor of a more pro-choice position, the issue of late-term abortion resonates in an entirely different way. Otherwise tepid and reluctant supporters of *Roe v. Wade* are often less supportive of a procedure that is often described as "gruesome, brutal, barbaric and uncivilized" (Goldman 2004). The move to place late-term abortions at the center of the debate reached its apotheosis in November of 2003 when President Bush signed the partial-birth abortion ban bill into law. Placing his policy in the broader context of moral duty, Bush explained his support for the bill as one that increased the value of all human life. He referenced the circumstances of the procedure and then invoked the rhetoric of "compassionate conservatism":

> The facts about partial birth abortion are troubling and tragic, and no lawyer's brief can make them seem otherwise. By acting to prevent this practice, the elected branches of our government have affirmed a basic standard of humanity, the duty of the strong to protect the weak. The wide agreement amongst men and women on this issue, regardless of political party, shows that bitterness in political debate can be overcome by compassion and the power of conscience. And the executive branch will vigorously defend this law against any who would try to overturn it in the courts. (Bush 2003b)

The terms of the Bush administration's support for a partial-birth abortion ban cannot be easily missed. Adversaries of the ban are not simply opponents on a policy issue; rather, they are opposed to the "basic standard of humanity." During the first term, this was a constant refrain from many leaders in the Republican congressional leadership. For example, Trent Lott, the Republican Senate minority leader at the time, described the opposition to a ban on late-term abortion as being concentrated on the nation's two coasts: "Where the meat is in the sandwich, the rest of America, these are pretty mainstream ideas" (VandeHei 2002). Such rhetoric allowed Bush to publicly censure the most outspoken proponents of abortion rights while avoiding the perception of being opposed to all legalized abortion. He went on to attach the significance of the ban to traditional images of American exceptionalism:

> America stands for liberty, for the pursuit of happiness and for the unalienable right of life. And the most basic duty of government is to defend the life of the innocent. Every person, however frail or vulnerable, has a place and a purpose in this world. Every person has a special dignity. This right to life cannot be granted or denied by government, because it does not come from government, it comes from the Creator of life. (Bush 2003b)

Bush concluded his remarks at the bill signing by referencing one of the single most consistent opponents of abortion from the Democratic Party, a direct slap at the opposition party's liberal wing: "The late

Pennsylvania Governor Robert Casey once said that: when we look to the unborn child, the real issue is not when life begins, but when love begins. This is the generous and merciful spirit of our country at its best" (Bush 2003b).

Experts are divided as to the extent of the ban on existing abortion practices. There are approximately 1.3 million abortions performed in the country each year. The ban could possibly effect as many as 130,000 but perhaps would outlaw as few as 5,000 (Goldman 2004). Clearly, then, the ban, while very popular and symbolically important among the Christian Right, would have only a minor impact in reducing the total number of abortions in the United States. Democrats were at a loss as to how to frame the issue and no fewer than 17 Democratic senators deserted the party and voted to institute the ban (Stolberg 2003b). Democratic pollsters such as Celinda Lake conceded that the nation was in favor of banning late-term abortions and yet found themselves cross-pressured due to their desire not to see women, whose health might be at risk, compelled by law to take their pregnancies to term (Stolberg 2003b).

By articulating his support for the ban as an element in the quest to establish a "culture of life" in the country, Bush put Democrats on the defensive with a once solid constituency—practicing Roman Catholics. On numerous occasions, Pope John Paul II, who indefatigably led the Church's opposition to both capital punishment and abortion, described a total ban on abortion as a question of promoting a culture of life (VandeHei 2005). The president deliberately associated himself with such sentiments. While speaking at Catholic University in 2001, he remarked that Pope John Paul II "is never more eloquent than when he speaks for a culture of life" (Bush 2001a). Bush was successful in his first term in appealing to Roman Catholic voters, who, despite having a coreligionist on the 2004 ballot, gave their vote to Bush. By shifting the focus to the specifics of partial-birth abortion, Bush met with clear success in his effort to respond to the Christian Right while continuing to occupy the center-right of American politics.

Embryonic Stem-Cell Research

No issue better points to the changing pantheon of Christian Right issues than the question of whether or not embryonic stem cells can be used for medical research. This controversy goes to the heart of the debate regarding the beginning point of life. At issue is whether the use of embryonic stem cells might lead to an overall devaluing of life by making abortion profitable. At the beginning of his administration, Bush was faced with the issue of whether or not to allow federal funding of stem-cell research. Further complicating matters was the division within the evangelical community itself. Prominent social conservatives such as former senator Connie Mack (R-FL) and Senator Orrin Hatch (R-UT) publicly spoke in favor of stem-cell research. Congresswoman Jennifer Dunn (R-WA) collected the signatures of 30 of her Republican House colleagues encouraging Bush to fund research (Thomas and Clift 2001). Further, Health and Human Services Secretary Tommy Thompson was a strong supporter of stem-cell research despite having a solid pro-life record as the former governor of Wisconsin. Vice President Richard Cheney expressed his concern that should a total ban go into place, the United States might fall behind the Europeans in searching for the cures for a number of diseases (Thomas and Clift 2001). The public was overwhelmingly in favor of stem-cell research.

At the same time, many in the pro-life community tended to view stem cells as more than just potential life and instead as actual life deserving to be protected. Public intellectuals such as Francis Fukuyama urged caution, citing the possibility that stem-cell research might, in fact, be but one more step down the road to our "post-human future" (Fukuyama 2003).

Such a complex issue would require careful consideration of the ethical as well as the political ramifications. President Bush seemed genuinely caught between the need to provide hope for the many citizens with debilitating diseases that might be rendered cured by medical advances and the need to honor his pledge to protect human life at whatever stage it existed. Throughout the summer of 2001, Bush met with a number of key advisors, religious as well as scientific, in order to reach a decision. A month before his nationally televised speech, he met with Dr. Leon Kass and Dr. Daniel Callahan, both medical ethicists, and asked the two directly whether or not stem cells, at that stage of development, could be considered human life. Bush was told that given the fact that all human life began at such a stage, the answer was probably yes. It was at that point that he floated a compromise. Was it possible to both honor the sacredness of human life while also advancing science if only existing stem-cell lines were used? Bush received a reluctant nod from both men (Fineman, Rosenberg, and Brant 2001). On August 9, 2001, in a nationally televised speech, the president articulated the moral dilemma he faced:

> My position on these issues is shaped by deeply held beliefs. I'm a strong
> supporter of science and technology, and believe they have the potential

for incredible good—to improve lives, to save life, to conquer disease. Research offers hope that millions of our loved ones may be cured of a disease and rid of their suffering. I have friends whose children suffer from juvenile diabetes. . . . I also believe human life is a sacred gift from our Creator. I worry about a culture that devalues life, and believe as your President I have an important obligation to foster and encourage respect for life in America and throughout the world. And while we're all hopeful about the potential of this research, no one can be certain that the science will live up to the hope it has generated. (Bush 2001c)

He then articulated a middle-of-the-road solution on stem cells, one designed to throw a carrot to the scientific community while at the same time giving the Christian Right hope that all federal funding might be ended for future stem-cell research derived from human embryos:

As a result of private research, more than 60 genetically diverse stem cell lines already exist. They were created from embryos that have already been destroyed, and they have the ability to regenerate themselves indefinitely, creating ongoing opportunities for research. I have concluded that we should allow federal funds to be used for research on these existing stem cell lines, where the life and death decision has already been made. Leading scientists tell me research on these 60 lines has great promise that could lead to breakthrough therapies and cures. This allows us to explore the promise and potential of stem cell research without crossing a fundamental moral line, by providing taxpayer funding that would sanction or encourage further destruction of human embryos that have at least the potential for life. (Bush 2001c)

Although many of the leading figures of the Christian Right such as Jerry Falwell, Pat Robertson, and James Dobson supported Bush's decision, not everyone on the Christian Right was satisfied. Many in the religious community were disappointed that Bush did not end all funding of stem-cell research. Some groups such as the Eagle Forum, Family Research Council, the Prison Fellowship, the Traditional Values Coalition, and the United States Conference of Catholic Bishops were vehement in their opposition. A spokesperson for the Concerned Women for America (CWA) even suggested that stem-cell research is the moral equivalent of Nazi medical experimentation on holocaust victims (Goodstein 2001).

Two events that occurred in 2004 had the effect of vaulting stem-cell research back into the national debate: President Reagan's death on June 6 from complications from Alzheimer's disease, a neurological affliction, and actor Christopher Reeve's death on October 10 due to complications from his paralysis. Advocates contend that restorative neuroscience, of which stem-cell research is a part, could potentially help cure or provide better treatment for people suffering from both Alzheimer's and paralysis (Dolgin 2003).

Ron Reagan's (2004) speech at the Democratic National Convention demonstrated the important place the debate had taken on the national agenda, as the son of the iconic Republican president spoke in favor of allowing stem-cell research:

> There are those who would stand in the way of this remarkable future, who would deny the federal funding so crucial to basic research. They argue that interfering with the development of even the earliest stage embryo, even one that will never be implanted in a womb and will never develop into an actual fetus, is tantamount to murder. A few of these folks, needless to say, are just grinding a political axe and they should he ashamed of themselves. But many are well-meaning and sincere. Their belief is just that, an article of faith, and they are entitled to it. But it does not follow that the theology of a few should be allowed to forestall the health and well-being of the many. And how can we affirm life if we abandon those whose own lives are so desperately at risk? (Reagan 2004)

George W. Bush's compromise in the stem-cell debate is typical of many decisions he made during the first term. He brings religious views and convictions into the equation, but it would be a mistake to view his policy decisions as fully reflecting the convictions of the Christian Right. In fact, Bush's stem-cell policy had the effect of dividing many in the religious community, further evidence of his pragmatic approach on some of the hottest ethical topics. Most often, what Bush offers the Christian Right is the assurance that it will be consulted—an important source of power but hardly a blank check to make policy.

Same-Sex Marriage

Few issues have evoked as intense a response as the question of whether gay and lesbian couples should be allowed to legally marry. Gay rights in general have been gaining increasing attention in American politics. On one side of the debate is the extent to which the state can sanction one particular form of intimacy over any other and thereby privilege one kind of union over others. The Supreme Court decision in *Bowers v. Hardwick* (1986), where the Court refused to recognize homosexuality as a suspect classification deserving of heightened protection under the

Fourteenth Amendment, remains precedent. Proponents of gay rights, however, argue that the constitutional right to privacy should be extended to their community as well. Marriage, in this view, should be regarded as a private contract binding two consenting adults (Johnson 2005). Thus, the issue pits two classical positions, tradition and liberal autonomy, against one another.

In the trade-off between tradition and social libertarianism, the Republican Party has increasingly moved in the direction of supporting tradition. This would stand to reason given the increasing power of the Christian Right, but the dilemma for President Bush formed on other lines as well. On the one hand, conservatives have a long history of supporting states' rights. Since the days of the New Deal, conservatives have consistently pointed to what they saw as a dangerous devaluing of the Tenth Amendment and the centralization of national policy. The problem for Bush is the difficulty in maintaining support for this traditional plank in the conservative political constellation while supporting the demands of social conservatives for a national amendment to define marriage as pertaining strictly to one man and one woman. The "Full Faith and Credit Clause" of the Constitution requires states to accept marriages performed in other states. Like abortion and stem-cell research, Bush struggled to find a political path that might satisfy not simply the right and the middle, but different factions of conservatives.

Initially, Bush seemed content to leave gay marriage in the hands of state legislatures; however, Christian Right leaders, along with their congressional allies, steadily increased their demands. In 2003, the issue was propelled into the national limelight by the decision of lower courts to allow for same-sex marriage, as well as the *Lawrence v. Texas* case in which the Supreme Court struck down a Texas statute criminalizing sodomy involving two persons of the same gender. Led by senators John Cornyn (R-TX) and Rick Santorum (R-PA), Senate Republicans began urging the White House to publicly throw its support behind a constitutional amendment to protect the traditional definition of marriage (Gilgoff 2003; Stolberg 2003a).

At a Rose Garden ceremony in the summer of that year, President Bush began articulating the middle passage. When asked whether he supported an amendment, he replied, "I am mindful that we're all sinners" (Bush 2003a). He thus struck a tone that would be recognized in the evangelical community. Bush went on to add, "And I caution those who may try to take the speck out of their neighbor's eye when they got a log in their own. I think it's very important for our society to respect each individual, to welcome those with good hearts, to be a welcoming country" (Bush 2003a). By using religious references, Bush appeared conciliatory and tolerant without alienating his supporters. He did not leave the matter there, however. Bush reaffirmed his support for the traditional definition of marriage: "I believe a marriage is between a man and a woman. And I think we ought to codify that one way or the other" (Bush 2003a).

Christian Right leaders began pressing the president to be even clearer in his rhetoric and by the beginning of 2004, they were openly warning the White House that their supporters would need a firmer commitment on the part of the administration if they hoped for a strong turnout in the upcoming elections (Kirkpatrick 2004a). From the outset of the first term, Karl Rove, Bush's key political advisor, had envisioned the need to mobilize social conservatives for the 2004 campaign. According to Rove, as many as 4 million would-be Republican voters stayed away from the polls in 2000 (Nather 2004). Their support would be crucial for ensuring reelection. In February 2004, Bush placated the Christian Right by announcing his support of a constitutional ban on same-sex marriage. Denouncing "activist judges" and "local officials who ignore the law," Bush called on Congress to respond:

> Marriage cannot be severed from its cultural, religious and natural roots without weakening the good influence of society. Government, by recognizing and protecting marriage, serves the interests of all. Today I call upon the Congress to promptly pass, and to send to the states for ratification, an amendment to our Constitution defining and protecting marriage as a union of man and woman as husband and wife. The amendment should fully protect marriage, while leaving the state legislatures free to make their own choices in defining legal arrangements other than marriage. (Bush 2004a)

While the president's comments were popular with many evangelicals, the political payoff from his stand on gay rights is difficult to gauge. For those most fervently in favor of the position, it is doubtful that their votes were truly up for grabs. What is more likely is that the intensity level increased for those already supporting Bush. Nonetheless, it is a mistake to lump all evangelicals together in a monolithic block. James Guth advised that whereas evangelicals do share a general worldview that would tend to view homosexuality as a sin, the views of Northern Reformed tradition conservatives were less likely to be enthusiastic about the political stand of the White House than their Southern counterparts (Kirkpatrick 2004a).

Many Christian Right leaders were disappointed in the immediate reaction of their parishioners. Instead of the intense reaction in support of Bush's initiative, the pews seemed rather still just months after the announcement. Richard Land, a leading spokesman for the Southern Baptist Convention (SBC), spent much of 2003 and 2004 warning the Bush White House that the rank-and-file members of his denomination were outraged by the efforts of many in the gay community to secure the right to marry. To his surprise, however, there had yet to be a large and enthusiastic response from many congregations of the SBC (Kirkpatrick 2004b).

While many on Capitol Hill expressed their opposition to gay marriage, they failed to fall into line behind the White House initiative. In the summer of 2004, with the nation already fully charged by the upcoming election, the Senate failed to shut off debate on the question, effectively killing the chances for passing the proposed amendment. Most disappointing to the White House was the failure to secure all of the votes from members of the GOP Senate caucus. Six Republicans voted with the Democrats in the procedural vote, while only three Democrats deserted their partisan colleagues (Dewar 2004). Although the measure failed, Bush had forged a strong symbolic bond with his base. Bush continued to tout his support for a marriage amendment. John Kerry, by contrast, distanced himself from the debate, even to the point of skipping the procedural vote that ultimately ended the legislative life of the proposal.

Some social conservatives, in the meantime, expressed their displeasure with the Bush administration for failing to secure passage of the amendment. "Social conservatives are not happy," reported Tony Perkins, president of the Family Research Council (Nagourney and Kirkpatrick 2004). Perkins reflected the thinking of many in the movement who considered Bush's support for the amendment to be at best tepid. This came as a surprise to some leaders in the movement, especially given the high level of opposition to gay marriage as gauged by numerous public opinion polls. The question of Bush losing evangelical voters, however, was never really in doubt. Those disappointed in the perceived lack of support for the constitutional amendment were unlikely to jump to Kerry. The fear on the part of the Bush's political advisors was that the failure to actually deliver the amendment might dampen turnout.

Disappointment among evangelicals only deepened late in the campaign when President Bush seemed to tack to the middle and endorse civil unions: "I don't think we should deny people rights to a civil union, a legal arrangement, if that's what a state chooses to do," remarked Bush in an ABC *Good Morning America* interview (Bumiller 2004). He went on to make clear that while he viewed the question of civil unions as a state matter, the word marriage itself should be reserved only for heterosexual couples. The distinction Bush was making was satisfactory to many Christian Right groups but not for all. For example, while the Alliance for Marriage supported Bush's position, the Concerned Women for America was outspoken in its opposition: "Civil unions are a government endorsement of homosexuality," declared Robert Knight, director of the Culture and Family Institute of CWA. Generally, the president's allies in the Christian Right muted their criticism and, while less than satisfied with the failure to pass the constitutional amendment and the late endorsement of civil unions, pledged their support for turning out as many evangelicals to the polls as possible (Stone and Vaida 2004).

Following his reelection, Bush appeared reluctant to spend more political capital on the issue of a marriage amendment. From the view of the White House, other policy matters were of greater concern. Bush's comments in an interview that "nothing will happen" regarding a constitutional amendment created a maelstrom on the right. Christian Right leaders who supported him in 2004 were "deeply concerned" by the president's comments and seeming lack of enthusiasm to push the marriage amendment (Easton 2005). The Arlington Group, a coalition that includes many of the leaders of the Christian Right, sent Karl Rove a letter threatening to withhold support of the administration's Social Security reform plan unless Bush provided the "same energy to preserving traditional marriage" as he was expending to overhaul Social Security (Kirkpatrick and Stolberg 2005). When Tony Perkins was asked to estimate, on a scale of one to ten, the level of discontent with the Bush White House on matters of social policy, he replied it was around an eight (Kirkpatrick and Stolberg 2005). Amidst this firestorm, Bush reversed course. White House Press Secretary Scott McClellan moved promptly to reassure Christian Right activists:

> The President is very firm in his belief that marriage is a sacred institution between a man and a woman, and he is concerned about steps that have been taken by activist judges. That's why the President believes it's necessary for us to move forward on a constitutional amendment to protect the sanctity of marriage. He's going to continue speaking out about the importance of protecting the sanctity of marriage and moving forward on a constitutional amendment. And he continues to urge Congress to act on that. (McClellan 2005)

One week later, in his 2005 State of the Union address, Bush went on record supporting the marriage amendment: "Because marriage is a sacred institution and the foundation of society, it should not be redefined by activist judges. For the good of families, children, and society, I support a constitutional amendment to protect the institution of marriage" (Bush 2005). Though the amendment received only two sentences in a speech in which Social Security reform composed nearly 25 percent, Bush, at least, supported publicly the effort.

Ultimately, Bush wavered little on the question of gay marriage. He was consistently opposed to altering the traditional definition of heterosexual marriage and yet, one can see the moderation in the administration's position, especially as the election neared. This indicates that the much vaunted strategy of turning the election of 2004 into a "base" election, while true in some respects, fails to capture the subtle distinctions Bush made in order to appeal to moderates in his own party and middle-of-the-road independents.

Faith-Based Initiative

At the heart of President Bush's compassionate conservatism is the faith-based initiative. Through this initiative, religious-based groups are eligible for federal funds to deliver a variety of social services. In this policy area, Bush was able to co-opt the claims of the Left and seize the middle ground. Since at least the New Deal, liberals have decried the lack of conservative commitment to fighting poverty. Conservatives routinely responded that antipoverty policies were ineffective. In recent years, the debate has turned to a comparison of state-directed agencies versus their religious counterparts (Donaldson and Carlson-Thies 2003). By advocating a faith-based approach, Bush was able to join the traditional conservative critique of welfare liberalism while simultaneously supporting the objectives of that same system and shoring up conservatism's credentials for fighting poverty and inequality.

Citing a Texas drug rehabilitation program as his model, President Bush appointed John Dilulio, a political scientist at the University of Pennsylvania and a Democrat, to oversee the policy proposal early in the term. The legislation that was ultimately proposed, however, was loaded with what Dilulio himself regarded as "political non-starter" provisions that almost guaranteed defeat (Sullivan 2003). Undeterred by roadblocks on Capitol Hill, Bush proceeded to push the program forward through a series of executive actions. Regardless of the legislative setbacks, the president's policy proved to be relatively popular at the end of his first term.

As is the case with most policy proposals, there was a political angle to Bush's support. On the one hand, by supporting church-sponsored programs, the appearance of lowering the wall of separation between church and state could be made manifest, a move that would endear the president to many social conservatives. On the other hand, it would go far toward ameliorating the view that Republicans have little concern for the poor and disadvantaged. Finally, it was hoped that the strongest payoff would be among the nation's Roman Catholics and African Americans, constituencies with traditional homes in the Democratic Party (Clymer 2001). Late in Bush's first term, research confirmed the strong support the administration enjoyed among many targeted groups. Latino Protestants, a key swing group, voiced support for faith-based initiatives at a higher level than any other group (62 percent), with Black Protestants only slightly less supportive (61 percent) (Green 2004, Table 25).

Bush was in need of shoring up his support among Catholics at the beginning of his term. Memories of his 2000 appearance at Bob Jones University, a fundamentalist Protestant campus where the founder once referred to the Catholic Church as a "satanic cult," lingered (Postman and Brunner 2000). The proposal would have the benefit of staking out a new middle ground in the debate regarding the relationship between religion and government. Critics, however, raised the alarm that Bush's proposals, far from being a benign approach to providing social services, would require the poor to recite some religious confession in order to receive assistance. "This is an end run around Congress that will allow groups to get taxpayer money and discriminate as they hire only people of their own religion," said Representative Barney Frank (D-MA) (Leonard 2002).

In some ways, such opposition played into the hands of White House political advisors who quickly turned such rhetoric into the charge that the Democrats were a party openly hostile to religion. "In government, we're still fighting old attitudes, habits and rules that discriminate against religious groups for no good purpose," proclaimed Bush (Bush 2002). The rhetoric of religious persecution in America falls on willing and receiving ears in many parts of the evangelical community. Bill Fried, an op-ed columnist, observed at a faith-based social services summit in 2004 that the talk of public policy was routinely interrupted by the consistent narrative that the wall between church and state has been lowered too far. Secular humanists, according to one speaker, were intolerant and trying to banish religion from American society (Fried 2004). For Bush's critics, it is this culture war angle that is most disturbing. While Bush has used the language of "us and them" in the context of the War on Terror, the fear is that such language might eventually permeate the discussions of the faith-based initiative (Fried 2004).

Democrats throughout the first term were wary that the White House was using the initiative to shore up vulnerable House and Senate candidates, especially during the mid-term elections. They pointed to the fact that Representative Ann Northrup (R-KY), who holds a swing district centered in traditionally Democratic Louisville, was awarded a $5 million grant for predominantly African American neighborhoods including a $400,000 grant for a church-based community center. Seminars sponsored by the White House on faith-based and community funding were also held in South Carolina to reach out to African American ministers before the Senate race to replace Strom Thurmond (Edsall and Cooperman 2002).

While the faith-based initiative has had only limited success receiving congressional support, the political implications of the policy are difficult to overestimate. It once again highlights the partisan divide in the country with Democrats raising objections about the entangling nature of the arrangements while Republicans were urging "new thinking" in regards to the nation's social policy (Edsall and Cooperman 2002). The political possibilities of reaching beyond this traditional divide point to nothing short of a possible realigning of the nation's political landscape in favor of the GOP. By opposing the Bush administration's faith-based initiative, Democrats were placed on the defensive, seeming to support programs and approaches that admittedly have not ended poverty. In this sense, Bush was able to cut a path between conservatives in his own party, who oppose activist government, and liberal Democrats, whose defense of existing programs ironically painted them as conservatives.

Bush's faith-based initiative has received opposition from some unexpected quarters: religious groups. It is a mistake to view the Christian community, and even the evangelical community for that matter, as being uniformly in support of a state-church united front in the fight against social ills. While traditionalists in all denominations tend to be more supportive of the policy, Mainline Protestants are more evenly divided. There are numerous theological controversies that are engaged when the issue of state and church cooperation is raised. There is the fear that the church might have to avoid proselytizing in order to receive funding, thus diluting the religious mission of the church. Minority religions are also less sanguine about the Bush administration's policy, sensing a resurgence of officially sanctioned Christian hegemony.

The administration failed to put the initiative fully into effect, although Bush could boast that more than a billion dollars in increased funding was flowing to religious charities at the end of his first term than at the beginning (Sullivan 2003). The policy of aiding religious programs designed to combat social ills served as yet more evidence of the effort to alter the nation's political landscape and to firmly situate Bush and his party in a more favorable political position.

Bush, the Christian Right, and the New Vital Center

At first glance, George W. Bush's relationship to the Christian Right would seem to offer explanation as to why he has become such a polarizing figure in American politics. His opposition to late-term abortion rights, support for the faith-based initiative, opposition to embryonic stem-cell research, and support for a constitutional amendment prohibiting same-sex marriage would all seem to indicate why many in the Christian Right are so supportive while liberals and secularists are more suspicious. On closer examination, however, it becomes apparent that Bush's support for the Christian Right agenda is not that simplistic. Conservative social initiatives have often taken a backseat to his support for economic proposals such as tax cuts and deregulation. It would be difficult, therefore, to describe Bush's efforts on behalf of the Christian Right to be a redefinition of the Republican Party's issue priorities.

More importantly, the substance of Bush's social issues proposals is far from ideologically pure. In fact, Bush has used the social issues agenda of the Christian Right to facilitate a kind of triangulation in American politics. He has creatively carved out new middle space in many of the perennial debates and has therefore satisfied all but the most zealous of his supporters, while at the same time holding onto the support of more secular voters. By refocusing the debate regarding abortion away from the issue of rights and strictly on late-term or partial-birth, he has placed pro-choice advocates on the defensive. By securing the use of existing stem-cell lines, the Bush administration was able to steer a middle course in that policy area as well. By the same token, his early support of a constitutional amendment banning same-sex marriage was arguably a safe position to take given the lack of necessary congressional support and thus a real chance of an amendment making it out of Congress. Finally, perhaps no area more directly symbolizes Bush's efforts as the faith-based initiative. He was able to gain support from traditionally Democratic constituencies while also satisfying the desires of many conservatives for a rolled-back welfare state.

In assessing George W. Bush's successes in these areas, it is apparent that he is not the mere mouthpiece of the Christian Right, as some critics allege. Bush has used a pragmatic, center-right approach to appealing to his conservative base. His success in maintaining high levels of support with these constituencies demonstrates the continuing willingness of the American people to respond to religious appeals as long as they appear as manifestations of a middle-of-the-road civil religion and not the agenda of the theological fringe. Further, the success enjoyed by Bush in his center-right strategy reveals important insights into the Christian Right as well. While many evangelicals have demonstrated levels of intractability while engaged in the theological controversies of their respective denominations, there appears to be far more support for pragmatic coalition building on the national political stage.

Given the media focus on the Christian Right's role in Bush's 2004 election victory, the danger for Bush in his second term is that Christian Right activists and leaders may not be as willing to accept his pragmatism. After all, Bush is a lame duck who no longer has the excuse that he must moderate for electoral positioning; rather, those in the Christian Right may expect to see Bush's "true colors" now that the pressure of facing reelection has passed. Bob Jones III, president of Bob Jones University, typifies this sentiment of expectation in a postelection congratulatory letter to Bush:

In your re-election, God has graciously granted America—though she doesn't deserve it—a reprieve from the agenda of paganism. You have been given a mandate. We the people expect your voice to be like the clear and certain sound of a trumpet. Because you seek the Lord daily, we who know the Lord will follow that kind of voice eagerly. Don't equivocate. Put your agenda on the front burner and let it boil. You owe the liberals nothing. They despise you because they despise your Christ. Honor the Lord, and He will honor you. . . . Undoubtedly, you will have opportunity to appoint many conservative judges and exercise forceful leadership with the Congress in passing legislation that is defined by biblical norm regarding the family, sexuality, sanctity of life, religious freedom, freedom of speech, and limited government. You have four years—a brief time only—to leave an imprint for righteousness upon this nation that brings with it the blessings of Almighty God. . . . On occasion, Christians have not agreed with things you said during your first term. Nonetheless, we could not be more thankful that

God has given you four more years to serve Him in the White House, never taking off your Christian faith and laying it aside as a man takes off a jacket, but living, speaking, and making decisions as one who knows the Bible to be eternally true. (Jones 2004)

Cracks in the coalition have already appeared—the furor over Bush's initial reluctance to support another marriage amendment is but one example. The hullabaloo that developed over Senator Arlen Specter's (R-PA) comments that the president should be cautious in his future judicial appointments is another. Though the Christian Right lost that battle and Specter became chair of the Judiciary Committee, it is obvious that the Christian Right was emboldened following the election. And certainly the movement was very pleased with Bush's eventual choices for two Supreme Court openings. It is interesting to note, however, that the Bush administration's first major policy push of the second term did not involve a values issue but rather Social Security reform, providing even further evidence that Bush is determined to chart his own course.

The Koerner painting that hung in the Texas governor's mansion when Bush was governor now hangs in the White House. The image of the Methodist circuit riders is interesting given Bush's governing experience. There is no doubt that Bush views himself and his administration as tasked with "keeping the charge" of promoting, through public policy, the values of the Christian Right; however, he has chosen to ride a more careful path between those who subscribe to a traditional view of American society and those whose views are more secular. To date, Bush's center-right strategy has allowed him to successfully spread the political gospel while not becoming a casualty of the culture war. Only time will tell whether or not he continues to ride the same path of pragmatism, or even stays on the horse, championing the values agenda.

References

Akron v. Akron Center for Reproductive Health. 1983. 462 U.S. 416.

Begley, Sharon. 2001. "Cellular Divide." *Newsweek*, July 9.

Bowers v. Hardwick. 1986. 478 U.S. 186.

Broder, David S. 1996. "Dole's Sunny Disposition." *Washington Post*, March 11.

Buchanan, Patrick J. 1992. "1992 Republican National Convention Speech." August 17, Houston, TX. http://www.buchanan.org/pa-92-0817-rnc.html (accessed March 12, 2005).

Bumiller, Elisabeth. 2004. "Bush Says His Party Is Wrong to Oppose Gay Civil Unions." *New York Times*, October 26.

Bush, George W. 1995. "Memo: 'A Charge to Keep Have I." April 3. http://www.pbs.org/wgbh/pages/frontline/shows/jesus/readings/ chargetokeepmemo.html (accessed March 12, 2005).

———. 2001a. "Remarks by the President at Dedication of the Pope John Paul II Cultural Center." March 22. http://www.whitehouse.gov/news/releases/ 2001/03/20010322-14.html (accessed March 11, 2005).

———. 2001b. "Remarks by President Bush and His Holiness Pope John Paul II." July 23. http://www.whitehouse.gov/news/releases/2001/07/20010723-1.html (accessed March 11, 2005).

———. 2001c. "Remarks by the President on Stem Cell Research." August 9. http://www.whitehouse.gov/news/releases/2001/08/20010809-2.html (accessed March 11, 2005).

———. 2002. "President Bush Implements Key Elements of His Faith-Based Initiative." December 12. http://www.whitehouse.gov/news/releases/2002/ 12/20021212-3.html (accessed March 8, 2005).

———. 2003a. "President Bush Discusses Top Priorities for the U.S." July 30. http://www.whitehouse.gov/news/releases/2003/07/20030730-1.html (accessed March 12, 2005).

———. 2003b. "President Bush Signs Partial Birth Abortion Ban Act of 2003." November 5. http://www.whitehouse.gov/news/releases/2003/11/ 20031105-1.html (accessed March 8, 2005).

———. 2004a. "President Calls for Constitutional Amendment Protecting Marriage." February 24. http://www.whitehouse.gov/news/releases/2004/ 02/20040224-2.html (accessed March 12, 2005).

———. 2004b. "President and Mrs. Bush's Remarks at Ask President Bush Event with Small Business Owners." August 13. http://www.whitehouse. gov/news/releases/2004/08/20040813-7.html (accessed March 10, 2005).

———. 2005. State of the Union Address." February 2. http://www. whitehouse.gov/news/releases/2005/02/20050202-11.html (accessed March 12, 2005).

Cannon, Lou, and David Broder. 1980. "Newly Combative Reagan Places Sights on Bush in New Hampshire Race." *Washington Post*, February 10.

Carson, Brad. 2004. "Vote Righteously!" *New Republic*, November 22.

Carter, David. 2004. *Stonewall: The Riots that Sparked the Gay*. New York: St. Martin's.

Clymer, Adam. 2001. "Bush Aggressively Courts Catholic Voters for 2004." *New York Times*, June 1.

CNN Exit Polls. 2004. http://www.cnn.com/ELECTION/2004/pages/results/ states/US/P/00/epolls.0.html (accessed March 13, 2005).

Corn, David. 2003. *The Lies of George W. Bush: Mastering the Politics of Deception*. New York: Crown.

Curtius, Mary. 2004. "Urged Judicial Remarks Stir Conservatives." *Los Angeles Times*, November 5.

Dean, Howard. 2003. "Address to Democratic National Committee WinterMeeting." February 21. http://www.crocuta.net/Dean/Transcript_of_Speech_to_DNC_Winter_Meeting.htm (accessed March 12, 2005).

Dewar, Helen. 2005 [SHOULD BE 2004]. "Ban On Gay Marriage Fails." *Washington Post*, July 15.

Dolgin, Janet L. 2003. "Embryonic Discourse: Abortion, Stem Cells, and Cloning." *Florida State University Law Review* 31 (Fall): 101–162.

Donaldson, Dave, and Stanley Carlson-Thies. 2003. *A Revolution of Compassion: Faith-Based Groups as Full Partners in Fighting America's Social Problems*. Grand Rapids, MI: Baker Books.

Easton, Nina J. 2005. "Mood Dampened For Conservatives." *Boston Globe*, January 20.

Edsall, Thomas B. 2000. "Gore, Democrats Face Challenges in Wooing South." *Washington Post*, September 28.

Edsall, Thomas B., and Alan Cooperman. 2002. "GOP Using Faith Initiative to Woo Voters." *Washington Post*, September 15.

Fineman, Howard, Debra Rosenberg, and Martha Brant. 2001. "Bush Draws A Stem Cell Line." *Newsweek*, August 20.

Fornek, Scott. 1996. "Who Should Wield Power?" *Chicago Sun-Times*, October 29.

Frank, Thomas. 2004. *What's the Matter with Kansas: How Conservatives Won the Heart of America*. New York: Metropolitan Books.

Fried, Bill. 2004. "Good Faith and Bad Faith." *Boston Globe*, August 6.

Fukuyama, Francis. 2003. *Our Posthuman Future: Consequences of the Biotechnology Revolution*. New York: Picador USA.

Gilgoff, Dan. 2003. "Gays Force the Issue." *U.S. News & World Report*, August 18.

Gilgoff, Dan, and Bret Schulte. 2005. "The Dobson Way." *U.S. News & World Report*, January 17.

Goldman, John J. 2004. "Abortion Ban Ruled Unconstitutional." *Los Angeles Times*, August 27.

Goodstein, Laurie. 2001. "Abortion Foes Split Over Plan on Stem Cells." *New York Times*, April 12.

Gorski, Eric. 2004. "Dobson Shifts Power to Focus on the Politics." *Denver Post*, November 14.

Green, John C. 1996. "A Look at the 'Invisible Army': Pat Robertson's 1988 Activist Corps." In *Religion and the Culture Wars: Dispatches from the Front*, edited by John C Green, James L. Guth, Corwin E. Smidt, and Lyman A. Kellstedt. Lanham, MD: Rowman and Littlefield.

——— 2003. "The Jesus Factor: John Green Interview." *Frontline*, December 5. http://www.pbs.org/wgbh/pages/frontline/shows/jesus/interviews/green.html (accessed March 12, 2005).

Green, John C. 2004. "The American Religious Landscape and Political Attitudes: A Baseline for 2004." *Fourth National Survey of Religion and Politics*, March–May 2004, Ray C. Bliss Institute of Applied Politics University of Akron. http://pewforum.org/publications/surveys/green-full.pdf (accessed March 13, 2005).

Green, John C., Corwin E. Smidt, James L. Guth, and Lyman A. Kellstedt. 2004. "The American Religious Landscape and the 2004 Presidential Vote: Increased Polarization." *Fourth National Survey of Religion and Politics, Post-Election Sample*, November–December 2004, Ray C. Bliss Institute of Applied Politics University of Akron. http://pewforum.org/publications/surveys/postelection.pdf (accessed March 13, 2005).

Grove, Lloyd. 1995. "How to Triangulate an Oval Office." *Washington Post*, November 28.

Hamilton, Pamela. 2005. "Bob Jones U. President to Retire." *State*, January 20.

Hunter, James Davison. 1992. *Culture Wars: The Struggle to Define America.* New York: Basic Books.

Hutchinson, Fred. 2004. "The Emerging Republican Majority." November 8. http://www.renewamerica.us/columns/hutchison/041108 (accessed March 15, 2005).

Hyde, Henry. 1996. "Henry Hyde's Plea to Override President Clinton's Veto of the Partial-Birth Abortion Ban." September 19. http://www.nrlc.org/news/2003/NRL01/hyde.html (accessed March 11, 2005).

Johnson, John W. 2005. *Griswald v. Connecticut: Birth Control and the Constitutional Right to Privacy.* Lawrence, KS: University Press of Kansas.

Jones, Bob III. 2004. "Congratulatory Letter to President George W. Bush from Dr. Bob Jones III." November 3. http://www. publicdomainprogress. info/2004/11/congratulatory-letter-to-president.html (accessed March 12, 2005).

Judis, John B., and Ruy Teixeira. 2002. *The Emerging Democratic Majority.* New York: Scribner.

Kellstedt, Lyman A., John C. Green, James L. Guth, and Corwin E. Smidt. 1996. "Has Godot Finally Arrived? Religion and Realignment." In *Religion and the Culture Wars: Dispatches from the Front*, edited by John C Green, James L. Guth, Corwin E. Smidt, and Lyman A. Kellstedt. Lanham, MD: Rowman and Littlefield.

Kirkpatrick, David D. 2004a. "In Fight Over Gay Marriage, Evangelicals Are Conflicted." *New York Times*, February 28.

——— 2004b. "Backers of Gay Marriage Ban Find Tepid Response in Pews." *New York Times*, May 16.

——— 2005. "In Secretly Taped Conversations, Glimpses of the Future President." *New York Times*, February 20.

Kirkpatrick, David D., and Sheryl Gay Stolberg. 2005. "Backers of Gay Marriage Ban Use Social Security as Cudgel." *New York Times*, January 25.

Kneeland, Thomas E. 1980. "Bush Feels Free to Differ With Reagan." *New York Times*, July 28.

Lawrence v. Texas. 2003. 539 U.S. 558.

Leonard, Mary. 2002. "Bush Eases Way for Religious Charities." *Boston Globe*, December 13.

Lind, Michael. 2003. *Made in Texas: George W. Bush and the Southern Takeover of American Politics*. New York: Basic Books.

Martos, Joseph J. 2004. *May God Bless America: George W. Bush and Biblical Morality*. Arizona: Fenestra Books.

McClellan, Scott. 2005. "Press Briefing by Scott McClellan." January 25. http://www.whitehouse.gov/news/releases/2005/01/20050125-2.html#8 (accessed March 12, 2005).

Miller, Mark Crispin. 2004. *Cruel and Unusual: Bush/Cheney's New World Order*. New York: W.W. Norton.

Morris, Richard S. 1999. *Behind the Oval Office: Getting Reelected against All Odds*. Los Angeles, CA: Renaissance Books.

Nagourney, Adam, and David D. Kirkpatrick. 2004. "Urged by Right, Bush Takes On Gay Marriages." *New York Times*, July 12.

Nather, David. 2004. "Social Conservatives Propel Bush, Republicans to Victory." *CQ Weekly*, November 6, 2586-2591.

Phan, Katherine T. 2004. "Bush's Tolerance of Civil Unions Spurs Ambivalent Reactions." *Christian Post*, October 27. http://www.christianpost.com/article/society/1118/full/bushs.tolerance.of.civil.unions.spurs.ambivalent.reactions/1.htm (accessed March 12, 2005).

Planned Parenthood v. Ashcroft. 1983. 462 U.S. 476.

Planned Parenthood v. Casey. 1992. 505 U.S. 833.

Postman, David, and Jim Brunner. 2000. "Bush Apologizes for School Visit." *Seattle Times*, February 28.

Reagan, Ron. 2004. "Ron Reagan's Remarks at the Democratic Convention." *USA Today*, July 29.

Sawyer, Jon. 1999a. "Ashcroft Nears Summit of His Political Climb." *St. Louis Post-Dispatch*, January 3.

——— 1999b. "Ashcroft Rejects 'Ambition,' Says He Won't Seek Presidency." *St. Louis Post-Dispatch*, January 6.

Schleifer, Yigal. 2000. "Playing the Jesus Card." *Jerusalem Post*, January 17.

Schlesinger, Arthur M., Jr. 1997. *The Vital Center: The Politics of Freedom*. London: Transaction Publishers.

Sheler, Jeffrey L., Caroline Hsu, and Angie C. Marek. 2004. "Nearer My God to Thee." *U.S. News & World Report*, May 3.

Singer, Paul. 2004. "Reaching Out." *National Journal* 36 (4) (December 4): 3604–3606.

Slater, Wayne. 2003/2004. "The Jesus Factor: Wayne Slater Interview." October 30, 2003 and January 8, 2004. *Frontline*. http://www.pbs.org/wgbh/pages/frontline/shows/jesus/interviews/slater.html (accessed March 12, 2005).

Slevin, Peter. 2005. "Battle on Teaching Evolution Sharpens." *Washington Post*, March 14.

Stolberg, Sheryl Gay. 2003a. "White House Avoids Stand on Gay Marriage Measure." *New York Times*, July 2.

Stolberg, Sheryl Gay. 2003b. "Bill Barring Abortion Procedure Drew on Backing from Many Friends of Roe v. Wade." *New York Times*, October 23.

Stone, Peter, and Bara Vaida. 2004. "Christian Soldiers." *National Journal* 36 (4) (December 4): 3596–3603.

Sullivan, Amy. 2003. "Faith Without Works?" *Washington Monthly*, October.

Thomas, Evan, and Eleanor Clift. 2001. "Battle for Bush's Soul." *Newsweek*, July 9.

Tolchin, Martin. 1980. "Conservatives First Recoil, then Line Up Behind Bush." *New York Times*, July 18.

VandeHei, Jim. 2002. "GOP Looks to Move Its Social Agenda." *Washington Post*, November 25.

——— 2005. "Freedom, Culture of Life United Bush and Pope." *Washington Post*, April 7.

Wead, Doug. 2003. "The Jesus Factor: Doug Wead Interview." *Frontline*, November 18. http://www.pbs.org/wgbh/pages/frontline/shows/jesus/interviews/wead.html (accessed March 12, 2005).

Whitman, Christine Todd. 2005. *It's My Party, Too: The Battle for the Heart of the GOP and the Future of America*. New York: Penguin.

Chapter Seven

The Politics of Faith-Based Initiatives

Amy E. Black and Douglas L. Koopman

Texas Governor George W. Bush's top three campaign pledges during his 2000 presidential campaign were to cut federal taxes, to reform federal education policy, and to expand faith-based initiatives. Upon his election, the new president set out his strategies for legislative success in these three areas. Victories came fairly quickly on bills involving the first two ideas. Major tax reform became law in early June 2001, and the "No Child Left Behind" education act became law a few days before the forty-third president celebrated his first anniversary in office. No similar good fortune came to faith-based legislation. Indeed, no significant faith-based bills became law in George W. Bush's entire first term—a failure on which most media attention has focused. The faith-based initiative did make progress, but such gains have come almost completely through behind-the-scenes executive branch action.

This is the essential truth of President Bush's faith-based initiative in his first term—publicly perceived failure but behind-the-scenes success. The cause for this mixed record has much to do with the political appeal of the faith-based initiative to both Republicans and Democrats, and to the interests and factions that both major political parties must work with and against in the Washington, DC, policy environment. After briefly describing the president's faith-based initiative and its goals, this chapter summarizes the political aspects of the faith-based initiative and then focuses on the story of the faith-based initiative within the executive branch. It concludes by offering a brief outlook for the faith-based initiative in a second George W. Bush administration.

Three-Part Presidential Initiative

President George W. Bush's faith-based initiative has always been, in fact, a package of legislative proposals and administrative strategies, all focused on the goal of expanding the variety of religiously affiliated social services that receive financial help from the federal government to meet social needs. It has three basic parts—regulatory reform, targeted technical assistance, and tax reform—each meeting a separate objective to help religious social service providers that seek federal dollars to assist their work.

Regulatory Reform

The first part of the faith-based initiative is to change current government practices—sometimes explicit in law but far more frequently the result of written and unwritten administrative rules—that exclude certain groups from getting government support in selected government programs because these groups are, in a variety of ways, "too religious." Sometimes faith-based groups have been discouraged by government from even applying for federal funds because, for example, their name or location appears religious. Some have programs that combine overtly religious elements with nonreligious programming, while others blend the two together in an inseparable mix. The operators of many such programs have been discouraged from seeking federal funds because of the dangers of excessive entanglement between religion and government. While some claim that discouraging applications from these groups helps preserve the wall of separation between church and state, the Bush administration sees these written and unwritten rules as perpetuating discrimination against religion.

One proposal that President Bush pushed early in the first term to combat this antireligious discrimination was legislation whose major provision expanded "charitable choice" to nearly all federal social service programs. Charitable choice provisions require federal administrators of covered programs to allow new categories of religious organizations to apply to provide federally funded services on the same basis as other providers, if the providers agree to follow a few guidelines keeping religious and nonreligious elements distinct in their programs. The federal government was already authorized to implement charitable choice language in four different laws when Bush came to office. The language had first been inserted in the 1996 welfare reform act, but it had barely been debated in Congress because welfare reform was dominated by much larger issues. Similar language was later added to three other pieces of legislation enacted in the Clinton years; each time the provision attracted only the briefest and most cursory attention by Congress. Even though included in four Clinton-era laws, the outgoing administration had done nothing to encourage bureaucratic compliance with charitable choice. The situation gave the new Bush administration an opportunity to breathe life into already enacted but dormant charitable choice provisions while also seeking their expansion to more federal programs. The first they could do through executive branch policy; the second required legislation.

Targeted Technical Assistance

A second part of President Bush's faith-based initiative provides technical assistance to equip smaller social service providers when they are allowed to compete for federal funds. Smaller groups often lack the administrative structure and expertise to make qualified applications for federal funds. Thus, the faith-based initiative proposed to help in two ways. A first step asked Congress to provide "compassion capital funds" to small community- and faith-based groups so they could develop or hire the necessary expertise. These special funds would be targeted at smaller, newer, and volunteer-intensive groups that are, in large part, faith-based entities. At the same time that Congress could provide some funding, the executive branch could use its own resources to assist newcomers to the federal grant process and build networks with faith-based and community organizations to encourage participation.

Supporters of this part of the faith-based initiative argue that the federal government should actively assist smaller organizations to avoid antireligious bias and to encourage provision of the most effective and efficient social services. Compassion capital funds help "level the playing field," making fairer the competition between experienced federal partners and those who are not yet providing government-funded services but should be at least be allowed to apply to do so. Because these funds are not reserved for faith-based groups alone, they are less controversial. Congress did approve small amounts of compassion capital funds in the first Bush term, and the administration has used these funds extensively for outreach to faith-based and community social service providers.

Tax Reform

The third part of the president's faith-based initiative package, tax reform, sought to assist all charitable groups through new tax incentives.

The most costly element of this third emphasis was a charitable contribution tax deduction for taxpayers who do not itemize deductions; under current practice only taxpayers who complete and return a separate itemized deduction page with their tax returns can take such deductions. These large and costly tax provisions were not included in the 2001 tax reform bill; because of deep and persistent federal deficits it seems unlikely they will be enacted in a second Bush term.[1]

President Bush described the entire bundle of proposals—expanded charitable choice, compassion capital technical assistance, and costly broad tax incentives—as his faith-based initiative, even though the objectives and proposals are distinct from each other and address different problems.

Establishing Faith-Based Offices

Bush signaled the high priority of his faith-based initiative by some of his earliest actions as president. On January 29, 2001, he announced his first two executive orders. The first order created a new office in the Executive Office of the president, the White House Office of Faith-Based and Community Initiatives (WHOFBCI), which was created to take the "lead responsibility in the executive branch to establish policies, priorities, and objectives, for the government's efforts to enlist, expand, equip, empower, and enable the work of faith-based and community groups."[2] According to the founding executive order, this White House Office was to carry out 11 stated functions, including coordinating public education activities, showcasing innovation, and monitoring implementation of these new initiatives.

The second executive order created faith-based centers in five cabinet-level departments: Health and Human Services, Housing and Urban Development, Education, Labor, and Justice. Besides working to remove obstacles that inhibited faith-based and community organizations from providing government social services, these centers were charged with the duty of conducting "a department-wide audit to identify all existing barriers to the participation of faith-based and other community organizations in the delivery of social services."[3] Each cabinet center submitted audit reports to the WHOFBCI, which then compiled the data into "Unlevel Playing Field," a report released in August 2001 that detailed the various barriers to government cooperation with faith-based and community groups.[4] In two subsequent executive orders during his first term, Bush increased the number of departments served by satellites from five to ten.

Transition Frenzy

During the transition before Bush's inauguration, two staff assumed primary responsibilities for faith-based planning. Don Willett, a young attorney who worked in then governor Bush's policy office in Austin handling a wide range of issues including faith-based initiatives, came to Washington to begin shaping and planning the faith-based agenda for the new administration. He enlisted the help of Don Eberly, a former Reagan official and activist in the civil society movement, who had volunteered to assist Willett with the transition work on faith-based policies.

With little direction from political advisors, Willett and Eberly began to design the structure and duties of the White House Office that Bush had promised on the campaign trail. Willett recalled these stressful days: "Roughly half the normal transition time was robbed by the recount wars, so things were incredibly crunched and compressed, especially for senior staff. . . . They were juggling innumerable balls and each one was critically important, so the daunting task of recommending the design of this culturally consequential office, from a blank sheet of paper and with only the vaguest of campaign descriptions, fell to me and my volunteer colleague, Don Eberly."[5]

Although the faith-based team created the promised separate White House Office along with centers in some cabinet-level agencies, insufficient time to research options and consider their impact created internal problems. "Because it happened so fast, without the benefit of laying some groundwork about how the cabinet centers would relate to the White House Office," one cabinet center director described, "the role for the office, the director, or the Secretary was not always clearly defined."[6] The newly appointed cabinet secretaries were, in essence, given faith-based offices in their agencies, complete with directors, and were told to begin their work.

Choosing the Original Director

In addition to the short time table for the creation of the White House Office and the administration's faith-based policies, Bush waited until almost the last minute to name the Office's director. A matter of days before the January 2001 executive orders, Bush offered the director's job to John J. DiIulio, Jr., a respected university professor and self-identified Democrat who had advised Bush on faith-based and other domestic issues during the campaign. DiIulio did not seek the position, and he likely agreed to serve only because of his own personal commitment to the issue and his respect for the president. When he did agree to serve, he said that he would only serve six months and while serving would commute between his Philadelphia home and Washington, DC. Without the benefit of time to learn the external and internal political landscapes, the WHOFBCI staff was often harried and disorganized. The office moved into its original suite in the Old Executive Office Building by the February deadline, but it would be many more weeks before the staff even had business cards.

Initial Isolation

The initial decision to create a separate White House Office situated outside the preexisting White House structure was likely an organizational mistake. The WHOFBCI was too weak and too disconnected from key White House staff to provide the support, expertise, and political muscle needed to champion the faith-based initiative's legislative details and lobbying strategy. Although staffed with experts who understood the complexities of faith-based proposals, the original WHOFBCI lacked personnel with much experience on Capitol Hill or in communications strategy. The typical White House structure includes offices of Legislative Affairs, Communications, Public Liaison, Domestic Policy Council, and others that could have helped guide a successful faith-based initiative. These established departments did not work effectively with the new WHOFBCI. The staff of the WHOFBCI and the rest of the White House largely followed different and distinct career tracks. The WHOFBCI had experts on the details of various elements of the initiatives and an open Democrat at its head; the other White House offices were staffed by political loyalists to George W. Bush from Texas and close Bush allies with Washington, DC, experience. The staffing decisions created tension and lack of coordination, which in turn harmed efforts to promote an accurate understanding of the faith-based initiative inside and outside the administration, and particularly in Congress. One congressional aide described White House efforts from the vantage point of many on Capitol Hill: "The White House was very disorganized. They needed a full-fledged lobby effort on the Hill. The WHOFBCI did not seem to know the details (of legislation); they needed a more broad effort. They had good people but not the right people."[7]

Hastily created behind the scenes and cloaked in uncertainty, the WHOFBCI nonetheless opened with much public fanfare. Bush kept his campaign promise to create an office, and the quick and bold move suggested the faith-based initiative would be a centerpiece of the new Bush administration. The mechanism for administrative reform was in place.

Motivations to Support Faith-Based Initiatives

Despite the difficulties designing faith-based strategy in the transition, the initial outlook for faith-based legislation and the WHOFBCI seemed good. Proponents from both the Republican and Democratic camps made strong altruistic and political arguments in support of the faith-based initiative.

Altruism

The central altruistic argument is that intensely religious social services and treatments are at least as effective as, and probably even superior to, conventional secular treatments and services that traditionally receive federal funds. One claim is that religion can help intended beneficiaries. Religiously grounded treatment methods may more completely address the causes of many social problems, supporters say. A religious conversion or a more intentionally religious lifestyle may improve outcomes for a set of individuals who would not otherwise be helped. A second claim is that religious organizations offer better services. Overtly religious persons may, for example, be more willing to work longer or harder for less pay or bring a greater concern for or understanding of the problems a client faces. Although the evidence for these claims was not conclusive at the beginning of President Bush's first term and is still in doubt, these arguments are based on the altruistic reason of making federally funded social service treatments more effective in their primary goal of addressing human needs. President Bush himself clearly seems primarily motivated by these altruistic reasons—and openly speaks about his own personal religious transformation as a confirming story.

Politics

There are also nonaltruistic, political, reasons to support faith-based initiatives. One such reason stems from the close competition between the two major parties for national majority status. Democrats and Republicans have been at virtual parity at the national level for nearly three decades. Such an extended period of equality is actually quite unusual, for in the almost 150-year history of Republicans and Democrats one or the other is usually a fairly reliable majority. From after the Civil War until the early decades of the twentieth century, the Republican Party dominated; the Depression of the 1930s ushered in a Democratic majority until the late 1960s, when fissures caused by the Vietnam War and civil rights legislation fractured the once solid Democratic South. History implies that the GOP should have reestablished itself in the 1970s as a reliable majority. That did not happen, in part because of Richard Nixon and Watergate, and then either because of, or in spite of (depending on one's reading of recent political history), Ronald Reagan and his legacy of purer social and economic conservatism.

The 1990s brought confusion to the picture. Republicans dominated the presidency since 1968 but lost the office in 1992. Democrats held the Congress from the 1950s to the 1990s, but in 1994 Republicans won both House and Senate majorities for the first time in 40 years. In 2000, both Republicans and Democrats had reasonable prospects of gaining full control of the elected branches of government.

Each party's leaders said nice things about the faith-based initiative as one strategy to achieve majority status. Republican elites thought that the initiative might allow them to attract a few more highly religious African American and Hispanic voters; gaining only a few more percentage points in these groups would assure a GOP majority. In addition, Republican support for social services might attract a few more ethnic white Catholic voters and keep in the fold upper-income suburban women, the "soccer moms" who were starting to vote Democratic by significant margins because they saw the GOP becoming too socially conservative. The faith-based initiative also seemed a good idea to Republican strategists trying to change their party's caricature as beholden to white evangelical Protestant males. The initiative's overt support for intense and vocal religion seemed consistent with the views of the white Protestant base, yet its emphasis on aiding the poor and needy would help attract supporters outside this base.

Some Democratic elites, mostly from the moderate Democratic Leadership Council (DLC), thought that supporting faith-based initiatives was a good idea for their party too. It might help inoculate the 2000 ticket of Al Gore and Joseph Lieberman's ticket from lingering character concerns about sitting President Bill Clinton. In addition, a frequent internal critique of the Democratic Party was that the public was becoming increasingly convinced that national Democratic leaders seemed uncomfortable with religious language and with issues important to deeply religious voters, many of whom had been regular Democratic voters.[8] While that voice seems larger after the 2004 elections, it was already being heard inside the Democratic Party in the run-up to 2000.

Politics in the Legislative Arena

Both parties have slowly changed their composition in the past few decades, each becoming more ideologically uniform. New recruits have made Republicans more solidly conservative and overtly religious and Democrats more uniformly liberal and secular. In addition, party elites such as convention delegates, elected officials, and grassroots leaders tend to be more ideologically extreme than the average party voter.[9]

These differences within and between the parties are muted during campaigns as each party appeals to undecided middle-of-the-road voters. It is commonplace to note that the faith-based initiative's advocacy in the campaign by both Al Gore and George W. Bush can be explained by its appeal to middle-of-the-road voters. Equally true, but less frequently noted, is that the faith-based initiative's mixed record after 2000 can largely be explained by the change of venue to "inside-the-Beltway" policy making that is more easily dominated by more extreme interest group leaders.

For Republicans, most recent intraparty fights have been between economic conservatives with long ties to the party who emphasize economic reform and limited government, and social conservatives with shorter historic ties to Republicans who focus on cultural issues such as abortion, homosexuality, and the family. Intraparty GOP support for the faith-based initiative is broad, but each camp has different reasons for that support. More "purist" religious conservatives like the fact that it promotes religion in the public square. Demographically, perhaps more devout Catholics and deeply religious ethnic minorities might be more attracted to the GOP. More traditionalist Republican "pragmatists" support it as it promises more effective government services; demographically, the traditional upper-class business constituency might find faith-based initiatives attractive for this reason. There was an early decision in the Bush administration—opposed by most in the faith-based office—that the faith-based legislative strategy needed the full support of the party's traditional religious allies among the interest group community.

This decision turned out to be a mistake. The long-term goal of most "purists" is greater official support for orthodox religion in the public square, so they seek what they define as a "neutral" government view of religion over against what they perceive as current widespread antireligious bias. The faith-based initiative could, and did for a short time, become for them a handy tool in this bigger battle. During the intense and failed legislative fight of early 2001, purists helped shape the details of H.R. 7, the faith-based bill introduced in the House that sought to expand charitable choice provisions. The resulting bill was far more conservative than the outline sketched in Bush's campaign, and observers noted the rightward movement of the legislative language. The outnumbered Republican pragmatists and most Democrats chafed at the tone of the bill, and controversies arose about whether the federal government would be directly funding religious programming or directly paying employees not fully covered by antidiscrimination provisions normally followed by federal contractors. Later modifications to the legislation in its quick but contentious journey through the House changed some of the substance, but few of the rapidly formed impressions, of faith-based legislation.[10]

Most purists mistakenly thought that a House bill to their liking would rally public support for faith-based initiatives. A strong advocate of this view was Marvin Olasky, a faith-based advisor for Governor Bush, who wrote, "I see the faith-based initiative as something that could be taken directly to the people of what remains a religious country."[11] Indeed, some deeply Catholic groups and a few conservative ethnic minorities (particularly some high-profile African American pastors) were sympathetic to the initial legislation. But in retrospect, it seems far more accurate to state that the early purist victories doomed the chances for longer-term faith-based legislative success by disregarding the need to build a broad interest group coalition. Purists seemed unconcerned about the political realities of a closely divided House and Senate, a skeptical media still learning about faith-based issues, and the uncertainty of future Supreme Court rulings on their arguments. The president himself hinted strongly his far more pragmatic perspective. On his first lobbying trip to the Hill regarding the House bill, he stressed the pragmatists' argument about faith-based effectiveness, describing how he personally "saw it work . . . in places where hope had been lost." The president reportedly told Republicans in a private meeting that the faith-based initiative was "so important to me that I want you to overlook some of the details and get it done."[12]

The Quiet Path of Administrative Reforms

When viewed solely through the lens of congressional action, the faith-based initiative appeared dead. But the high-profile attention in Congress created an ideal environment for the administration to make progress behind the scenes promoting regulatory reform and technical assistance through executive branch actions.

The legislative strategy had run aground by summer of 2001 and, after sporadic attempt through 2002, was later virtually abandoned. Initial impressions had cemented, poisoning the well in a closely divided Washington. Ironically, the longer-term administrative success of the faith-based initiative is likely due in part to the political shift among purists. By moving their support away from faith-based legislation and toward other political issues more easily understood as advancing their primary goal of promoting overt religion in the public square, purists left the more pragmatic faith-based actors to attend to the further implementation of an initiative still at the center of the president's personal agenda.

Most of the implementation of the faith-based initiative in the executive branch occurred after the media spotlight moved to other issues. To the extent that the national media followed faith-based work at all, the central WHOFBCI received the attention. Although this office was a central point of faith-based expertise, it was often distracted by legislative battles and media inquiries. While reporters focused on what the WHOFBCI was or was not accomplishing directly, the five original faith-based offices created in executive branch departments were quietly busy rewriting regulations and removing government barriers to partnerships with religious organizations.

Satellite Office Structure

Staff in the satellite offices reported to both the WHOFBCI and their respective cabinet secretaries. The nature of the relationship between the staff of each of these satellite offices, the cabinet secretary (or the attorney general, in the case of the Department of Justice), and the White House varied across agencies and over time as each key player learned to negotiate the complexities in the structure of their own departmental bureaucracies. All of the center directors kept in regular contact with the WHOFBCI, just as they also reported to their secretaries to achieve the goals and expectations of their agency.

Although each office had some flexibility in identifying and confronting the unique challenges of its host department, all shared in the same charge to conduct an annual audit of department coopera-tion with faith-based groups. Describing the program audits, then director John DiIulio explained, "This is easily the most crucial, but least well-understood, part of our mission. It's about paving the path to civic results through greater government solicitude for faith-based and community organizations."[13]

The WHOFBCI released its first five-department audit, "Unlevel Playing Field: Barriers to Participation by Faith-based and Community Organizations in Federal Social Service Programs," on August 16, 2001.[14] Compiling data received from all five cabinet centers, the report laid the groundwork for future efforts to change bureaucratic patterns. The document attempted to measure the amount of federal funding that went to faith-based and community organizations and then described "a federal system inhospitable to faith-based and community organizations," discussing how the existing grant system allowed current grantees to receive funding each year without demonstrating their effectiveness and essentially shut out new orga-nizations from receiving grant money. As the report concluded,

> The Federal Grants process, despite a few exceptions and a growing sensitivity to and openness towards both faith-based and community groups, does more to discourage than to welcome the participation of faith-based and community groups. . . . Too much is done that discour-ages or actually excludes good organizations that simply appear "too religious"; too little is done to include groups that meet local needs with vigor and creativity but are not as large, established, or bureaucratic as the traditional partners of Federal Government.[15]

The release of this report was an important milestone for the WHOFBCI, as it documented barriers to participation and provided a blueprint for potential executive branch action.

While the media focused on the high stakes legislative battle just concluded in the House and the potential for Senate legislative action, the cabinet centers continued their work off the radar screen of major media. Communicating regularly with the staff of the WHOFBCI, each office had a good measure of autonomy to facilitate partnerships with faith-based and community organizations. To accomplish their goals, cabinet center staff designed and implemented outreach efforts, created new grant programs targeting new partnerships, and began the slow but influential process of rewriting regulations to assist in "leveling the playing field."

Cabinet center staff, speaking off the record, disagreed among themselves about the impact of the high-profile and emotionally charged debate over faith-based legislation in Congress. While some found that the increased attention and controversy complicated the work of their offices, others argued that the congressional debate in some ways freed them. The House of Representatives was the focus of most of the public attention, debate, and hostilities on faith-based issues, so cabinet center work received little notice or scrutiny. Although not without its challenges, the work of the satellite offices was one of the greatest successes of the faith-based initiative.

Progress on the Faith-Based Initiative: A Timeline

In the year after Bush assumed the presidency, many external events affected work promoting his faith-based agenda. Events often outside of the control of the policy's supporters shaped the progress of faith-based efforts and informed the public debate.

Waning White House Interest

Although Bush's senior policy advisors gave the faith-based initiative prime billing in the first weeks of the administration, White House focus on faith-based initiatives was short-lived. The WHOFBCI was always "on issue" but other offices in the administration turned to other policy priorities. Although some officials we interviewed insist that the faith-based initiative was always an important administration priority, much evidence suggests this was not the case. For example, one staff member whose boss was a vocal supporter of faith-based legislation in Congress assessed the situation: "Legislative affairs, Domestic Policy Council, OMB—they didn't care about this. Point blank, it wasn't a priority for them. They weren't trying to kill the bill; it just wasn't important."[16]

Some observers argue that key White House officials actively disliked the issue and therefore avoided it, but a more accurate assessment is probably that the issue suffered mostly from neglect. With so many issues competing for scarce time and resources, the White House could not concentrate full attention on every proposal. Advisors fight for even a few minutes of the president's time as they try to move forward programs they believe are most important. The original faith-based director, John DiIulio, admitted that he should have been more aggressive in demanding time on the president's schedule. The president himself even raised the issue with DiIulio, who noted, "When the president called me, each time, he would say, 'How come you're not getting on my dance card?'" [17] After initial activity, most traditional religious interest groups aligned with the GOP turned their attention to other new issues that arose, such as defending traditional marriage or protecting public religious symbols such as the "under God" clause in the Pledge of Allegiance. The faith-based initiative continued to hold some appeal to devout Catholics and deeply religious racial and ethnic minorities but, by itself, the initiative seemed to have little power to move large numbers of these demographic groups toward the GOP.

Even as members of the White House staff varied in their levels of interest and support for faith-based proposals, the president never wavered in his personal support. Rooted in his faith commitment and his reliance on faith to overcome a drinking problem, Bush believes whole-heartedly that faith-based organizations can meet needs in ways that traditional government programs often cannot. Former cabinet center director Elizabeth Seale, who began working with Bush on the faith-based issue back in Texas, described the president's commitment as heartfelt: "The story in Texas speaks volumes. . . . What I've seen in him—he has a tender heart for people in need. . . . He engages one-on-one and he connects with people. It causes him pain to experience people's needs and at the same time to feel like there are barriers in place that keep the needs from being met. Our problems aren't cut and dried; religion can do what policy cannot." [18]

To many unfamiliar with the complexity of the issue, faith-based proposals appeared reasonably simple and relatively noncontroversial. Those who worked on the policy, however, were all too aware of the complicated political environment surrounding the faith-based initiative. In all likelihood, most of the key policy advisors in the West Wing were completely unprepared for the faith-based firestorm that was brewing.

The DiIulio Departure

On August 17, 2001, the day after the WHOFBCI released the "Barriers" report, John J. DiIulio, Jr., announced he would be stepping down as director of the office, citing personal and health reasons. White House insiders knew, and a few early media reports acknowledged, that DiIulio had only agreed to serve six months, but the announcement still managed to send shockwaves across Washington. The first departure of a high-ranking member of the Bush administration drew significant media attention, and the exit of a Democrat in a Republican administration added to the drama.

Although DiIulio's departure followed the timeline he had announced in advance, frustrations with internal and external politics surrounding the faith-based issue likely contributed to his resignation. Having spearheaded the office during the rancorous debate over a House bill he could not fully support, DiIulio was physically and emotionally exhausted. The outlook for faith-based legislation in the Senate was bleak. Perhaps most importantly, however, he and his staff had completed the "Unlevel Playing Field" report, a document DiIulio that believed was crucial for identifying the barriers facing faith-based and community organizations and laying the groundwork for future executive branch action.

Observers on the left and the right awaited the Bush administration's next move to see whether a new director would steer the office in a different direction or attempt to stay the course. Before President Bush could name a successor, however, the events of September 11, 2001, shocked the nation and transformed White House priorities.

September 11, 2001

Likely no single event affected the work of the WHOFBCI and the direction of faith-based initiatives more profoundly than the tragedy of September 11, 2001. Stunned by the events of that day, the direction of the administration changed. John Bridgeland, who was the head of the Domestic Policy Council at that time, describes the impact of that day: "Then September 11 hits. For all of us at the Domestic Policy Council we went from domestic policy to domestic consequences [of the terrorist attack]. It totally changed our lives."[19] No longer free to reflect and build a policy agenda, the White House staff needed "all hands on deck" to assess the potential external threat and take any action possible to secure the nation. Foreign policy took front and center stage; domestic proposals not directly related to homeland security slid to the background.

A New Start with a New Director

After many months in which direct efforts to promote the faith-based initiative made very little progress, President Bush introduced Jim

Towey as the new director for the WHOFBCI on February 1, 2002. Recommended for the job by the president's brother, Florida Governor Jeb Bush, Towey had an impressive background. A committed Catholic with a bipartisan resume, Towey's experience varied widely. He served as Republican Mark Hatfield's legislative director, headed the Department of Health and Rehabilitation Services under Democratic Florida Governor Lawton Chiles, founded and ran the nonprofit group Aging With Dignity, and served as legal counsel to Mother Teresa for 12 years. Conservative organizations responded positively to Towey's appointment, and most opponents of the faith-based initiative did not publicly criticize the selection.

When Towey began his work at the White House, some changes had already been made. In the absence of a director, the WHOFBCI had been told to report to the domestic policy staff that was better integrated into the White House Office structure. Although Towey retained a few of the first year's staff, he chose to build a team of his own for the WHOFBCI and inspired "house cleaning" at the satellite offices. Under Towey's watch, the office took more direct control of the agency centers. As the new director explained, "We want to know what they're up to so we can make sure that the left hand and the right hand are in sync. . . . It's the president's initiative first and foremost."[20]

While continuing to promote a legislative agenda and regulatory reforms, the WHOFBCI under Towey began conducting outreach programs designed to provide technical assistance reaching thousands of organizations nationwide. Beginning in late 2002, the WHOFBCI sponsored a series of free conferences held in various regional centers across the country. At these gatherings, the White House Office networked with religious and community leaders to educate them about the federal grant process and encourage partnerships where appropriate. The office also created vast databases of thousands of community leaders interested in and likely supportive of their work.

In addition to using the faith-based offices to promote regulatory reform and conduct outreach, the Bush administration has used other means of presidential power to bolster the goals of the initiative. As congressional debate about religious hiring practices intensified, Bush issued an equal protection executive order that reiterated fundamental protections including the ban on discrimination against beneficiaries of government grants, the prohibition of funding worship or proselytizing with federal funds, and protection for faith-based organizations that use religious criteria in hiring.[21]

Looking Ahead: Faith-Based Initiatives in Bush's Second Term

As the previous discussion demonstrates, political battles in Congress and the administration's focus on foreign policy in the aftermath of September 11 slowed, but did not halt, the progress of the faith-based initiative in Bush's first term. Given President Bush's personal commitment to this issue, however, programs designed to encourage the work of faith-based organizations will continue to be a priority in Bush's second term. Experience from the first four years will affect decisions for the following four, so we expect the faith-based issue to take a different form than what we saw at the beginning of Bush's first term in office.

Legislative Prospects

While the prospect for ambitious faith-based legislation that comprehensively rewrites the church-state boundary is slim, some version of tax credits for charitable donations and legislative ratification of a version of President Bush's equal protection executive order is still possible. Nonetheless, President Bush does not seem willing to allow other more ambitious domestic policy ideas such as Social Security reform to completely overshadow the initiative. In his 2005 State of the Union address, Bush reiterated his commitment to assisting faith-based and community groups and then proposed a new nationwide outreach effort to assist at-risk youth to be led by his wife, Laura. This marks the first time the popular First Lady has overseen a policy-oriented program, increasing the likelihood that the new program will receive media attention and may even get favorable treatment in Congress.

Staying the Executive Branch Course

The administration likely still feels some of the sting from the legislative failures and the often rancorous debate in Congress, so we expect the more controversial pieces of the agenda will proceed through quiet regulatory reform. It still remains a personal priority of President Bush, and Republican officials clearly see it as a means, as new Republican National Committee Chair Ken Mehlman said upon assuming his position, to "bring new African American faces and voices into our party."[22] By keeping the issue out of the media spotlight most of the time, faith-based proponents in the executive branch can continue clearing access for faith-based groups. Eight years of focused attention will leave a long legacy of change.

Coordination between the faith-based office in the White House and its satellites solidified and progressed under Director Jim Towey, so this structure will continue to play a central role in furthering the faith-based agenda. The recent announcement of Towey's promotion to assistant to the president, the highest level of staff with direct reporting responsibility to the president, confirms his importance in the administration and bodes well for continued progress in Bush's second term.[23]

Not all executive branch agencies are equally suited to host a faith-based office, but the Bush administration still has departments where faith-based offices could logically be added. In addition, new cabinet members who assume positions in agencies with preexisting faith-based offices will be able to incorporate that agenda from the start, which should create more consistent cooperation and coordination than in the first term.

Other signs indicate that the strategy to pursue regulatory reform and offer technical assistance has helped faith-based groups that want to partner with the government. As recent reports from the grant process indicate, faith-based organizations now have increased access to and success competing for federal grants. For example, an early 2005 White House report given to the mainstream media asserted that selected programs in five federal agencies awarded $1.7 billion to faith-based groups in fiscal year 2003, approximately 8 percent of the $14.5 billion total spent in these programs.[24]

We expect these trends to continue with slow but steady increases in federal dollars going to faith-based organizations. Not all types of religious social service providers are equally suited to participate in the complete spectrum of government programs, and secular providers will continue to seek and win important government contracts. Given this context, faith-based organizations as a category will never receive a majority (or anything even close) of federal grant monies but are likely to see increased influence and representation.

Leaving a Judicial Legacy

What will likely be the most intense and most far-reaching battles of the faith-based initiative are in progress in the federal courts as a series of cases test the interpretation of the First Amendment religion clauses.[25] Knowing that much of the work so far on the faith-based initiative could all but disappear with a few key judicial opinions, those concerned about protection of religious organizations will look for help by securing friendly judicial appointments, especially those to the Supreme Court. Although media reports like to tell of an abortion litmus test for evaluating judicial nominees, we expect the Bush administration will focus at least equally on prospective nominees' views of the Constitution's two religion clauses. Many recent landmark Supreme Court decisions on church and state issues have been 5 to 4 rulings; any change in the composition of the Court could shift the balance away from the Bush administration's goals.

Conclusion

As seen in this chapter, George W. Bush's faith-based initiative followed a rocky path from the initial frenetic activity surrounding its introduction through its stabilization as an important, albeit background, piece of the president's domestic agenda. Although faith-based legislation failed to become law during Bush's first term, the initiative was not a failure as many commentators named it. When faced with congressional impasse, Bush furthered his faith-based initiative through executive action. As the battle raged on Capitol Hill, staff in the WHOFBCI and at the cabinet centers quietly began to change regulations, earmark money for faith-based organizations, and generally transform the relationship between the executive branch and religious groups. The implementation of the initiative in the executive branch faced some setbacks, but the story of regulatory reform and administrative action appears a qualified success.

Notes

1. Due to space constraints, we will focus our attention on the other two pieces of Bush's faith-based initiative. For a fuller discussion of the failure of the tax proposals, see chapter 4 of Amy E. Black, Douglas Koopman, and David K. Ryden, *Of Little Faith: The Politics of George W. Bush's Faith-Based Initiatives* (Washington, DC: Georgetown University Press, 2005).
2. "Executive Order: Establishment of White House Office of Faith-Based and Community Initiatives," WhiteHouse.gov, January 29, 2001, http://www.whitehouse.gov/news/releases/2001/01/20010129-2.html (accessed March 3, 2003).

3. "Executive Order: Agency Responsibilities with Respect to Faith-Based and Community Initiatives," WhiteHouse.gov, January 29, 2001, http://www.whitehouse.gov/news/releases/2001/01/20010129-3.html (accessed March 3, 2003).

4. "Unlevel Playing Field: Barriers to Participation by Faith-Based and Community Organizations in Federal Social Service Programs," WhiteHouse.gov, August 16, 2001, http://www.whitehouse.gov/news/releases/2001/08/unlevelfield.html (accessed August 30, 2001).

5. Don Willett, interview by Amy Black, telephone conversation, August 15, 2002.

6. Confidential interview by Amy Black.

7. Confidential interview by Amy Black and Doug Koopman.

8. See, e.g., Anna Greenberg and Stanley B. Greenberg, "Adding Values," *American Prospect* 11, no. 19 (August 28, 2000): 28. This journal has been an especially lively forum for the Democratic Party's debate on how it should interact with more traditional and often explicitly religious themes and policies.

9. This argument is made by Geoffrey Layman in *The Great Divide: Religious and Cultural Conflict in American Party Politics* (New York: Columbia University Press, 2001). We find the general outlines of his argument quite helpful in explaining some of the partisan aspects of the faith-based story.

10. For a fuller discussion of the faith-based legislative process in 2001 and 2002, see, especially, Black, Koopman, and Ryden, *Of Little Faith*, chapters 3 and 4.

11. Marvin Olasky, "Sounds of Silence: Bush Initiative Gets through the House, but What Now?" *World*, August 4, 2001, www.worldmag.com/world/issue/08-04-01/closing-2.asp (accessed December 2, 2001).

12. Thomas B. Edsall and Dana Milbank "Blunt Defense of 'Faith-Based' Aid," *Washington Post*, March 8, 2001, A8.

13. John J. DiIulio, Jr., "Compassion 'In Truth and Action': How Sacred and Secular Places Serve Civic Purposes, and What Washington Should—and Should Not—Do to Help," speech delivered before the National Association of Evangelicals, Dallas, TX, March 7, 2001, www.whitehouse.gov/news/releases/2001/03/20010307-11.html (accessed March 3, 2003).

14. "Unlevel Playing Field."

15. Ibid.

16. Confidential interview by Amy Black and Douglas Koopman, June 27, 2002.

17. John J. DiIulio, interview by Amy Black, Philadelphia, PA, December 9, 2002.

18. Elizabeth Seale-Scott, interview by Amy Black, Washington, DC, September 23, 2002.

19. John Bridgeland, interview by Amy Black, Washington, DC, December 6, 2002.

20. Meghan Twohey, "Bush Cleans House, Takes Charge of Faith Team," *Federal Paper*, September 23, 2002, 24.

21. "Executive Order: Equal Protection of the Laws for Faith-based and Community Organizations," WhiteHouse.gov http://www.whitehouse. gov/news/releases/2002/12/20021212-6.html (accessed November 3, 2005).

22. "Republican National Committee Chairman Ken Mehlman's Remarks to RNC Winter Meeting," U.S. Newswire, January 10, 2005, http://www. usnewswire.com (accessed January 20, 2005).

23. "Personnel Announcement," WhiteHouse.gov, http://www.whitehouse. gov/news/releases/2005/01/20050113-8.html (accessed January 29, 2005).

24. Laura Meckler, "Records Show $1 Billion Given to Faith-Based Groups," Associated Press, January 3, 2005.

25. For more details on the constitutional issues affecting faith-based policies and the cases working their way through the federal courts, see Black, Koopman, and Ryden, *Of Little Faith*, chapter 6.

Chapter Eight

Buying Black Votes? The GOP's Faith-Based Initiative

Michael K. Fauntroy

Introduction

The Republican and Democratic parties are in pitched battle for supremacy in American politics. Their efforts have taken on heightened significance in recent years as national elections have become more closely contested, forcing both parties to seek additional ways to attract new supporters. Over time, a political maxim has developed: Democrats must do a better job with evangelical voters to win national elections, and Republicans must win more minority votes to maintain their recent success. This maxim has driven both parties to court voters that they have traditionally conceded to the opposition. The Republican Party has a particularly difficult task as it relates to African Americans, a segment of the electorate with which it has had very limited electoral support. And despite the Grand Old Party's (GOP) recent electoral successes and contemporary dominance, they may actually have a more difficult task ahead in overcoming its inability to win black votes.

Led by Republican National Committee Chairman Ken Mehlman, and with the support of many Republican strategists around the country, the party has recently placed greater emphasis on winning black votes. Republican control of the federal government has given it a substantial reservoir of possibilities to direct public policy that is in line with its ideological beliefs and, at the same time, potentially attractive enough to win black votes. This chapter relies on elite interviewing and an examination of the historical record to examine the most prominent Republican policy initiative in recent years that can be seen as an attempt to accelerate Republican policy initiatives and win black votes—the faith-based initiative. This chapter examines the GOP's use of the federal faith-based initiative to overcome its perennial poor standing in the black community and maintain their political success.

It also explores the extent to which these policies have borne any fruit in terms of increased numbers of black voters.

The GOP and the Black Vote

The GOP's relationship with black voters has undergone a remarkable evolution since the party's founding. Indeed, the contemporary relationship between African Americans and the Republican Party has taken nearly a 180-degree turn in the decades following the GOP's birth. Upon its founding, the Republican Party took a progressive, liberal stance on racial issues, most notably supporting civil rights and the limiting the expansion of slavery. Even though the GOP was not willing to go as far on the slavery issue as antislavery parties such as the Liberty Party and the Radical Abolitionist Party, Republican policy positions earned a political debt from African Americans that was repaid with consistent and overwhelmingly high levels of support throughout much of the balance of the nineteenth century. Organizations such as the New England Colored Citizens Convention endorsed the Republican Party and urged its followers to as well.[1] The overwhelming black support for the GOP was a response to the call by "Radical Republicans," for black freedom and equality and the reconstruction of Southern society. Republican platforms during the late nineteenth century called for the enforcement of the Fourteenth and Fifteenth amendments, the protection of "honest voters," and the free exercise of every citizen's "civil, political, and public rights."[2] Congressional Republicans "led investigations of fraud and violence in Southern elections and accused Southern Democrats of holding their seats illegally."[3]

GOP Loses Black Support

Since its Reconstruction high point of support in the African American community, the GOP has been on a more than 100-year decline. Some of it was their own doing, such as the Reconstruction-era decision to back away from some of the founding principles of racial equality for blacks, which ended Reconstruction and led to the reestablishment of a rigid, race-based segregated society. Also notable was the party's late nineteenth and early twentieth-century purge of blacks from the party during the "lily White movement."[4] In a precursor to the party's rightward shift in the 1960s, the lily White movement resulted in changes in rules throughout the South (and in other parts of the country) that removed African Americans from leadership positions throughout the party and removed rank-and-file blacks, virtually all of whom had been loyal to the party that supported their freedom and equality, from "membership" in the party.

Additionally was the 1960s-era decision by the GOP to woo and embrace Southern racial conservatives who were becoming disenchanted with a Democratic Party that was increasingly supportive of racial equality. As more racial conservative voters and elected officials switched their allegiance to the Republican Party, the GOP became less hospitable and attractive to African American voters.

Some of the African American shift was also due to Democratic Party efforts to win black voters through increasingly progressive civil rights legislation from the New Deal and throughout the 1960s. This move put the Democratic Party in the same position as the Republicans a century earlier to reap large numbers of black voters. Another favorable factor was the support and promotion of African American candidates for elected office. These and other factors have created an environment in which Republican presidential candidates win about 1 in 10 black votes, an astounding reversal from the GOP's heyday in the black community.

Why the GOP Needs More Black Support

Republicans have been able to ride this political "trade" of voters (African Americans for white Southerners) to national prominence and success over the last generation or so. However, demographic projections going forward suggest that the GOPs traditional reliance on white voters may soon not be enough to win national elections, because America's minority populations are growing at a greater rate than whites. According to Census Bureau projections, America will cease to be a majority white nation in the middle of the twenty-first century. The political implications behind these demographic changes are significant, particularly if political parties remain tied in only to their traditional voter bases. Consequently, the GOP needs to make more inroads into minority populations or risk subjugation to political also-ran status. Yes, the party has had better success with Hispanic voters than with African Americans. However, given that there is a smaller percentage of Hispanics registered to vote, GOP success with this voting bloc is insufficient to continue to overcome its poor standing with black voters.

This changing demographic places more pressure on the GOP to win minority voters who have, traditionally, been unsupportive or undersupportive of the party. An unfavorable response by the party to this new pressure is risky and has some Republicans concerned about the future of the party. As South Carolina Senator Lindsay Graham indicated in the wake of the 2004 election, "If we continue to lose 90 percent of the African American vote—and I got 7 percent—if we continue to lose 65 percent of the Hispanic vote, we're toast; just look at the electoral map."[5] Senator Graham's black support level is representative of what most white Southern Republicans get from African American voters—and the overwhelming majority of GOP candidates only do marginally better. No Republican member of the 109th Congress received more than 30 percent of the black vote in his or her 2004 general election. Republicans comprise fewer than 50 of the more than 9,000 African American elected officials in the United States.[6] The demographic change represents a double-edged sword for the GOP. It rose to prominence on racial conservatism that came under increasing pressure as the country became more racially diverse. As Louis Gould, historian and author of *Grand Old Party: A History of the Republicans*, noted, "[B]alancing the racial views of a predominantly Southern leadership with the changing demographics of a more ethnically and racially diverse nation did not prove easy as the twentieth century ended; a party that did not reach out to minorities could find itself at a permanent electoral disadvantage."[7] The test, therefore, for the GOP, then, is how to reach out to black voters and maintain the support of its base—some of which has been racially primed to vote Republican?

There is no larger upside for the GOP than with black voters, because African American voters have been more resistant to the party than any other voting bloc. It has been 62 years since a Republican presidential candidate received at least 40 percent of the African American vote. Indeed, President Bush did twice as well with gay voters in 2004 (23 percent) than with African Americans (11 percent).[8] Only twice since then has a GOP presidential nominee received at least 30 percent of the African American vote. Since Barry Goldwater's 1964 presidential campaign that signaled the conservative takeover of the party, no GOP candidate has received more than 15 percent of the African American vote. President George W. Bush, the current party leader, received 11 percent of the African American vote in 2004 after four years in office. That figure represents a 3 percentage point increase over his 2000 performance and was seen as a disappointment for the party and worrisome relative to its future with black America given that Bush nominated African Americans to unprecedented positions in his cabinet, including Colin Powell as secretary of state and Condoleezza Rice as national security advisor and, later, secretary of state.

The GOP has sought to overcome its poor standing in the black community in ways large and small. Upon his election to the presidency, George W. Bush talked openly of working hard to turn around the perception of him and his party. The 8 percent of the black vote he received in 2000 was a far cry from the totals he received in two Texas gubernatorial races. He won 15 percent of the black vote in his 1994 campaign and 27 percent in his 1998 reelection bid.[9] These performances lead many to believe that Bush could usher in a new era for the Republican Party in the black community if he were able to translate his Texas black support nationally. That did not happen and now the GOP finds itself in a near desperate search for more black votes. Republican strategists are well aware of the demographic data going forward and are seeking to craft policies that will be attractive to black voters. And, while it may now appear that all is electorally well for the GOP, the demographic signs alone point to a difficult future for the "Party of Lincoln" if it cannot expand its electoral voting base.

What Is the Faith-Based Initiative and Why Is It Popular among Republicans?

The faith-based initiative refers to a Bush-initiated policy shift that opens federal government contracting to church-based organizations. The policy change emanated from the conservative religious and political argument that too many government and government-supported social service delivery programs are ineffective and, religious service providers argue, can be better and more effectively run by church-based groups. These groups have been legally precluded from competing for government contracts on the grounds that such participation violates the distinction between church and state.

The legislative history of the federal faith-based initiative begins with the Republicans' welfare reform legislation—the Personal Responsibility and Work Opportunity Reconciliation Act of 1996.[10] That legislation contained the "charitable choice" provision that allowed for federal funding of religious institutions. The provision required that state-administered vouchers under the Temporary Assistance for Needy Families (TANF) must be redeemable to religious organizations that provide social services on the same basis as nongovernmental service providers and that no requirements can be made on those religious groups that impair "the religious character of the organization and without diminishing the religious freedom of TANF beneficiaries." This legislation also explicitly permits states to use charitable, religious, or private organizations "to provide services under other programs such as food stamps, Medicaid, Supplemental Security Income, and child support enforcement."[11]

President Bush's interest in and support for an increased role for religious organizations was well established prior to his 2001 inauguration. His public pronouncements of his own religious beliefs made clear that he believed faith-based organizations could and should play a larger role in society and should be eligible for governmental funding for service provision purposes. While governor of Texas, he created an advisory task force on faith-based community service groups to study an expanded role for religious organizations to receive state funding for its service programs. He also issued an executive order to selected state agencies requesting plans on how "charitable choice" would be implemented by those agencies.

Bush's embrace of state funding for religious service providers may have been a factor in the decision of a group of Black Ministers Association of Houston and Vicinity to endorse his 1998 gubernatorial reelection campaign. While Bush was relatively popular among African Americans, for a Republican, and cruising to reelection, this endorsement was notable in that it broke with political tradition—the group historically endorsed Democrats—and that the group saw befriending Bush as a potential boon to their attempts to receive state faith-based grants.

In one of President Bush's first major acts, he signed two executive orders in a large White House ceremony that marked the start of his push to do nationally what he did in Texas regarding faith-based government funding. Bush, flanked by prominent black ministers including two former members of Congress, noted that his administration would "look first to faith-based programs and community groups, which have proven their power to save and change lives," to meet social needs in America.[12] The first executive order created a White House Office of Faith-Based and Community Initiatives. The second created centers in five federal agencies—Justice, Housing and Urban Development, Health and Human Services, Labor, and Education—to ensure greater cooperation between the government and the independent sector by reporting on regulatory barriers to working with nonprofit groups, making recommendations on how these barriers can be removed.[13]

Regulatory changes effectuated by President Bush's faith-based initiative, a prominent part of his 2000 campaign, has made religious organizations eligible for federal grants for which they were previously ineligible, including services for drug treatment and other social programs. The regulatory changes were seen as a precursor to legislative initiatives supported by Congressional Republicans. From the outset, these plans were seen as a potential magnet for African American voters, particularly since the first major meeting Bush had on the subject, held in the month prior to his inauguration was attended by 30 religious leaders from around the nation with black clergy making up a plurality of the group.[14]

Why Do Republicans Support the Initiative?

The faith-based initiative has been popular with Republicans for two main reasons. First, there is broad philosophical agreement among the GOP's core constituency of Christian conservatives that religious organizations should have access to the federal funds made available through this initiative. Related to this is the fact that those voters who identify themselves as Christian conservatives want a stronger religious presence in the operation of government. Making federal funds available for religious organizations is a substantial and concrete step in that direction. It is a political winner for Republican elected officials who want to use government resources to maintain their political dominance. According to one study, "[M]ore than 90 percent of Americans believe in God; roughly two-thirds say religion is important in their lives and almost 40 percent attend worship services regularly."[15] Given this and other political realities, it may be impossible for the GOP to avoid conflicts between church and state.

Second is patronage politics. Like Tammany Hall and the Daley Machine, the faith-based initiative can be seen as a venue to reward like-minded loyal supporters with grants and contracts. Republican supporters and beneficiaries of the initiative, then, have a vested interest in seeing federal grants to religious organizations becoming a deeply ingrained aspect of governmental operations. On this issue, church-based service providers seek a place at the table that can, ultimately, rival other industries and contractors for government funding. The Christian Right, which has no real profile in areas such as defense and energy contracting or environmental services, for example, can access government funding through social service delivery. Once in the door, they can advocate that more funding is needed and expand the amount of governmental funding that goes to their social service programs. Republican support for this new way of doing business, then, helps to ensure future access to program grants.

The Faith-Based Initiative in the Context of Other GOP Attempts to Win Black Votes

The faith-based initiative is not the first policy conceived by Republicans with winning black votes in mind. Indeed, it joins Nixon-era plans such as the "Black Capitalism" program and the Philadelphia Plan and more recent school choice proposals as Republican-driven policies that were created with at least an ancillary goal of drawing more black support.

President Richard Nixon's Black Capitalism campaign was a political initiative that emerged from his 1968 presidential campaign to halt growing black radicalism that began to emerge in the wake of the rise of the Black Power movement and the riots, anger, frustration, and hostility that gripped much of the African American community in that summer following the assassination of Reverend Dr. Martin Luther King, Jr.[16] As scholars Weems and Randolph noted in their study of Black Capitalism, "Nixon viewed an uncontrolled Black Power movement as a major threat to the internal security of the United States."[17] That view was informed by his advisors, many of whom categorically rejected black claims of being victimized. The advisors were motivated more by the need to comfort conservatives nervous about the potential for expanded black rioting than by trying to deal honestly with the reality of black life in America. According to Dean Kotlowski, author of *Nixon's Civil Rights: Politics, Principle, and Policy*, some Nixon advisors neglected white racism and blamed its black victims.[18]

The nation was angry. White conservatives were upset about crime and violence and wanted government to step in and stop it. They did not know or care about the economic, social, and political repression that led many African Americans to America's streets angrily demanding change. African Americans were frustrated that after years of the Civil Rights Movement, change was slow or nonexistent. That, coupled with the assassination of Dr. King, led many African Americans to take a more militant approach to the larger white society. It was within this context that Nixon embraced Black Capitalism and voiced a message that combined repression (the use of force, if necessary, to end street rioting to appease white conservatives) with reform (new economic opportunities to appease black nationalists).[19]

In that way Black Capitalism may be seen as an attempt to co-opt the nationalist, "Black Power" wing of the African American community—a group of activists who were gaining popularity throughout black America. The initiative promised to increase black entrepreneurship and wealth by growing small black businesses. The plan would have an ancillary benefit for the Republican Party that by accelerating the inclusion of African Americans into the national economy there was a greater likelihood that that would lead to greater black support for the Republicans economic policy grounds. As one Nixon aide noted, "[E]verything we can do to increase minority business holdings, minority home ownership, and more jobs for minorities, will in the long run mean more to the minorities and help increase our political favor."[20]

Although Nixon's initiative may be seen as a legitimate attempt to craft policy favorable to African Americans, it drew numerous critics within the black community. Many viewed the initiative as an attempt to segregate the national economy and limit opportunities to black communities, thereby leaving the rest of the economy—larger and more lucrative—to white entrepreneurs. Further, some critics believed that Black Capitalism would merely set up black businesses to be taken over, ultimately, by larger white businesses, particularly in an area such as apparel manufacturing. Andrew Brimmer, then a member of the Federal Reserve Board, noted that black businessmen should not "count on nationally oriented manufacturing firms leaving the Negro market to Negro entrepreneurs" and called the initiative "one of the worst digressions that has attracted attention and pulled substantial numbers of people off course."[21] An additional criticism of the plan was that it would only benefit African Americans who were already middle class and upper class.

The Philadelphia Plan was the name given to the first federal affirmative action plan. It was developed by the Department of Labor to address racial discrimination in Philadelphia's construction industry that, like most around the nation, was heavily influenced by labor unions that controlled who worked and who did not. The unions had job-assignment arrangements with builders that made it easier to lock out minority craftsmen. Also, "father-son traditions [passing down jobs from father to son] and guildlike patterns in the American Federation of Labor had largely excluded minorities from apprenticeships and union membership, and, hence, from high-wage construction jobs."[22]

The goal of the plan was to make the proportion of African Americans in each trade equal to their 30 percent proportion of metropolitan Philadelphia's workforce.[23] While the plan was localized to Philadelphia, it ultimately became the model for affirmative action programs around the nation. The plan was an expansion of and built on Johnson administration's efforts to enforce Executive Order 11246, which required contractors to engage in affirmative action to assure equal employment opportunity. The Johnson administration's requirements to end, or at least limit, racial discrimination in employment were ultimately ruled violations of federal contract law. The ruling, made near the end of the Johnson administration, left Johnson little time to respond and left many to conclude that such redress for racial discrimination would not be allowed or pursued with Nixon entering the White House.

Nixon resurrected the plan, a surprise to many given his 1968 presidential campaign as an opponent of racial quotas, school busing, and other attempts to use law to address structural racism. These positions earned Nixon a great deal of animus in the black community and made him, perhaps, the president least likely to advocate policy changes that could be seen as "problack." Hugh Davis Graham suggests four reasons for Nixon's support of the plan: "1) a new etiology of social disadvantage that implied more radical remedies; 2) clientele control of civil rights agencies; 3) Nixon's commitment to affirmative action preferences; and 4) the intervention of federal courts in social policy."[24] Nixon's positions in this regard were also guided by his experience as vice president, chairing President Eisenhower's Committee on Government Contracts, which was designed to end bias in firms doing business with the government. Nixon concluded that "bias was a waste of urgently needed manpower" and that equal opportunity was "the right thing to do."[25]

A consistent point of concern to many African Americans has been the quality of education their children receive. Generations ago, the concern and fight was against underfunded, segregated schools. Now, the concern and fight is over reversing the low levels of achievement amongst African American students. African American performance in America's public schools is among the worst in the nation, and many of the states with the highest dropout rates also have large African American populations.[26] While there are a number of reasons for the disparity that are not necessarily a function of the school system, such as the need for a young person to quit school to work full time to help support the family, the fact that black achievement is not where it could be has created frustration and presented opportunities to call for a movement away from the status quo. School choice is one alternative in this regard.

African Americans have historically dropped out of school at higher rates than whites. While official dropout data show that the African American dropout rate has been relatively stable—in the low- to mid-teens—there are many public school districts around the nation in which more black students drop out of school than graduate. Unofficial estimates place African American dropout rates far higher than official state data. According to Education Trust, a Washington, DC-based education think tank, nearly half of African American high school students in North Carolina do not graduate and 75 percent of African American males do not graduate the Indianapolis, Indiana, public schools.[27] Of the 40 states and the District of Columbia, which provided data for a 2004 Urban Institute study on school dropout rates, 13 had an African American dropout rate of at least 50 percent.[28] New York had an African American graduation rate of 35 percent. These graduation results have a deleterious impact on African American employment (those without high school diplomas have fewer options than those who graduate and, additionally, go on to college), social stability, and other characteristics of a healthy community.

Failing public schools have had a profound and deleterious impact on the black community. African Americans comprise nearly half of the 2 million people incarcerated in U.S. prisons and most of those are high school dropouts. There is a multitude of social science research that demonstrates the role education plays in one's life. The better one is educated, the more opportunities one has including a relatively stable employment future. The poorer the education, the fewer opportunities that person may have. Without education, employment opportunities are limited and neighborhoods suffer and run the risk of destabilization. Chronic high unemployment has been shown to have devastating effects on communities. As Wilson noted in his 1996 study of the effects of unemployment *When Work Disappears*, "[M]any of today's problems in the inner-city ghetto neighborhoods—crime, family dissolution, welfare, low levels of social organization, and so on—are fundamentally a consequence of the disappearance of work."[29] Blacks are unemployed at higher rates than whites.

These programs were all trumpeted as policy initiatives that could solve political problems. They were unable to sustain any long-term success and were unable to meet the political potential seen therein. Therefore, the faith-based initiative is but the latest in a number of

Republican attempts to craft policies that could be ideologically acceptable *and* potentially attractive to African American voters.

Why Does the GOP See the Faith-Based Initiative as an Inroad to the Black Community?

Although the faith-based initiative was not created solely to win black votes, it has struck a chord with some blacks. That the faith-based initiative has been seen as a potential political winner in the African American community is indisputable. Some Republican operatives and activists see it as the best policy tool yet for bringing down political barriers between the party and black voters. According to Republican pollster Frank Luntz, "I will tell you absolutely that if he continues on this road of alternative charities and faith-based assistance, that is the first successful effort I've seen to penetrate the black mindset that has worked."[30] Luntz also noted that African Americans "are the most faith-based segment of the population there is, and they not only appreciate what Bus is doing, but they support it."[31] Further, African American Republican activists see it similarly.[32]

John Pitney has effectively evaluated the Republican use of political issues design to undermine a political opponent.[33] According to Pitney, Republicans accelerated their search and use of political issues as "frames," "wedges," "magnets," and "silver bullets" after three consecutive presidential election victories left Republicans in 1990 with fewer seats in the U.S. House and Senate, fewer governorships and control of fewer state legislative chambers than in 1980—the year of the "Reagan Revolution."[34] Republicans further concluded that a greater emphasis had to be placed on issues that drive voters—either to the GOP or from the Democrats—and that focusing primarily on candidate recruitment was insufficient to win closely contested races. Framing an issue in a certain way or advocating policies that can split the opposition or attract new voters, or finding the magic single issue or event that can settle an election by itself can make or break a party as it seeks to win elections. The faith-based initiative is the quintessential "wedge/magnet" issue in that it combines, either directly or indirectly, some of the most controversial issues in American politics: the separation of church and state, social welfare policy, race, and federal budgeting.

According to Pitney, a wedge issue "splits the opposition causing a large share of its supporters to switch sides or withdraw from battle" while a magnet issue "is a positive policy stand that attracts voter support and inspires people to take part in politics."[35] The faith-based initiative splits the Democratic Party to the extent that it purports to positively change negative social ills while it, at the same time, injects religion more deeply into government. This circumstance pits those whose orientation is most acutely focused on solving social problems against those who feel strongly about maintaining the separation between church and state. In many cases, both of these groups tend to be Democrats. It also forces Democrats to defend a position that can be framed as opposed to remedying social problems that acutely effect its base voters—African Americans. The faith-based initiative also wedges the black church communities, many of whom vote Democratic but are open to questioning their political allegiances.

For many of these same reasons, the faith-based initiative is a magnet for black voters. It has the potential to draw in new religious voters into the political process that may have been reticent about engaging in politics. This is particularly the case with African Americans who are very religious and have been socialized, through the Civil Rights Movement and other venues, to see government funding of religious organizations as reasonable. It may also move undecided voters and "soft" Democrats across the political line of demarcation. As Pitney noted, magnet issues, if successful in shifting voters, can have positive long-term political implications: "[D]uring the 1930s, Franklin Roosevelt endowed the Democratic Party with its own magnet issues: Social Security, labor rights, job creation, and rural electrification."[36] These issues put the Democrats in the political forefront for two generations. Republicans believe that the faith-based initiative can have the same positive impact for the GOP that these policies had for the Democrats.

Republicans see the faith-based initiative as a potentially attractive opportunity to win black voters for two reasons. First, there are high levels of religiosity in the African American community and a related perception of an untapped vein of social conservatism in the black community that many Republican activists see as in line with that of the GOP on "moral" issues. Second, there is a consistent, long-standing need for social services in much of the black community. These two characteristics of African Americans have long led Republican strategists to believe that blacks were "ripe for the picking" by the GOP. While theoretically true, this theory overlooks the decades-long history of negative public policy and symbolic politics perpetrated against African Americans by the GOP.

High African American Religiosity and Perceived Social Conservatism

Republican political strategists cite high levels of religiosity in the African American community as evidence that blacks will support the faith-based initiative and, by extension, be more open to the GOP. John Dilulio, the first director of the White House Office of Faith-Based and Community Initiatives, noted in a 2001 speech to the National Association of Evangelicals that 86 percent of African Americans believe that religion can help "answer all or most of today's problems."[37] The African American Civil Rights Movement was largely led by black religious leaders who were long entrenched community leaders. Many of those religious leaders had built in constituencies that made them natural choices to move into politics. African American Republican activists and candidates for office have indicated that they see religion as the key to GOP success in the black community.[38]

Coupled with this high African American religiosity is the belief held by many that there are wide swaths of conservatism by blacks on many social issues including, but not limited to, same-sex marriage and abortion. According to a 2004 Joint Center for Political and Economic Studies poll, 49 percent of African Americans oppose both marriage and civil unions for same-sex couples—a figure 8 percentage points higher than the general population.[39]

Need for Social Services

There is now, and will likely continue to be, a market for social service delivery, particularly in the African American community. The impact of a harsh criminal justice system that many African Americans believe unfairly treats them, deep-seated poverty and deprivation, poor educational options, the disappearance of inner-city jobs, family dissolution, poor health and access to health care facilities, and the general negativity that is associated with African Americans, among other variables, has created a dismal reality for millions of African Americans that too often leave them reliant on social services to survive.

Black unemployment is more than twice that of whites as is the proportion of African Americans living below the poverty level.[40] Two-thirds of all African American children are born out of wedlock. Nearly a third of black men in their twenties have criminal records, 12.6 percent of all black men between the ages of 25 and 29 are behind bars, and black males have a 32 percent chance of serving time in prison at some point in their lives (Hispanic males have a 17 percent chance; white males have 6 percent chance).[41] In some large American cities, half of all African American public school students do not graduate high school. The dropout issue has particularly significant long-term implications. Nearly 70 percent of all prisoners in state penitentiaries in America are high school dropouts.

Consequently, Christian Right service providers may see the faith-based initiative as an opportunity to plow vast fields of government contracting to engage in their activities while, at the same time, providing services to people who need help. There is a political irony in this. Conservatives have long criticized government social service programs for creating an environment of "dependency" on the government by those who seek such services. With faith-based programs, one can argue, the dependency will still exist, but it shifts from a direct relationship with government to one that becomes indirect, with church groups acting as the conduit.

How Have Republicans Used the Faith-Based Initiative for Political and What Impact Has It Had on Black Voters?

Republican political strategists have consistently denied that the faith-based initiative is a political endeavor. However, there is some evidence to suggest that there were some attempts to use the initiative as an entree to black ministers in the run-up to the 2004 election. According to one report, "[S]ome Black ministers reported receiving entreaties to attend White House meetings or faith-based conferences held around the country, some of them in hard-fought election states."[42] In addition, "about two-thirds of [White House Office on Faith-Based and Community Initiatives Director Jim] Towey's travel during the election year was to a dozen battleground states where he often met with community leaders and promoted the availability of federal funds for church-related social service projects."[43] In addition, large meetings to promote federal grants and grant-writing workshops were held in heavily contested states in September and October of 2004.

Some prominent African American church-based organizations have received large grants, and some of their leaders have been linked to the Republican Party. One Milwaukee pastor who supported Democrats including Bill Clinton and Al Gore in previous elections met with President Bush, received a $1.5 million in federal faith-based grants and, ultimately, endorsed Bush's 2004 reelection campaign. A Philadelphia church led by a pastor who gave the invocation at the 2000 Republican national convention and has long been a Bush supporter received $1 million in federal funds.[44] A Palm Beach, Florida-based group led by a Bush supporter received a $1.7 million grant to train smaller charities.[45]

It is virtually impossible to prove that these grants were solely responsible for these black ministers changing their political allegiances or increasing their already existent support for President Bush. However, the appearance of a quid pro quo leads some to believe that one actually exists and that perception fuels some of the criticism that the faith-based initiative is nothing more than a tax-payer-funded political payoff designed to, among other things, peel off black support for Democrats. It also raises concerns about the potentiality of black ministers being "on the take" for federal grants in exchange for their political support. And as more federal funding circulates through black communities, it may be increasingly difficult to separate which ministers support Republicans because they are aligned with the party on its issues, from those who support the party because they need to maintain access to federal funds.

While President Bush's performance among African Americans nationally rose but by 3 percentage points, his totals increased in some of the states that were large recipients of faith-based grants. In Florida, Bush won 13 percent of the African American vote in 2004, a 6 percentage point increase from 2000. In Ohio, he won 16 percent of the African American vote in 2004, a 7 percentage point increase from 2000. Given that presidential elections are actually individual state elections, the GOP does not need to significantly increase its national African American support levels to have a major impact on these contests.

Conclusion

It is too early to definitively conclude that the faith-based initiative is buying black votes. There is no "smoking gun" that proves beyond a reasonable doubt that the Bush administration is overtly directing funds to black ministers to buy their support (or their silence). However, there is anecdotal evidence to suggest that, at least minimally, there is an infrastructure in place that can achieve that goal. It is also clear that some black ministers, like people of any race, can be wooed as much by money as by issues. There is a long and unfortunate history of some black ministers acting for money in ways that may not reflect the best interests of their congregations.

The Republican Party clearly understands the political potential in federal funding of church-based groups and has coordinated some of its activities around using these grants as an entree into the African American community. As Reverend Louis Shelton, chairman of the conservative Traditional Values Coalition noted, "The political benefits are unbelievable. . . . The Democrats ought to have their heads examined for voting against this."[46]

The faith-based initiative and the distribution of its billions of dollars in grants offers the Republican Party the opportunity to engage African American voters in ways in which it had previously been unable. The focus on faith resonates with African Americans, many of whom could care less about the constitutional separation between church and state. There is a downside, however, for those black church-based organizations that accept these federal grants—their ready receipt of this funding ties them, whether they believe it or not, to those who provide the funding. So a group that has become accustomed to winning these grants and becomes reliant on these grants to operate their programs could find itself on the outside if an administration change results in a movement away from federal funding for religious organizations. The same could happen if court rulings place restrictions on these programs.

This raises some issues going forward that will require steps to remove politics from the distribution of grants to the greatest extent possible. For example, the regulatory changes allowing faith-based federal grants allow organizations to only hire employees who share their faith. In other words, it allows for religious discrimination. Another concern is that grants can be set aside only for religious organizations, thereby creating a stream of federal grants solely for the use of faith-based organizations. In this way, the federal government goes from "leveling the playing field" by allowing church-based groups to compete with secular organizations for grants to tilting the funding in favor of religious groups.

Notes

1. Herbert Aptheker, ed., *A Documentary History of the Negro People in the United States* (New York: Citadel Press, 1969); and Benjamin Quarles,

Black Abolitionists (New York: Oxford University Press, 1969), quoted in Hanes Walton, *Black Republicans: The Politics of the Black and Tans* (Metuchen, NJ: Scarecrow Press, 1975), 15.

2. Vincent P. De Santis, "The Republican Party and the Southern Negro, 1877–1897," *Journal of Negro History*, 15, no. 2 (April 1960): 73.

3. Ibid., 73.

4. The premier study of this period was written by Hanes Walton, *Black Republicans: The Politics of the Blacks and Tans* (Metuchen, NJ: Scarecrow Press, 1975).

5. Dan Balz and John F. Harris, "Some Republicans Predict Upheaval within the Party: Concerns Include Changing Electorate, Lack of Heir Apparent," *Washington Post*, September 4, 2004, A8.

6. David Bositis, "Black Elected Officials: A Statistical Summary, 2000," Joint Center for Political and Economic Studies, Washington, DC, 2002; and David Bositis, "African Americans and the Republican Party, 1996," Joint Center for Political and Economic Studies, Washington, DC, 1997. See also Darryl Fears, "GOP Makes 'Top Priority' of Converting Black Voters," *Washington Post*, December 25, 2003, A4. It should be noted that many public offices around the country are nonpartisan, so while it is likely that there are additional African American Republicans holding office, they were not elected as Republicans.

7. Louis Gould, *Grand Old Party: A History of the Republicans* (New York: Random House, 2003), 489.

8. CNN exit poll data, November 2004 presidential election, http:// www.cnn.com/ELECTION/2004/pages/results/states/US/P/00/epolls.0. html (accessed April 4, 2007).

9. R. W. Apple, Jr., "Courting of Voting Bloc Poses Question of Motive," *New York Times*, August 2, 2000.

10. P.L., 104–193."Personal Responsibility and Work Opportunity Reconciliation Act of 1996."

11. Joseph P. McCormick, 2nd, "George W. and the Souls (and Votes) of Black Folk," lecture and Power Point presentation at the Black Political Thought Lecture Series, DePauw University, Greencastle, IN, April 1, 2002.

12. President George W. Bush, "Remarks by the President in Announcement of the Faith-Based Initiative," The White House, January 29, 2001.

13. Ibid.

14. Dana Milbank and Hamil Harris, "Bush, Religious Leaders Meet: President-Elect Begins Faith-Based Initiative, Reaches for Blacks," *Washington Post*, A6.

15. David Masci, "Religion and Politics," *CQ Researcher*, July 30, 2004, 639.

16. Robert Weems and Lewis Randolph, "The National Response to Richard M. Nixon's Black Capitalism Initiative: The Success of Domestic Detente," *Journal of Black Studies*, 32, no. 1: 66.

17. Ibid.

18. Dean Kotlowski, *Nixon's Civil Rights: Politics, Principle, and Policy* (Cambridge, MA: Harvard University Press, 2001), 128.
19. Ibid., 127.
20. Ibid., 134.
21. Weems and Randolph, "The National Response to Richard M. Nixon's Black Capitalism Initiative," 76, quoting Andrew Brimmer, "Trouble with Black Capitalism," *Nation's Business*, 57: 78–79 and Kotlowski, *Nixon's Civil Rights*, 139.
22. Hugh Davis Graham, "The Origins of Affirmative Action: Civil Rights and the Regulatory State," *Annals of the American Society of Political and Social Science*, v. 523 (September 1992): 56.
23. Ibid., 57.
24. Ibid.
25. Kotlowski, *Nixon's Civil Rights*, 99, quoting transcript of press interview by Nixon, October 25, 1955.
26. Diana Jean Schemo, "Graduation Study Suggests That Some States Sharply Understate High School Dropout Rates," *New York Times*, September 17, 2003.
27. Daria Hall, "Getting Honest about Grad Rates: How States Play the Numbers and Students Lose," *Education Trust*, June 2005; and Michael Dobbs, "States' Graduation Data Criticized: Independent Study Shows Disparities," *Washington Post*, June 24, 2005.
28. Christopher Swanson, "Who Graduates? Who Doesn't? A Statistical Portrait of Public High School Graduation, Class of 2001," *Urban Institute*, February 2004.
29. William Julius Wilson, *When Work Disappears* (New York: Vintage Books, 1996), xiii.
30. Julie Mason, "Bush Turns Up Heat in Effort to Win Over Black Voters," *Houston Chronicle*, March 3, 2001, 1.
31. Ibid.
32. Michael Steele, interview by author, tape recorded, Washington, DC, December 9, 2005; Andre Cadogen, interview by author, tape recorded, Washington, DC, and West Palm Beach, FL, May 3, 2005; Bill Calhoun, interview by author, tape recorded, Washington, DC, and Dallas, TX, June 23, 2005; Niger Innis, interview by author, tape recorded, New York, NY, March 18, 2005 and March 30, 2005; Peter Kirsanow, interview by author, tape recorded, Washington, DC, and Cleveland, OH, July 19, 2005; J. C. Watts, interview by author, tape recorded, Washington, DC, October 12, 2005; Alvin Williams, interview by author, tape recorded, Washington, DC, June 29, 2004; and Armstrong Williams, interview by author, tape recorded, Washington, DC, July 22, 2005.
33. See, John Pitney, "Frames, Wedges, Magnets, and Silver Bullets: Republican Strategies," in *American Political Parties and Constitutional Politics*, ed. Peter Schram and Bradford Wilson (Lanham: Rowman and Littlefield, 1993).
34. Ibid., 119–120.

35. Ibid., 122–123.

36. Ibid., 123–124.

37. John J. Dilulio, Jr., Speech before the National Association of Evangelicals, Dallas, TX, Wednesday, March 7, 2001, citing data from George Gallup, Jr., "Religion in America: Will the Vitality of Churches Be the Surprise of the Next Century," *Public Perspective* (October–November 1995): 4. See also George Gallup and D. Michael Lindsay, *Surveying the Religious Landscape: Trends in U.S. Beliefs* (Harrisburg, PA: Morehouse Publishing, 1999).

38. Michael Steele, interview by author, tape recorded, December 9, 2005, Washington, DC; Andre Cadogen, interview by author, tape recorded, May 3, 2005, Washington, DC and West Palm Beach, FL; Bill Calhoun, interview by author, tape recorded, June 23, 2005, Washington, DC and Dallas, TX; Niger Innis, interview by author, tape recorded, March 18, 2005 and March 30, 2005, New York, NY; Peter Kirsanow, interview by author, tape recorded, July 19, 2005, Washington, DC and Cleveland, OH; J. C. Watts, interview by author, tape recorded, October 12, 2005, Washington, DC; Alvin Williams, interview by author, tape recorded, June 29, 2004, Washington, DC; and Armstrong Williams, interview by author, tape recorded, July 22, 2w005, Washington, DC.

49. Joint Center for Political and Economic Studies, "National Opinion Poll—Politics," released October 19, 2004.

40. Unemployment data from the Bureau of Labor Statistics, "Table A-2. Employment Status of the Civilian Population by Race, Sex, and Age," February 2006, http://www.bls.gov/news.release/empsit.t02.htm (last accessed April 4, 2007); poverty data from the Census Bureau, "Current Population Survey," 2002 and 2003, http://www.census.gov/prod/2003 pubs/p60-222.pdf (last accessed, April 4, 2007).

41. The Sentencing Project, "Facts about Prisons and Prisoners," May 2005, quoting Bureau of Justice Statistics data. According to the Sentencing Project, African American women comprise the fastest growing segment of America's prison population.

42. Peter Wallsten, Tom Hamburger, and Nicholas Riccardi, "Bush Rewarded by Black Pastors' Faith—His Stands, Backed by Funding of Ministries, Redefined the GOP's Image with Some Clergy," *Los Angeles Times*, January 18, 2005.

43. Ibid.

44. See Lew Daly, "Compassion Capital," *Boston Review*, April–May 2005.

45. Wallsten, Hamburger, and Riccardi, "Bush Rewarded by Black Pastors' Faith."

46. Ibid.

Chapter Nine

Life Issues: Abortion, Stem-Cell Research, and the Case of Terry Schiavo

Ted G. Jelen

Introduction

One of the centerpieces of the administration of George W. Bush has been the emphasis on the "culture of life" that has marked the rhetoric, and, to a slightly lesser extent, the policies of the Bush presidency. As several of the other essays in this volume suggest, one of the priorities of the presidency of the George W. Bush has been the mobilization of cultural conservatives around issues involving morality. George W. Bush has arguably taken the traditionalist side in the "culture war" (Hunter 1991; but see Williams 1997 and Fiorina 2005). Issues involving the sanctity of human life such as abortion, euthanasia, and stem-cell research are central to the values of the leadership of groups such as Christian Coalition, Focus on the Family, and Concerned Women for America. Moreover, the phrase "culture of life" has been credited to Pope John Paul II and earlier to Cardinal Joseph Bernardin (Bernardin 1988). President Bush's use of the phrase may thus have resonated rhetorically with U.S. Catholics as well.[1]

Arguably, issues such as abortion and other "life" issues are extremely important to cultural conservatives because these issues provide possible counterarguments to libertarian assertions of personal autonomy. In the United States, a core value is personal freedom, and advocates of diverse positions on issues of personal morality are advantaged to the extent that such positions can be framed as describing autonomous individuals exercising personal freedom (Jelen 2005). For example, opponents of gay marriage have had some difficulty creating a counterframe to the assertion that free, consenting, adults should be allowed to make their own choices about marriage, without interference from the state. Indeed, support for gay rights generally has been increasing, in large part because of the increased visibility of the libertarian frame (Wilcox and Norrander 2002).

With respect to the life issues that form the focus of this chapter, the personal liberty frame can be challenged by pointing out that there are other possible "persons," possibly bearing rights, whose interests need to be considered. With respect to an issue such as euthanasia, there is no doubt that the entity whose life is to be terminated is a person, who very likely has done nothing to deserve her fate (as opposed to convicted murderers or enemy soldiers). Issues such as abortion and stem-cell research pose fascinating (and perhaps intractable) moral and ethical challenges precisely because the identity of persons bearing rights is contested. Thus, the rhetorical importance of these life issues is considerable, since proponents of "pro-life" (broadly construed) issue stances can advance arguments consistent with the dominant value of the American political culture.

Thus, it seems clear that life issues are important to many cultural and religious conservatives, and that cultural and religious conservatives constitute an important part of George W. Bush's political base. Nevertheless, it is the thesis of this chapter that, as president, George W. Bush has provided rhetorical support for pro-life positions on the life issues considered here. However, even when questions of foreign policy and capital punishment are excluded from the analysis, the substantive record of the second Bush administration has been one in which "matters of life and death" are balanced by other considerations, and that President Bush's support for even this limited version of the culture of life is scarcely unequivocal.

Abortion

Clearly, an important aspect of the presidency of George W. Bush has been the administration's policies surrounding the issue of abortion. Some of the most visible policy decisions of the first Bush term have dealt with the question of abortion, and discussion of Bush's nominations to the U.S. Supreme Court in 2005 have been dominated by the abortion issue. Nevertheless, the Bush record on abortion has been one of studied ambiguity (or, more charitably, balance).

As presidential candidate and president, George W. Bush has provided a set of mixed signals on the issue of abortion. On the pro-life side of the ledger, Bush has offered praise for "pregnancy crisis centers," which are widely regarded as institutions that discourage abortion. Conversely, Bush has repeatedly criticized the *Roe v. Wade* decision, but has never called for its outright reversal. Further, as elaborated below, President Bush has sent mixed signals with respect to his nominations for the U.S. Supreme Court, and, as elaborated below, has invoked the *Dred Scott* decision, which has enormous symbolic importance to the pro-life movement (Kirkpatrick 2005a). President Bush's policies on abortion can generally be characterized as incrementally pro-life. That is, the Bush administration has consistently used its executive authority to discourage abortion and to withhold government support for institutions and policies that facilitate abortion. However, President Bush has stopped well short of proposing or implementing policies that would drastically curtail abortion rights.

Upon being inaugurated as president in 2001, George W. Bush immediately reinstated the "global gag rule," which proscribes funding from the U.S. government for international groups that provide abortion services or abortion counseling. This policy, termed the Mexico City Provision (after the cite of a population conference in 1984) had been previously used by presidents Ronald Reagan and George H. W. Bush and had been rescinded by President Clinton (Blackman 2001).

In 2003, President Bush also signed a bill banning the practice of intact dilation and extraction, a late-term abortion procedure popularly known as partial-birth abortion. A similar bill had been vetoed by President Clinton, because it lacked an exception for the protection of maternal health. George W. Bush signed the bill, despite the continued lack of a maternal health exception and despite the fact that similar laws passed by state legislatures had already been held unconstitutional, because of the lack of such a provision (*Stenberg v. Carhart* 2000).[2]

In 2004, the Food and Drug Administration (FDA) rejected making "Plan B" (the so-called morning after pill, which prevents pregnancy when taken after sexual intercourse) available without a prescription ("FDA Rejects Non-Prescription Pill for Now" 2004). This decision contradicted the FDA's scientific advisors, who had found the drug safe, and who had suggested that the drug would be useful in preventing many abortions (Alonso-Zalvidar 2005). The decision was widely interpreted as a concession to cultural conservatives, who feared that the easy availability of Plan B would encourage sexual promiscuity among teenagers. Journalistic accounts of the decision have emphasized that Commissioner Marc McClellan (a Bush appointee) may have overruled the judgment of FDA staffers and an advisory panel of experts (Kaufman 2005).

Conversely, while candidate Bush repeatedly expressed reservations about RU-486 (a so-called abortion pill, the FDA continued to permit the use of the drug during the Bush administration. While Heath and Human Services Secretary Tommy Thompson ordered a review of the safety of the drug (Pear 2001), the use of RU-486 has continued to be legal during the Bush presidency.

It is in the area of appointments to the U.S. Supreme Court that the Bush administration's ambiguous approach to the abortion issue is most apparent. In his election campaigns of 2000 and 2004, George W. Bush was persistently asked questions about the sorts of justices he would appoint to the Supreme Court if elected. Bush consistently endorsed the idea of appointing conservative justices, who would interpret the law rather than create law by judicial fiat. Bush repeatedly criticized activist justices, who had allegedly written their personal preferences into constitutional law. Bush also stated that he would not impose a "litmus test" on prospective nominees to the Supreme Court, which was widely understood to mean that Bush would not require justices who opposed abortion rights. Conversely, Bush pointed to justices Antonin Scalia and Clarence Thomas as models for the type of justices he favored. Both Scalia and Thomas have vociferously criticized the *Roe v. Wade* decision and urged that the *Roe* precedent be overturned. In the presidential debates in his 2004 campaign against John Kerry, Bush also asserted that he would not appoint justices who would issue *Dred Scott* type rulings. Of course, the Supreme Court's ruling in *Dred Scott v. Sanford* (1857) is among the most notorious in the history of the Court. Pro-life activists routinely compare *Roe* to *Dred Scott*, and Bush's remarks were widely interpreted as a signal to the right to life movement. Thus, candidate Bush's public pronouncements about Supreme Court nominations and abortion were studiously vague (and to some pro-life activists infuriatingly Delphic), but clearly intended to signal Bush's opposition to legal abortion.

In 2005, President Bush had the opportunity to fill two vacancies on the U.S. Supreme Court. After the death of Chief Justice William H. Rehnquist, Bush appointed John Roberts as chief justice. Roberts was confirmed rather easily by the U.S. Senate. To fill the seat of retiring Associate Justice Sandra Day O'Connor, Bush first appointed White House Counsel Harriet Miers. After a few weeks, Miers withdrew her candidacy in the face of persistent criticism of her qualifications, as well as some reservations among conservatives about her ideological leanings. Bush then named Appellate Court Justice Samuel Alito to fill the O'Connor seat. In all three appointments, President Bush appeared to have avoided candidates who have taken clear positions in opposition to *Roe v. Wade*. While both Roberts and Alito have argued in favor of restrictions on abortion as advocates, neither has established a judicial record of outright hostility to abortion rights (Kirkpatrick 2005a). Indeed, both justices have suggested that, in general, they plan to be deferential to legal precedents, implying that they would be unlikely to overturn *Roe* (Stout 2005). Comments made by Chief Justice Roberts during his confirmation process have suggested that he regards himself as a judicial craftsman, rather than a justice with broad ideological commitments (Holland 2005).

The rationale underlying these selections is not entirely clear. One possibility is that President Bush avoided making highly controversial choices, because the vacancies on the Supreme Court occurred during a period in which his personal popularity was rather low. Another possibility involves the narrowness of the Republican majority in the U.S. Senate in 2005, and the desire of President Bush to avoid protracted confirmation battles. Finally, it is possible that Bush's failure to nominate justices who are publicly committed to overturning *Roe* may reflect the relatively low priority President Bush places on the issue of abortion, relative to questions concerning the war in Iraq or the future of social security. Indeed, some analysts have suggested that the Bush administration is more concerned with questions of federal-state relations, especially as such constitutional issues apply to questions of economic regulation (Rosen 2004). What is clear, however, is that President Bush has not taken the opportunity to nominate more ideologically conservative or pro-life justices such as Janice Rogers Brown or Priscilla Owen.

When appointing justices to federal courts below the level of the Supreme Court, the Bush record has been more mixed. Bush's appointees to federal circuit and appellate courts have been generally conservative (Carp, Manning, and Stidham 2004), and some of his more ideologically strident appointees (such as Brown or Owen) have attracted opposition from liberals within and outside the U.S. Senate. However, despite the existence of some highly visible confirmation fights, a large majority of Bush's appointees to the federal bench have received Senate approval, and Bush appears to have made a conscious effort to increase the demographic diversity of federal judges (O'Brien 2004).

To date, then, the legacy of the Bush administration on the abortion issue has been somewhat mixed. While the policies of the executive branch during the Bush administration have generally discouraged information about and access to legal abortion, President Bush has not made a serious attempt to roll back the precedent set in *Roe v. Wade*, or to appoint justices likely to overrule the 1973 decision. Politically, this set of actions may be regarded as politically astute. Specific policies designed to discourage abortion may resonate with activists who care deeply about the issue but may exist "below the radar" for the populace whose attention to abortion politics is not as intense.

Stem-Cell Research

Another aspect of the politics of life issues that has been a recurrent source of controversy during the Bush presidency has been the use of fetal tissue for medical research. Of course, the potential for medical advances using genetic research have been apparent for about a generation, and, indeed, were the subject of a presidential commission, whose existence spanned the Carter and Reagan administrations (Evans 2002a).

Public support for genetic medical research is difficult to measure and is often contingent on the manner in which a survey question is posed (Evans 2002b). Nevertheless, the prospects of curing or treating intractable diseases such as Alzheimer's or diabetes has clearly created new constituencies for what is popularly termed stem-cell research and has altered the dynamic of public discourse on issues pertaining to human life. The simplest formulation of an enormously complex issue might be to suggest that the raw material for such medical research (and, ultimately, medical treatment) often comes from human embryos, which may have been generated outside the womb. For persons convinced that human life begins at the moment of conception, the use of such embryos for medical purposes poses an extremely serious ethical problem.

In August of 2001, President Bush announced his policy with respect to federal funding of embryonic research. Bush's policy was essentially to split the difference between those who favored such research for the potential medical benefits and those who opposed such science on ethical or religious grounds. Bush announced that he would permit federal funding for research on existing stem-cell lines but would ban federal funding for the creation of new lines ("Remarks by the President on Stem Cell Research" 2001).

In his speech, President Bush claimed that there existed over 60 stem-cell lines, but this claim proved controversial. Other scientists suggested that there were as few as 22 existing lines and that several of these had been rendered useless for research because of contamination (Tumulty 2005). Thus, there was no consensus concerning the research possibilities for stem-cell research under President Bush's carefully crafted compromise.

The stem-cell controversy evoked a number of diverse reactions among state governments and within the Republican Party. A few state governments such as California and New Jersey enacted legal protections intended to permit stem-cell research. In California, Governor Swartznegger proposed a referendum that provided $3 billion (to be funded by state bonds) to support stem-cell research. Similar measures have been proposed in other states such as Florida and Massachusetts. Conversely, one state (South Dakota) bans stem-cell research completely, and a number of other states have enacted restrictions to make such research extremely difficult (Chu 2005).

Stem-cell research has also been something of a wedge issue for Republicans at the federal level. Legislation has been proposed in both the House and the Senate, which would expand opportunities for federal funding by permitting funding for research on embryos created in vitro (Tumulty 2005). The Senate version was sponsored by Majority Leader Bill Frist, a conservative on most life issues such as abortion and euthanasia and a possible presidential candidate for 2008 (Stolberg 2005). Conversely, Kansas Senator Sam Brownback, another 2008 GOP presidential hopeful, has attempted to attract the support of conservative Christians by supporting bans on embryonic stem-cell research and human cloning (Kirkpatrick 2005b).

Thus, at this writing, President Bush's carefully crafted compromise on stem-cell research appears to be unraveling and may create an important division within the Republican Party. While limitations on stem-cell research are clearly consistent with the pro-life message of the GOP, the medical promise of stem-cell research has likely created new constituencies for these scientific efforts. The medical technology that stem-cell research may empower could alter the frame by which life issues such as abortion and euthanasia are debated in future American politics (Jelen and Wilcox 2003; Burns 2005).

Euthanasia: The Case of Terry Schiavo

Several aspects of the culture war coalesced around the Terry Schiavo case in 2005. The tragic circumstances surrounding Ms. Schiavo's death brought the issue of passive euthanasia (or, more colloquially, the "right to die") to the center of public debate and ultimately proved to be something of a political embarrassment for President Bush and his brother, John Edward ("Jeb") Bush, the governor of Florida at that time.

Of course, the issue of euthanasia has been a contentious one in American politics for several decades. In the early 1990s, Dr. Jack Kevorkian achieved notoriety for performing assisted suicides for patients regarded as terminally ill. Kevorkian was eventually convicted of second degree murder, after several acquittals and challenges to the constitutionality of laws prohibiting physician-assisted suicide.

In 1994, the state of Oregon enacted (by referendum) the first law explicitly permitting physician-assisted suicides for mentally competent, terminally ill patients. A series of legal challenges have prevented the law from taking effect, and the Bush administration sought to invalidate the law as a violation of federal statutes. In October of 2005, the U.S. Supreme Court heard oral arguments concerning the right of a state government to enact such a law under the Tenth Amendment to the U.S. Constitution. At this writing, the Court has not issued a ruling.

It is against this legal and political background that the public controversy over the fate of Terry Schiavo took place. In 1990, perhaps as a result of habitual bulimia, Schiavo went into what physicians termed "a persistent vegetative state." After being kept alive for several years, her husband, Michael Schiavo, requested removal of her feeding tube, asserting that Terry would not wish to be kept alive by artificial means. He petitioned a Florida state court for permission to terminate her life support. Terry's parents opposed the petition, and, after over a year of litigation, a Florida state judge granted Michael Schiavo's petition.

Terry's parents, Robert and Mary Schindler, appealed this ruling to the state court of appeals in Florida and filed a suit in federal court. Governor Jeb Bush of Florida filed an amicus brief on behalf of the Schlinders. When these appeals were denied, the feeding tube was removed in October of 2003 (Frank 2005).

It is at this point in the narrative that the involvement of Governor Jeb Bush and President George W. Bush became most visible. After the Florida Supreme Court denied the Schindler's petition, the Florida state legislature, at Governor Bush's urging, passed a measure popularly known as Terry's Law. This measure, which permitted the governor to order the reinstatement of Terry Schiavo's feeding tube, was praised publicly by President Bush. After the passage of Terry's Law, the feeding tube was reinstated, and Michael Schiavo filed a lawsuit, alleging that the law was unconstitutional.

In 2004, the Florida Supreme Court ruled Terry's Law unconstitutional, and the U.S. Supreme Court refused to hear the Schlinder's appeal in January of 2005. A month later, Florida Judge George Greer ordered the feeding tube removed. In March of 2005, the U.S.

Congress passed a bill that would provide the Schlinders access to federal courts. President George W. Bush flew in from Texas to sign the bill, even though he could have signed the bill in Crawford. President Bush made a public show of signing the bill at approximately 1:00 a.m. on March 21, to illustrate the urgency that he attached to the measure.

The actions of the Congress ultimately proved futile. Terry's parents submitted several appeals to state and federal courts between March 23 and March 26, but all were denied (Tumulty 2005). With no legal appeals remaining to the Schiavos, Terry's tube was not reinstated, and she died on March 31, 2005.

The Terry Schiavo case might well have remained a contentious, but private, family tragedy, were it not for the intervention of elected officials and the news media. Throughout the legal appeals processes, numerous public demonstrations were held in support of Terry Schiavo's "right to life." One prominent Catholic clergymen termed the removal of Terry's feeding tube "a modern crucifixion" (Eisenberg 2005). Several news reports emphasized the fact that Michael Schiavo had entered into a new romantic relationship after his wife had been comatose for over a decade, and a few news reports contained allegations of spousal abuse by Michael. On the other side of the controversy, Senator Bill Frist (a physician) was subjected to criticism and some ridicule by late-night television comics for his assertion, based on viewing videotape, that Terry Schiavo was conscious and aware of her situation. News reports also emphasized that Thomas DeLay (a conservative Republican and supporter of the Schlinder's appeals) had participated in a decision to withhold life support for his comatose father.

Despite the highly visible protests against allowing Terry Schiavo to die, the decision of several elected officials (including Jeb and George W. Bush) to intervene in the case was not a popular one. A poll conducted by *Time* magazine shortly after Terry's death showed that large majorities of both parties opposed Congress' intervention in the Schiavo matter, and that the motives of elected officials were based on political calculations rather than moral principles. Over 70 percent of those polled disapproved of President Bush's involvement in the case (Eisenberg 2005).

While I am in no position to assess the motives of anyone connected with the Schiavo case, it seems clear that the actions of George W. and Jeb Bush, as well as Republican members of Congress, are consistent with the culture of life that President Bush has repeatedly endorsed. Nevertheless, any sober political assessment of the Bush's intervention

in the Schiavo case would conclude that the intercession of the governor
of Florida, the Congress, and the president of the United States had
backfired. While it seems unlikely that the Schiavo case will have electoral repercussions in 2006 or 2008, it seems clear that the pro-life
rationale that underlay the participation of public officials in this
matter was not persuasive to many Americans. Indeed, one of the
long-term effects of the Schiavo case appears to have been to motivate
large numbers of Americans to create living wills, in which they
request not to be kept alive by extraordinary means if they become
terminally ill (Eisenberg 2005).

George W. Bush and the Culture of Life: An Assessment

I have shown elsewhere (Jelen 1990, 2006) that there does not appear
to exist a constituency for what Cardinal Joseph Bernardin (1988) has
termed a "consistent ethic of life." Even if issues such as capital punishment and military spending (in which the persons to be killed may
be regarded as morally culpable) are excluded, there is little support
for a general culture of life, in which the protection of "innocent life"
is a primary value. In the cases of abortion and stem-cell research, of
course, the identity of "persons" bearing rights is precisely at issue.
The question of whether human embryos constitute persons deserving
of legal protection is, of course, central to the debate over these issues
(but see McDonagh 1996). Nevertheless, the actions of the Bush
administration and the public reactions to these policies illustrate the
implausibility of the consistent life ethic to many Americans.

With respect to the abortion issue, research has shown that abortion
attitudes are quite stable (Jelen and Wilcox 2003, 2005; Sharpe 1999)
and, indeed, may be becoming more conservative in the aggregate.
Many, if not most, Americans are "situationalists" who favor legal
abortion under some circumstances, but not others (Cook, Jelen, and
Wilcox 1992), and who may be uncomfortable with the easy availability of legal abortion (Saletan 2003). Given the distribution of public
attitudes on abortion, and given that abortion attitudes seem quite
stable at the individual level (Converse and Markus 1979), President
Bush's approach to the abortion issue may be politically astute, regardless of what one might think of the content of the policy. If one assumes
that pro-life voters are more attuned to the nuances of abortion
policy than other Americans,[3] Bush's approach of discouraging abortion
through highly specific policy decisions, while avoiding a frontal attack

on *Roe v. Wade*, may in fact achieve the goal of placating the Republican base of Christian conservatives, without occasioning a countermobilization among the large majority of Americans who believe abortion should be legal under at least some circumstances. Pro-life groups have been particularly attentive to the rhetorical possibilities contained in the question of "partial-birth" abortion (Saletan 2003). It is considerably more plausible to argue for the humanity of a fetus at seven or eight months than to suggest that a zygote is entitled to legal and constitutional protection. By focusing on what seems to many to be a gruesome aspect of the abortion issue, pro-life activists may have shifted attention away from the privacy rights of women to the ontological status of the fetus. As such, President Bush's support for legislation outlawing intact dilation and extraction is not likely to incur substantial political costs among moderates on the abortion issue, and may serve to shore up support among voters more committed to restricting access to legal abortion.

Such a mixed message becomes more difficult if the abortion issue assumes a prominent role on the national political agenda. President Bush's attempt to find a middle ground, which may be conceptually inconsistent but politically advantageous, may be challenged by the highly charged politics of nominations to the Supreme Court. Bush's centrist strategy appears to have been generally successful with the nominations of Chief Justice John Roberts and Justice Samuel Alito.[4] The effects of this strategy on the voting behavior of cultural conservatives (including devout evangelical Protestants) in 2006 and 2008 are not yet clear. While it seems unlikely that discontent with Bush's abortion policies, or his nominations to the Supreme Court, would cause many evangelicals to vote Republican, such questions may have depressed Republican turnout in the 2006 off-year elections, or provide an uncomfortable wedge issue for GOP presidential candidates in the 2008 primary elections. Nevertheless, one is inclined to credit the Bush administration with a high level of political acumen for its general handling of the abortion issue.

By contrast, the middle ground option seems to have been considerably less effective with respect to the issue of stem-cell research. Admittedly, this is a relatively new, complex issue, and President Bush (along with all other elected officials) is in uncharted territory where issues of biotechnology are concerned. Kristin Luker (1985) has reminded us that even highly emotional "moral issues" are often structured by the self-interests of those involved. Luker's analysis of the abortion issue suggests that the situations of homemakers and women who are members of the paid labor force provide gestalts about life, sexual morality, and gender roles that frame the abortion issue differently for diverse groups of women.

When this style of analysis is applied to issues of biomedical research, it seems clear that the promise of medical research involving fetal tissue is in the process of creating large new constituencies, whose political leanings are as yet undefined. Some surveys have shown that the idea of stem-cell research, as well as government funding for such efforts, is rather popular among the mass public (Harris Poll 2004), although surveys in this area seem quite sensitive to variations in framing and question wording (Evans 2002a, 2002b). From that static standpoint, Bush's attempt to find a middle ground on this issue may have been futile. Perhaps more importantly, the existence of large (and largely undermobilized) constituencies for the medical benefits that stem cell research may provide suggest that public opinion on this issue is likely to be quite unstable in the immediate future, and we may witness major changes in the distribution of public attitudes about these cutting-edge medical technologies.

Finally, the attempts by the Bush brothers to intervene in the case of Terry Schiavo must candidly be characterized as a failure, albeit one that seems unlikely to have long-term consequences. Public support for the "right to die" is generally quite high (Jelen 2006; Eisenberg 2005), and the public seems to have responded to the Schiavo case as an instance of that more general principle. President Bush's attempts at intervention in this matter were quite unpopular even among Republicans, and it seems likely that few members of the mass public connected the fate of Terry Schiavo to the more general principle embodied in the culture of life.

In general, then, the record of the Bush administration on life issues illustrates an important aspect of the consistent ethic of life. The conceptual connection between abortion, stem-cell research, and euthanasia is cognitively demanding and does not seem apparent to many ordinary citizens in the United States. Moreover, each issue involves considerations beyond questions of human life: in addition to the ontological status of the fetus, the abortion issue involves issues of gender roles, sexual morality, and individual autonomy (embodied in the phrase "right to choose"). Medical research involving fetal tissue holds out the promise of effective treatment (perhaps even cures) for a wide variety of diseases, while the euthanasia issue is centrally concerned with individual autonomy and questions of the "quality" of life. It is possible that these diverse considerations, unique to each issue, affect the structure of public attitudes as much as do "matters of life and death." If this is indeed the case, this may explain why

President Bush's (politically) successful strategy in dealing with the issue of abortion was not as effective when applied to medical research or the right to die.

Notes

1. Some observers may consider it ironic that an administration ostensibly committed to the sanctity of human life has pursued the war in Iraq, or has enthusiastically supported the death penalty. I leave it to others to sort out any possible potential contradiction.
2. The bill does contain a provision permitting the procedure if the woman's life is in danger.
3. This assumption is extremely controversial. See Cook, Jelen, and Wilcox 1992.
4. It should be noted that both Roberts and Alito voted to uphold the Congressional ban on "partial birth" abortions (*Gonzales v. Carhart*, 2007).

References

Alonso-Zalvidar, Ricardo. 2005. "Probe Finds FDA Deviated in Morning After Pill Decision." LATIMES.com (accessed November 14).

Bernardin, Joseph. 1988. *A Consistent Ethic of Life*. Chicago, IL: Sheed and Ward.

Blackman, Ann, 2001. "Bush Acts on Abortion 'Gag Rule.'" *Time*, January 21.

Burns, Gene. 2005. *The Moral Veto: Framing Contraception, Abortion, and Cultural Pluralism in the United States*. New York: Cambridge University Press.

Carp, Robert A., Kenneth L. Manning, and Ronald Stidham, 2004. "The Decision-Making Behavior of George W. Bush's Judicial Appointees." *Judicature* 88 (July–August): 20–28.

Chu, Jeff. 2005. "California Leads, but a Pack Follows." *Time*, May 23.

Converse, Philip E., and Gregory Markus. 1979. "'Plus Ca Change . . .' The New CPS Panel Study." *American Political Science Review* 73: 32–49.

Cook, Elizabeth Adell, Ted G. Jelen, and Clyde Wilcox. 1992. *Between Two Absolutes: Public Opinion and the Politics of Abortion*. Boulder, CO: Westview.

Eisenberg, Daniel. 2005. "Lessons of the Schiavo Battle." *Time*, April 4.

Evans, John H. 2002a. *Playing God? Human Genetic Engineering and the Rationalization of Public Bioethical Debate*. Chicago, IL: University of Chicago Press.

——— 2002b. "Religion and Human Cloning: An Exploratory Analysis of the First Available Opinion Data." *Journal for the Scientific Study of Religion* 41: 747–758.

"FDA Rejects Non-Prescription Pill for Now." 2004. *USA Today*, May 6.

Fiorina, Morris P. (with Samuel J. Abrams and Jeremy C. Pope). 2005. *Culture War: The Myth of a Polarized America*. New York: Pearson-Longman.

Frank, Mitch. 2005. "The Legal Struggle." *Time*, April 4.

Harris Poll. 2004. "Those Favoring Stem Cell Research Increases to a 73 to 11 Percent Majority." *HarrisInteractive*. http://www.harrisinteractive.com/harris_poll/index.aps?PID=488 (accessed March 2, 2006).

Holland, Jesse J. 2005. "Roberts: Precedent Settles Abortion Ruling." Associated Press, September 13. http://www.sfgate.com/cgi-bin/article.cgi?f=?n/a/2005/09/13/national/w072607D51.DTL (accessed March 1, 2006).

Hunter, James Davison. 1991. *Culture Wars* New York: Basic Books.

Jelen, Ted G. 1990. "Religious Belief and Attitude Constraint." *Journal for the Scientific Study of Religion* 29: 118–125.

——— 2005. "Political Esperanto: Rhetorical Resources and Limitations of the Christian Right in the United States." *Sociology of Religion* 66: 303–321.

——— 2006. "American Catholics and the Structure of Life Attitudes." *University of St. Thomas Law Review* 2: 397–420.

Jelen, Ted G., and Clyde Wilcox. 2003. "Causes and Consequences of Public Attitudes toward Abortion: A Review and Research Agenda." *Political Research Quarterly* 56: 489–500.

——— 2005. "Continuity and Change in Attitudes toward Abortion: Poland and the United States." *Politics and Gender* 1: 297–315.

Kaufman, Marc. 2005. "GAO: FDA Ruling on 'Morning After Pill' Was Unusual." *Washington Post*, November 16.

Kirkpatrick, David D. 2005a. "The Nation: A Wink and a Prayer: The Crisis of the Bush Code." *New York Times*, October 9.

——— 2005b. "Kansas Senator, Looking at Presidential Bid, Makes Faith the Bedrock of Campaign." *New York Times*, October 14.

Luker, Kristin. 1985. *Abortion and the Politics of Motherhood*. Berkeley, CA: University of California Press.

McDonagh, Eileen. 1996. *Breaking the Abortion Deadlock: From Choice to Consent*. New York: Oxford University Press.

O'Brien, David M. 2004. "Ironies and Disappointments: Bush and Federal Judgeships." In *The George W. Bush Presidency: Appraisals and Prospects*, edited by Colin Campbell and Bert A. Rockman. Washington, DC: CQ Press, 133–157.

Pear, Robert.2001. "Transition in Washington: Health and Human Services: Thompson Says He Will Order a New Review of Abortion Drug." *New York Times*, January 20.

"Remarks by the President on Stem Cell Research." 2001. http://www.whitehouse.gov/news/releases/2001/08/20010809-2.html (accessed March 1, 2006).

Rosen, Jeffrey. 2004. "How the Election Affects the Court: Supreme Mistake." *New Republic Online*. http://www.tnr.com/doc.mhtml?i-20041108&s=rosen110804 (accessed March 1, 2006).

Saletan, William. 2003. *Bearing Right: How Conservatives Won the Abortion War*. Berkeley, CA: University of California Press.

Sharpe, Elaine B. 1999. *The Sometime Connection: Public Opinion and Public Policy*. Albany, NY: SUNY Press.

Stenberg v. Carhart. 2000. 530 U.S. 914, 932.

Stolberg, Sheryl Gay. 2005. "Senate's Leader Veers from Bush over Stem Cells." *New York Times*, July 29.

Stout, David. 2005. "Supreme Court Pick Assures Key Senator on Abortion Views." *New York Times*, December 2.

"Terry Schiavo." 2005. http://www.nndb.com/people/435/000026457/.

Tumulty, Karen. 2005. "Why Bush's Ban Could Be Reversed." *Time*, May 23.

Wilcox, Clyde, and Barbara Norrander. 2002. "Of Mood and Morals: The Dynamics of Opinion on Abortion and Gay Rights." In *Understanding Public Opinion*, edited by Barbara Norrander and Clyde Wilcox. Washington, DC: CQ Press.

Williams, Rhys, ed. 1997. *Culture Wars in American Politics: Critical Reviews of a Popular Thesis*. Hawthorne, NY: Aldine de Gruyter.

Chapter Ten

Evangelical "Internationalists" and U.S. Foreign Policy during the Bush Administration

Kevin R. den Dulk

Introduction

Commentators in the immediate wake of the 2004 elections were in near unanimous agreement that the "values voter" had won the day; some even declared (with either a celebratory or dispirited tone) that the victory, though close, was decisive and long-term. The passage of 11 state ballot initiatives banning same-sex marriage as well as exit surveys showing "moral values" as more important to more voters than terrorism, Iraq, or jobs were among the pieces of evidence that pundits and pollsters combined into a story of morality-based mobilization across the United States. They also chose an exemplar of the values voter: evangelical Christians, eight in ten of whom voted for George W. Bush.

Mark J. Rozell and Corwin Smidt et al. in this volume discuss the relevance of moral values in the 2004 elections. For purposes of this chapter, the key feature of that discussion is the widely held assumption that values voters, and particularly traditionalist evangelicals, were motivated primarily by *domestic* policy concerns, chief among them old standbys such as abortion, indecency, and gambling, as well as new policy areas such as same-sex marriage. To be sure, evangelical energies were focused on these and similar issues during President Bush's first term and the 2004 campaign, as they have been since the emergence of the so-called Christian Right movement in the early 1980s.[1] My question in this chapter, however, is whether similar values-based concerns mobilized evangelicals during the first term to advance a *foreign* policy agenda—and if so, to what effect.

My general answer is that evangelicals—and particularly evangelical elites—did indeed pursue what might be called a "faith-based" foreign policy agenda, and they did so fervently and with similar results as their domestic agenda (i.e., with mixed results, with mixed success).[2] Evangelicals have also confronted international affairs in a wider range of policy areas than journalists and social scientists have typically explored, including the Israeli-Palestinian conflict, perhaps the most prominent of evangelical international concerns; the "War on Terror" overseas and the relationship between Islam and the West; human rights abroad, particularly religious freedom abuses; and global population issues such as abortion, contraception, and AIDS/HIV.[3] These policy issues, though often interrelated, nevertheless present distinctive areas of evangelical international concern.

Comparing evangelical involvement in these four areas illumines some broader features of evangelicalism's global outlook during the Bush presidency. In each of these areas evangelicals have rejected isolationism in favor of a foreign policy that is globally focused but generally unilateralist, partly motivated by distinctive theological convictions and aided by increasing strategic sophistication. Evangelical elites are not monolithic, however, in their understandings of international affairs, which can make for robust debate but can also present an obstacle to greater influence. Indeed, evangelical justifications for global engagement run the gamut, depending on the issues and personalities involved; some are focused on traditional piety, others on human (and therefore transnational) dignity rooted in the image of Christ, still others on the role of U.S. foreign policy in hastening endtimes expectations. In addition to this familiar Protestant penchant for theological diversity and infighting, evangelical leaders also face the daunting challenge that internationalism does not yet command the attention of the evangelical "grassroots" to the extent domestic issues do.

In light of these features of evangelical internationalism, it is no wonder that evangelical efforts, taken on the whole, have met some ambivalence within the Bush administration. On the one hand, Bush's team has recognized evangelicals as a key part of the president's governing base and an influential constituency in Congress. They are ignored at some political peril. Moreover, Bush's own religious experiences and inclinations, his use of religious imagery to describe international threats, and his openness to unilateralism resonate with many members of the Christian Right. On the other hand, the administration has had a somewhat uneasy relationship with evangelicals on international affairs. The lack of a united and mass-based mobilization within evangelicalism on global affairs has generally given the administration leeway to develop foreign policy with little fear of political repercussions. Bush's foreign policy is also subject to intense cross-pressures, including the ideological factionalism within the administration itself.

Internationalism, Global Christianity, and Religious Worldview

In May 2002, *New York Times* columnist Nicholas Kristof declared American evangelicals "the newest internationalists."[4] The discovery of evangelical engagement in international affairs apparently took him by surprise, and he anticipated that many in his readership—those "snooty, college-educated bicoastal elitists," as he put it—would be quite skeptical of his claim. Kristof's reaction may have been the result of a perception that evangelicals tend to international isolationism because they are blinkered to the world or downright contemptuous of it. Or perhaps he assumed that, to the extent evangelicals care about non-Americans, they perceive them as little more than potential converts.[5] Yet especially in response to religious persecution overseas, evangelicals were taking the lead in combating various global human rights abuses abroad—and had been doing so well before George W. Bush took his first oath of office. Aided by "strange bedfellow" coalitions, they helped to shepherd through Congress the International Religious Freedom Act of 1998 (requiring, among other things, the State Department to monitor religious freedom worldwide), the Trafficking Victims Protection Act of 2000 (authorizing strong sanctions against nations that countenance sex trafficking and other forms of forced servitude), and a debt relief authorization in 2000 ($400 million in debt relief for impoverished nations). During the Bush presidency they have successfully lobbied Congress to pass the Sudan Peace Act of 2002, which pressures the Sudanese regime to end that country's bloody internal (and partly religion-based) conflict, and evangelicals have continued to push for strong sanctions on North Korea, China, and other countries for their religious freedom abuses.

These *specific* efforts on human rights are new to evangelicals, but to suggest more generally that evangelicals are "new" internationalists reveals a lack of historical perspective. If one uses a capacious definition of "internationalist" that includes most forms of deliberate engagement with foreign nations, evangelical internationalism has ebbed and flowed over time. Indeed, modern American evangelicalism came of age during the cold war, when evangelical leaders regularly and forcefully denounced "godless" communism and supported U.S. efforts at containment. It is telling that President Ronald Reagan's famous speech in 1983 declaring the Soviet Union "an evil empire" was given at the annual convention of the National Association of Evangelicals.[6] Over the past few decades, many evangelical leaders have also been involved in policy debates over Israel, international family planning, and China's trade status, among other issues. While these leaders have often been unilateralist and highly skeptical about pursuing U.S. foreign policy through international coalitions, this strategic approach should not be confused with reactionary isolationism. On the contrary, on certain issues evangelical leaders have generally preferred energetic U.S. interventions abroad.

Survey data suggest that ordinary evangelicals today share their leaders' general global outlook. In fact, comparing their survey responses to their religious peers reveals that evangelicals are remarkably receptive to an active U.S. foreign policy. Among all identifiable religious groups except Jews, evangelicals Christians are the least likely—34 percent—to say that the United States should mind its own business in global politics, and this view is strongest among those evangelicals who are most likely to attend church services regularly and intensely identify with the faith.[7] Moreover, again with the exception of Jewish Americans, white evangelicals are the most likely (60 percent of all evangelicals, 69 percent among the most committed) to claim that the United States ought to play a special role in the world.[8]

These patterns of mass opinion—that the United States is not merely obligated to engage the world but also has a special role to play—suggests that evangelicals have a strong sense of American exceptionalism in international affairs. This perception is reinforced by a comparatively strong belief that God has provided the United States with special protection—a belief with deep roots in the history of American Protestantism, from the Puritan vision of America as a "city on the hill" to more contemporary understandings of the providential destiny of the United States as a "Christian nation."[9] Coupled with a deep-seated suspicion of international organizations, the belief in America's unique role in the world explains the unilateralism of many evangelicals. While it is important to note that a majority of highly committed evangelicals support working through international organizations—a fact often overlooked in scholarly portrayals of evangelical foreign policy beliefs[10]—a sizable minority of evangelicals— 44 percent—say that the United States ought to act unilaterally to keep the peace. No more than a third of any other religious grouping supports this latter position.[11]

There are many reasons for the general evangelical support of global engagement, but perhaps none is more important to contemporary politics than the dramatic demographic shifts in global Christianity. As a proportion of the world's population of Christians, at least half as many believers reside today in Europe and North America as in 1900.[12] At least 60 percent—and by one estimate as many as three-quarters[13]— of Christians live in developing or third world countries today, especially in the Southern Hemisphere. The change is so important that the historian Philip Jenkins calls non-Western Christianity the "next Christendom."[14] American evangelicals, with large numbers of missionaries and development workers in the field, are exposed directly to the social and economic deprivation non-Western Christians confront in daily life. Stateside Americans experience these hardships vicariously and consequently they have become more sensitive to the "suffering Church" abroad, as well as related policy issues ranging from the ravages of violent international conflict to the role of international population policy. The processes of globalization, most notably the speed and reach of modern communication technologies as well as Christian immigration into the United States, have ensured that the information flow from far-flung mission fields is continuous and substantial.

These demographic shifts are complemented by distinctive beliefs about morality and missions that provide evangelicals an intellectual resource for global engagement. In the most general terms, consider Pew Center findings in 2003 that 86 percent of evangelicals think that moral principles ought to guide American foreign policy, 62 percent claim that foreign policy ought to be "compassionate," and 55 percent say that religion ought to shape foreign policy—all of which are significantly higher percentages than any other reported demographic or political group.[15] The differences between evangelicals and other groups are sufficiently pronounced to suggest that a distinctively religious worldview explains the variation.

Moreover, evangelical opinion leaders, many of whom have the ear of the White House, have increasingly focused on global issues and religious justifications for political involvement on a global scale.[16] The proportion of feature articles focused on international affairs in *Christianity Today*, the most prominent evangelical magazine, has climbed from 3.6 percent in 2001 to 22.2 percent in 2005.[17] Editorialists at the magazine have repeatedly exhorted readers to see global political engagement as a mandate of faith, as revealed in a quote from a representative opinion piece in October 2001: "Christians are to love our neighbors. When our neighborhood expands to the globe, then we are called to love globally."[18] In addition, evangelical leaders such as Charles Colson and James Dobson have strongly urged their readers and listeners to take up various global causes beyond the older issues of Israel and the spread of communism. In 2007, the National Association of Evangelicals even weighed in (although with some resistance from Dobson and other evangelical leaders) on the issue of climate change in an initiative on global creation care. Think tanks, too, have emerged to push international engagement, including the faith-based Institute for Global Engagement, founded in 2000 by Robert Seiple, the former president of the relief organization World Vision and U.S. ambassador-at-large for International Religious Freedom from 1998 to 2000. The Institute publishes a journal, *The Review of Faith and International Affairs*, which seeks to encourage critical Christian thinking on international affairs, and Seiple himself has authored or edited several books that provide a Christian justification for addressing global issues.[19]

To be sure, evangelical elites often disagree theologically in specific areas such as Israel, terrorism, religious freedom, or global population policy. As I suggest below, these disagreements can not only soften the ostensibly hard edge of the Christian Right but can also diminish evangelical influence. Moreover, on global matters ordinary evangelicals are not necessarily theologically deep or politically mobilized on a mass scale. Nevertheless, intellectual efforts have raised awareness and laid the groundwork for long-term evangelical attention to U.S. foreign policy. These efforts also reframe the typical evangelical arguments for a global vision. Many evangelical opinion leaders are not motivated solely or even principally by missions-oriented purposes, though that remains important. Rather, they insist that evangelicals have *civic* (in addition to evangelistic) obligations to internationalize their worldview and to understand, as U.S. citizens, what their faith means for foreign policy.

Internationalist Strategies: Coalition Building and Other Approaches

As evangelicals have developed a theology (or theologies) of global engagement, they have become more sophisticated in their political strategies and tactics as well. This increasing attention to the imperatives of power politics should not be surprising. Through advocacy on a range of domestic issues from abortion to middle-class taxes, evangelicals have been learning the nitty-gritty of modern politics for over two decades. They have employed a variety of tactics in domestic politics, but in the arena of U.S. foreign policy there is no better case study of tactical sophistication than evangelicals' willingness to engage in coalition building.

The Israeli-Palestinian conflict, which is the most closely watched area in which evangelicals have sought to influence U.S. foreign policy, illustrates evangelicalism's openness to coalitions. Recent efforts to broker a peace agreement between Israel and the Palestinians have raised concerns among key supporters of Israel in the United States, including many evangelical leaders. In particular, the "road map" for peace, President Bush's plan for a series of mutual concessions leading to an eventual Palestinian state, has been subjected to vigorous public criticism by many of evangelicalism's top elites. But these same leaders have long realized that they would have to do more than bluster on cable television or in newspaper reports; accordingly, they sought out ready partners in their opposition to the administration's plans.

Conservative evangelicals found willing and able allies among American Jews, and a strange bedfellow coalition developed—a "mixed marriage," as *Newsweek* describes it—that has taken on new organizational forms during the Bush presidency.[20] In 2002, Ralph Reed, former executive director of the Christian Coalition, joined Orthodox Rabbi Yechiel Eckstein to form Stand for Israel as an outlet for churches and ordinary citizens to advocate for Israel's interests. The organization's emergence marked a turn in the political relationship between Jews and conservative evangelicals—a relationship that had been uneasy for decades and was widely perceived by religious and political leaders as an obstacle to even more effective pro-Israel mobilization of evangelicals. While "Christian Zionist" leaders in the United States had begun to develop relationships with Israeli political elites already in the early 1980s, many American Jews were concerned (and remain so) about the emerging partnership. The troubled relationship has often been soured by nonpolitical events, including the Southern Baptist Convention's declared goal in 1996 to step up evangelization of Jews, which met with widespread condemnation by Jewish leaders in the United States.[21]

But Eckstein, who chairs an ecumenical group called the International Fellowship of Christian and Jews that has worked on easing Jewish-evangelical tensions for over two decades, saw an opportunity for common cause on Israel. He had little trouble partnering with Reed, who had been instrumental in rallying the evangelical vote to support the Republican takeover of the Senate and House of Representatives in 1994 and knows well the power of evangelical mobilization in domestic politics. Today a GOP election strategist with his own consulting firm, Reed became convinced that evangelicals "have the potential to be the most effective constituency influencing foreign policy since the end of the cold war." Evangelicals, he declared, are "shifting the center of gravity in the pro-Israel community to become a more conservative and Republic phenomenon."[22]

Similar strange bedfellow coalitions have developed in other areas of U.S. foreign policy. Evangelicals have worked with the Vatican and, remarkably, Islamic countries on UN Population Fund initiatives. There have been numerous efforts since the 1970s to pressure American administrations to remove funding from UN family planning programs and even from agencies of the American government involved in morally controversial activities. From the 1970s to the present evangelical groups have been part of these efforts, but they rely heavily on other players, most notably the Holy See (which has a direct role in UN negotiations through its Permanent Observer status) and Catholic as well as Islamic countries.[23] These nations have often joined in coalition to fight attempts to include access to or information about contraception or legal abortion as part of UN population control measures. While leaders of evangelical organizations have occasionally been vocal participants in these negotiations—some have even gained credentialed nongovernmental organization status, allowing them direct access to family planning discussions—they do not appear to wield the influence of other religious traditions that can vote through the governments that they control. The imperative of coalition building, then, is decisively important for evangelicals, who use their nation-state allies to amplify their own voice.

Perhaps the most remarkable example of coalition building is the partnership of evangelicals with liberal Jews and feminists on human rights issues, particularly religious freedom and human trafficking. Allen Hertzke's *Freeing God's Children* is an excellent description and analysis of this phenomenon.[24] The coalition developed partly from the persistent urging of Michael Horowitz, a Jewish think tank lawyer who began a campaign to stop Christian persecution abroad in the mid-1990s. He targeted evangelical organizations with a plea letter, drafted a statement about religious persecution that was eventually adopted by the National Association of Evangelicals, and smoothed rivalries while assembling a remarkably diverse lobbying coalition that included a prominent place for evangelicals.

This "unlikely alliance," as Hertzke calls it, illustrates better than any other area of foreign policy the overall willingness of evangelical to suppress old animosities, at least temporarily, to advance common goals. Coalition building provides obvious advantages for agenda setting and policy making: by building a broader base of support, the president and other elected representatives will see a given issue as more important and be more attentive to evangelical concerns. Coalition building can also bring in new expertise, innovative ideas, wider legislative networks, and other resources of time, money, and energy. Evangelicals learned that these resources were indispensable in domestic policy making, and they brought that lesson with them to the foreign policy arena.

Evangelical Internationalists and the Bush Administration: Obstacles and Opportunities

Prospects within the Evangelical Tradition

The dual trends of increasing theological reflection and tactical sophistication suggest that evangelicals are emerging as serious contributors to American foreign policy. To be sure, many evangelical voices now resonate in certain quarters of the foreign policy establishment, and indeed they were coming to prominence even before the George W. Bush presidency. Yet certain key features within evangelicalism itself pose challenges to the effectiveness of its internationalist aspirations, including burgeoning evangelical efforts on human rights.

A key test for evangelical internationalism is lack of elite- or mass-level agreement about the appropriate approach to various global issues. There is a popular tendency, reinforced by some breathless media punditry, about the role of the Christian Right in the 2000 and 2004 elections, to perceive evangelicals as nearly monolithic and marching in political lockstep.[25] But just as there are real and substantive disagreements among evangelicals on domestic issues, so too contemporary evangelicals are rarely of one mind on how to view or implement specific foreign policies. On an abstract level, as I have shown, they overwhelmingly agree that they ought to have a global perspective guided by the general moral dictates of the faith. But on specifics the apparent consensus often falls apart. The disagreements can come down to theology or tactics, or both.

In terms of religious justifications for specific policies, what do both elite and ordinary evangelicals say? The complex answer is that a "faith-based" approach to particular foreign policies can take many forms; religious justifications are issue-dependent and often vary significantly based on subtle differences in theological first principles. Some evangelicals, for example, put the Israeli-Palestinian conflict in eschatological context by envisioning the presence of Jews in Palestine as a sign of Christ's second coming. A Pew survey in 2003 indicated that over 60 percent of white evangelicals support this "premillennialist" view of Israel,[26] and the strength of that view appears to explain why traditionalists in the evangelical camp—those most committed to Christian orthodoxy and religious activity—are the second most likely of all religious groupings (behind Jews) to support U.S. policy favoring Israel over the Palestinians.[27] The reverends Jerry Falwell and Pat Robertson, both staunch and long-standing supporters of Israel whose "Christian Zionism" has been openly courted by Israeli political leaders since the late 1970s, also hold versions of premillennialism and actively preach that perspective to their followers.[28]

Yet there are other voices. Although media and scholarly focus on evangelical eschatology is understandable, especially in the wake of the wildly popular Left Behind Series of end-times novels, this attention masks other explanations for evangelical support of a strong pro-Israel policy.[29] In fact, premillennialism is not the only theological perspective on Israel, nor is it the most salient. Some evangelicals place less emphasis on biblical prophecy, but nevertheless insist on a pro-Israel policy that reflects, as Richard Land of the Southern Baptist Convention recently explained, the biblical promise that "God blesses those who bless the Jews."[30] When this promise is a survey option set alongside end-times theology, nearly 60 percent of evangelicals choose the divine blessing of Israel instead of the Jewish role in ushering in the apocalypse, while only 28 percent select the latter as a reason for a pro-Israel policy.[31]

Another important group of evangelicals, mostly scholars and intellectuals with a less biblical literalist bent than the fundamentalist strain of evangelicalism, do not perceive support for Israel as a theological litmus test for the faithful at all. Indeed, they reject the idea that either biblical prophecy or biblical commands require a preference for the Israeli state in addressing Middle East conflict.[32] Richard Mouw, president of Fuller Seminary, and other evangelicals in this camp have insisted that there is no specific theological point that forbids or requires a Palestinian state, though general principles of justice requires a peaceful resolution that would privilege neither side.[33]

These differences of opinion, particularly at the elite level, have broken out into conflict via direct public advocacy over Middle East policy. The dueling letters of 2002 and 2003 between two sides of the evangelical leadership are illustrative of this internal division. In

July 2002, nearly 60 evangelicals, among them Richard Mouw, Robert Seiple, Tony Campolo (a popular speaker and teacher), and David Neff (editor of *Christianity Today*) wrote to President Bush to assure him that "the American evangelical community is not a monolithic bloc in full and firm support of present Israeli policy."[34] They invoked the Old Testament prophets (in contrast to apocalyptic and other "distorted" biblical interpretations) to suggest that God's justice rests on the Palestinian *and* Israeli sides of the conflict and that the United States must take an "evenhanded" approach to both. Many of these same leaders would support President Bush's road map for Middle East peace when it was proposed in the spring of 2003. In an apparent response to their fellow evangelicals—and in the midst of escalating violence in Israel, Gaza, and the West Bank—24 other evangelical leaders sent a letter to President Bush in May 2003 urging him to rethink his road map, which they described as "well-intentioned" but likely to cause "disaster." Written by Gary Bauer of American Values and signed by Jerry Falwell, Richard Land, Paul Weyrich (chair of the Free Congress Foundation), and D. James Kennedy (head of Coral Ridge Ministries), the correspondence targeted the language of their fellow evangelicals in the 2002 letter, insisting that "it would morally reprehensible for the United States to be evenhanded between Democratic Israel, a reliable friend and ally that shares our values, and the terrorist-infested Palestinian infrastructure that refuses to accept the right of Israel to exist."[35]

It is difficult to know the extent to which these letters and other forms of advocacy influenced the president's handling of the conflict, if at all. But we can say that President Bush has given both sides a little of what they wanted. On the one hand, the administration has retained (and, in the relative Israeli-Palestinian peace of early 2005, showed optimism about) the basic road map, which appeared to be one of the hopes of the first letter's authors. On the other hand, Bush effectively refused to negotiate since at least 2003 with the late Yasir Arafat, who embodied the Palestinian governing "infrastructure" that so worried the authors of the second letter, and the recent electoral success of Hamas has complicated matters even further.[36]

Similar disagreements emerged in the wake of the terrorist attacks on September 11, 2001 and the incipient War on Terror. At least one study of evangelical media suggests that while some evangelicals envision a mushrooming battle between the Islam and Christian West, others seek to distinguish a retributive war on international terrorists from a clash of civilizations.[37] The former position is characterized by the likes of Jerry Falwell and the evangelist Franklin Graham, whose provocative—even inflammatory—comments immediately after the September 11 attacks implied that Islam as a religion holds some responsibility for the destruction that day. In response to this way of thinking, Richard Cizik, vice president for Government Affairs at the National Association of Evangelicals, worried aloud that evangelicals had "substituted Islam for the Soviet Union" and that "Muslims have become the modern-day equivalent of the Evil Empire."[38] The disagreements are sufficiently important that the war in Iraq, which the Bush administration has framed as a key battle in the War on Terror, brought an ambivalent response from Cizik's organization, which refused to take an official stand.[39]

As with the Israeli-Palestinian conflict, we cannot know for certain whether the evangelical dispute over the status of Islam or evangelical ambivalence about the War in Iraq has shaped Bush administration policy. President Bush has, of course, repeatedly insisted that the United States is not targeting Islam in the War on Terrorism, but it is unlikely that he has said this simply because evangelicals told him to do so. Nor should we expect evangelicals to have much effect without a unified and coherent perspective on the matter.

There is perhaps more agreement among evangelicals in the area of religious persecution abroad. Evangelicals from various camps have leaned on the State Department in both the Clinton and Bush administrations to pressure and even sanction abusive regimes, thereby freeing Christians to practice their faith, opening doors to mission and relief efforts, and satisfying the demands of justice, which evangelicals link to every person's worth as God's image bearer.[40] Even in this context, tactical disagreements have emerged. For example, some look at legislation such as the International Religious Freedom Act as a means to identify and punish states that suppress religious freedom; others seek to use the act and other aspects of U.S. foreign policy to focus on promotion of religious freedom rather than punishment when freedom is absent.[41] Moreover, some have charged evangelicals with paying little attention when the Sudanese government shifted its genocidal campaigns from the largely Christian south to Darfur and the Muslim west.[42] But the relatively broad-based evangelical agreement that human rights ought to be a Bush administration agenda item seems to have had the desired effect.[43] Evangelical success on the human rights issue suggests that unity of purpose can foster effective political advocacy, especially in comparison to the mixed messages evangelicals have conveyed in other areas of foreign policy where they lack basic agreement.

While evangelical treatment of religious freedom and human rights reflects broad conceptions of human dignity, evangelical approaches to population control or HIV/AIDS harks back to their traditional emphasis on individual piety. In the context of international—and particularly UN—efforts to address population growth, evangelical pietism goes global. For example, consistent with the evangelical emphasis on traditional sexual morality and marriage, President Bush's $15 billion pledge to combat the global AIDS epidemic was met with demands by evangelical leaders to earmark a third of the funds for abstinence education.[44] Their efforts fit into a pattern of both unilateralism and moralist resistance to U.S. funding of certain reproductive policy initiatives that began with allocations to the United Nations Fund for Population Activities during the Reagan administration.[45] Other evangelicals have looked at global issues like the scourge of AIDS in Africa and begun to rethink such moralist commitments, most notably Rick Warren, the prominent megachurch pastor and bestselling author who has launched a crusade to address the crisis.[46] These reassessments may portend some points of conflict in the future.

In addition to these disagreements over the religious justifications for global engagement, evangelicals are beset by another obstacle to greater effectiveness: a lack of a full-scale "mass movement" on international issues. The international efforts of American evangelicals remain a largely elite-driven phenomenon. This is a relative claim: I do not suggest that ordinary evangelicals are wholly uninterested or inactive in global issues—far from it—but rather that evangelical advocacy groups with mass memberships have focused a great deal more attention on domestic rather than foreign policy concerns. This has been the case even during the first four years of the Bush administration, when international affairs took on a special relevance for the public and government alike. Without such mass mobilization on global issues, it is hard to imagine that these groups, which have been the engine of evangelical effectiveness over domestic policy in the past, will have comparable influence on foreign policy.

My analysis of evangelical mass movement politics starts with a simple assumption: if organizational leaders want their members to act, they will communicate their desires to their members through organizational channels. One piece of evidence is the communications media that evangelical leaders have established with their memberships in several of the major mass-based organizations, including news releases or organizational magazines associated with the Concerned Women for America, Christian Coalition, Focus on the Family, and the Family Research Council. As an illustration, figure 10.1 displays the results of a content analysis of statements, editorials, reports, and other communications in two distinct information sources from two

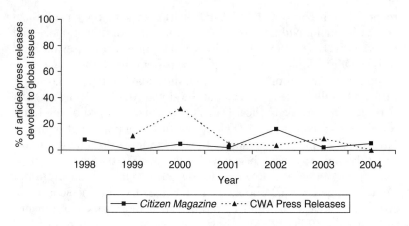

Figure 10.1   Evangelical Attention to Global Issues, 1998–2004

Source: Author's analysis of *Citizen Magazine* (http://www.family.org/cforum/citizenmag/) and CWA press releases (archived at www.cwfa.org).

different organizations: news releases from Concerned Women for America (CWA) and feature articles in a membership magazine (*Citizen*) from Focus on the Family. The figure shows that communications about global issues comprise a very small proportion of all communications to group members; the vast majority of the remaining communications focus on domestic issues.

The figure does show two small spikes—in 2000 for CWA, in 2002 for Focus on the Family's *Citizen*—which primarily represent responses to a debate about UN population funding and to the September 11 attacks, respectively. But in the aggregate these data indicate that there is *relatively* little attention to global engagement. The point comes in sharper focus when one compares these trends in communications about all global issues to just a single domestic issue. From 1999 to 2006, Concerned Women for America committed 13.2 percent of its releases to the sole issue of domestic same-sex relations and 14.4 percent to domestic abortion policy; in contrast, only 7.4 percent of its communications were devoted to global issues *of any kind*. From 1999 to 2006, 12.6 percent of *Citizen* magazine's articles addressed abortion domestically and 13.6 percent focused on same-sex relations in the United States, while only 7.3 percent of its articles were devoted to *all* global issues combined.[47] Communications from the Christian Coalition and Family Research Council reveal similar trends.

While there are numerous explanations for this lack of enduring attention to global issues, there is at least one straightforward reason: attention to domestic policy remains the primary way to meet the requirements of organizational maintenance. It is a truism of interest group mobilization that members are more likely to give consistently their time, energy, and money when they perceive that the issues are "local" and likely to have a direct effect on their lives. This localism continues to be decisively important to evangelicals, who are much more likely to take an interest in, say, local school board elections than funding for obscure UN programs.[48]

Of course, many of the issues that are most closely associated with the Christian Right in domestic policy making—abortion and other matters related to reproduction and sexual relations—have also been integrated into the foreign policy agenda of American evangelicals. Yet, while some scholars have referred to this latter focus as an effort to "globalize family values" (Buss and Herman 2003), the moral issues take on a distinctive cast when they move from the domestic to international arena. Quite often conflicts over abortion, contraception, and women's rights have flared during discussion of the ill effects of global population growth or disease outbreaks overseas—issues that are not as salient in domestic debates about reproductive rights or sexual morality. For example, Rick Warren's efforts, notwithstanding, evangelical Protestants are the least likely of all religious traditions to insist that AIDS/HIV should be a "high priority" of U.S. foreign policy. [49] Moreover, the breadth of the domestic agenda—not only abortion and abstinence but also education and school prayer, indecency and morality in the media, same-sex relations, and gambling, among others—is not reflected in the relatively narrow range of "family values" issues that evangelicals have confronted at the international level.

There have been hints of a mass movement on global issues. In the late 1990s, for example, *Christianity Today* chronicled "an enormous network" of small Christian Zionist organizations springing up across the country.[50] In addition, after a Palestinian suicide bombing in 2002, Bush gave a speech that seemed to equate the Israeli army's actions with Palestinian terrorists,' triggering a mobilizing effort by Bauer, Falwell, and Robertson that resulted in a flurry of hundreds of thousands of e-mails and letters from American evangelicals.[51] But the political relevance of these mobilizations appears to be intermittent. The strongest and most durable broad-based evangelical responses to global issues have been more spiritual than political. Prayer for the Persecuted Church, for example, assembles tens of thousands of churches every year to set aside time for prayer for Christian victims of persecution.[52] Such efforts may someday evolve into greater mass pressure on the U.S. government over human rights and other issues, but for now the organizers of the International Day of Prayer appear to have no such aspirations. Even their organizational partners— Christian Federation International and Voice of the Martyrs, for example—are advocacy groups that seek to generate funds and action within churches rather than the halls of Congress.

Prospects for Evangelical Internationalists outside the Tradition

Many of the obstacles and opportunities I have addressed thus far rest on the assumption that evangelicals, as a core constituency of George W. Bush, could have greater access to and influence over the administration's foreign policy agenda if they present a united and coherent perspective backed by mass mobilization. This assumption focuses on conditions internal to the evangelical community itself. But even if evangelicals could muster a broad internal agreement, their influence would not be assured. The Bush administration is cross-pressured from quarters outside of the evangelical tradition, and those pressures can and often do create tension with evangelical foreign policy preferences.

This tension is especially manifest in the various ideological factions that have sought to influence Bush's foreign policy decisions. Consider evangelical efforts to address human rights abuses. It may seem natural to look to various conservative perspectives for intellectual support of the evangelical internationalists, but Hertzke suggests that the arguments of human rights or moralist conservatives have not always fared well with conservatives of other stripes.[53] Economic conservatives, for example, worry that limits on trade with human rights abusers will close off important markets and put American business at a competitive disadvantage in an increasingly global economy. When the editor of *Christianity Today* declares that evangelicals must learn that "conservative politics need not mean captivity to business interests,"[54] he is confronting more than a tendency of some evangelicals to support national economic interests over human rights concerns. Many advisors in the Bush administration have similar tendencies.

Realist conservatives are also skeptical of moralist demands, fearing international impositions of human rights standards will upset international security and the delicate worldwide balance of power. A good illustration of this latter approach is Charles Krauthammer, a prominent *Washington Post* columnist who speaks for many other realists when he explicitly rejects "moral foreign policy." He is particularly dubious about the usefulness of religion in helping define what such a policy would be; in the context of international affairs, he writes, religion "will not tell, inform, or guide anyone about how to act collectively or individually."[55]

These are important sources of conservative support that have been largely closed off to evangelicals with human rights agendas, but another group—the so-called neoconservatives—counter economic and realist conservatives by insisting that democratization and human rights standards are good for both business and security. Moreover, the neoconservatives have been in the close orbit of the Bush administration, as we see in the lead-up to the Iraq War of 2003.[56] Paul Wolfowitz, a leading proponent of the war in his role as deputy secretary of Defense, has argued that "nothing could be less realistic than the version of the 'realist' view of foreign policy that dismisses human rights as an important tool of American foreign policy," and he also played a small role in addressing the human trafficking issue in his capacity as an academic dean before he went into government.[57]

These competing conservatisms can shift in their usefulness from one issue to another. While evangelicals with human rights interests may find common cause with neoconservatives, those who seek a pro-Israel policy may find support among the realists, who see a strong Israel as a "wedge" state that checks the power of surrounding nations. Moreover, the alliances can shift such that the same evangelicals who seek support from conservatives on one issue may oppose those same conservatives on a different one. Many of the same evangelicals who joined neoconservatives on human rights issues rejected the neoconservative arguments in favor of the war in Iraq.

Conservative factionalism within the administration is not the only challenge to effective evangelical internationalism. Evangelicals face the other obstacles and opportunities of foreign policy making that any other group must confront: the direction and intensity of American public opinion; the partisan and countervailing interest group pressure within Congress, and especially in the Senate; the bureaucratic norms and inertia of the State Department and the rest of the diplomatic corps; the scarcity of resources for foreign policy implementation; the interests and occasional intractability of other nation-states, allies and enemies alike; and the unpredictability of international events. These factors, among others, comprise a complex and highly fluid context for American foreign policy that is largely beyond the control of evangelicals to shape.

Conclusion

What do these features of evangelical internationalism, both within and outside the evangelical community, suggest for its future effectiveness in the Bush administration and beyond? First, we are unlikely to see evangelical elites revert into a reactionary isolationism, especially as they have begun to develop theological justifications for internationalizing their worldview. Compared to, say, the rich intellectual legacy of a global religious institution such as the Catholic Church, an evangelical theology of world-formative engagement is in its infancy. But the simple *recognition* that evangelicals, as *Christianity Today*'s Neff puts it, "sorely need deeper theological reflection on the nature of [global] political activity" is itself a step toward paying more attention to such a theology.[58] Coupled with the constant flow of information evangelicals receive from the mission field, this theological reflection could institutionalize a global vision, which could result in longevity in the evangelical focus on foreign policy.

Still, theological reflection will be ineffectual without overcoming the perception that all politics is local. Mass mobilization is possible, but only if the foreign policy agenda is reconceived as something more than a stepchild to the domestic agenda. Without greater mass mobilization, it is hard to imagine that evangelical influence over U.S. foreign policy will intensify. A regular conference call between evangelical elites and the White House is unlikely to bear fruit unless the administration is convinced that a substantial number of intensely interested citizens are standing behind those elites. Evangelical leaders may bypass mass politics and continue to have some sway by maintaining their coalitions. Evangelicalism's "unlikely alliances" with the Vatican, Islamic countries, Jews, and feminists for common cause have been impressive. Those coalitions, however, will be difficult to foster with bedfellows who are so remarkably strange.

Finally, even if evangelicals maintain their coalitions or mobilize the grassroots, it is an open question whether the administration will feel an urgent need to listen to them. On the one hand, evangelicals are a key electoral constituency of the president and the Republican Party. In an era of slim electoral margins, the evangelical voting bloc commands attention. On the other hand, President Bush is not running for office again, and hence may feel liberated to ignore even the most vociferous evangelical internationalists. Evangelicals are clearly not the only pressure point in foreign policy making, and their many disagreements about global engagement have likely made their collective voice less clear in specific foreign policies than in areas of domestic concern.

Notes

Portions of chapter 10 first appeared in "Evangelical Elites and Faith-Based Foreign Affairs," *The Review of Faith and International Affairs*, Spring 2006, pp. 21–29. www.cfia.org. Used by permission.

1. Political categorizations often convey too much and too little simultaneously, and so it is with the Christian Right, which paints with a broad ideological and religious brush. While I use terms such as Christian Right, Christian conservative, or evangelical conservative to denote a portion of the evangelical tradition in this chapter, I also show that the tradition as a whole includes diverse motivations, policy goals, tactics, and experiences.

2. Carin Larson and Clyde Wilcox, "The Faith of George W. Bush: The Personal, Practical, and Political," in Mark Rozell and Gleaves Whitney, eds., *Religion and the American Presidency* (New York: Palgrave Macmillan, 2007).

3. But see Walter Russell Mead, "God's Country," *Foreign Affairs*, 85, no. 5 (September/October 2006): 24–43;William Martin, "The Christian Right and American Foreign Policy," *Foreign Policy*, no. 114 (Spring 1999): 66–81; and Duane Oldfield, "The Evangelical Roots of American Unilateralism: The Christian Right's Influence and How to Counter It," in *Foreign Policy in Focus* (Silver City, NM: Interhemispheric Resource Center, 2004). With the exception of Mead's article, these studies, which are largely unsympathetic to evangelical efforts, also attribute more unity and influence to the Christian Right than I do in this chapter.

4. Nicholas D. Kristof, "Following God Abroad," *New York Times*, May 21, 2002, A21.

5. In a 2003 column, Kristof asserts that "many" Americans, when they hear the words "evangelical missionary," "conjure up an image of redneck zealots, forcing starving children to be baptized before they get a few crusts of bread." Nicholas D. Kristof, "God on Their Side," *New York Times*, September 27, 2003, A15.

6. For a transcript of the speech, go to http://www.americanrhetoric.com/speeches/ronaldreaganevilempire.htm (accessed March 17, 2007).

7. John C. Green, "The American Religious Landscape and Political Attitudes: A Baseline for 2004," Pew Forum on Religion and Public Life, Washington, DC, September 2004.

8. Ibid.

9. The Pew Research Center finds that 71% of white evangelicals believe that the United States has such divine protection, higher than any other religious group. The percentage does not suggest, however, that evangelicals believe that other nations receive no such protection. Pew Research Center and Pew Forum on Religion in Public Life, "Americans Struggle with Religion's Role at Home and Abroad," Pew Research Center/Pew Forum on Religion in Public Life, Washington, DC, March 2002, 7.

10. Oldfield, "The Evangelical Roots of American Unilateralism."

11. Pew Research Center and Pew Forum on Religion in Public Life, "Americans Struggle with Religion's Role at Home and Abroad," 31.

12. For a concise discussion of the demographics, see Allen D. Hertzke, *Freeing God's Children: The Unlikely Alliance for Global Human Rights* (Lanham, MD: Rowman and Littlefield, 2004).

13. Paul Marshall, *Their Blood Cries Out* (Dallas, TX: Word, 1997).

14. Philip Jenkins, *The Next Christendom: The Coming of Global Christianity* (New York: Oxford University Press, 2003).

15. Pew Research Center, "Foreign Policy Attitudes Now Driven by 9/11 and Iraq," Pew Research Center for the People and Press, Washington, DC, August 2004, 25.

16. See, e.g., Elizabeth Bumiller, "Evangelicals Sway the White House on Human Rights Issues Abroad," *New York Times*, October 26 2003, A1.

17. Based on the author's analysis of 368 feature articles from January 2001 to December 2005. Note that features include stories that are not necessarily explicitly "political" but nevertheless raise awareness about global issues.

18. Miriam Adeney, "Think Globally, Love Globally," *Christianity Today*, October 22, 2001, 14.

19. Robert Seiple, *Ambassadors of Hope: How Christians Can Respond to the World's Toughest Problems* (Downer's Grove, IL: InterVarsity Press, 2004); Robert Seiple and Dennis R. Hoover, eds., *Religion and Security: The New Nexus in International Relations* (Lanham, MD: Rowman and Littlefield, 2004). For an example from *The Brandywine Review of Faith and International Affairs*, see Mark T. Mitchell, "A Theology of Engagement for the 'Newest Internationalists,'" *Brandywine Review of Faith and International Affairs*, 1, no. 1 (2003).

20. Howard Fineman and Tamara Lipper, "A Very Mixed Marriage," *Newsweek*, June 2, 2003, 34.

21. Gustav Niebuhr, "Baptists Move on Two Fronts in New Effort to Convert Jews," *New York Times*, June 14, 1996.

22. David Firestone, "Evangelical Christians and Jews Unite for Israel," *New York Times*, June 9, 2002.

23. Doris Buss and Didi Herman, *Globalizing Family Values: The Christian Right in International Politics* (Minneapolis, MN: University of Minnesota Press, 2003). For selected newspaper accounts, see Peter Steinfels, "Beliefs," *New York Times*, March 18, 1995, 9; Laurie Goodstein, "Women's Work: New Options," *Washington Post*, August 27, 1995, A20; and Christopher Marquis, "U.S. Is Accused of Trying to Isolate U.N. Population Unit," *New York Times*, June 21, 2004, A3.

24. Hertzke, *Freeing God's Children*. See also Robert Booth Fowler, Allen Hertzke, Laura Olson, and Kevin den Dulk, *Religion and Politics in America: Faith, Culture, and Strategic Choices*, 3 ed. (Boulder, CO: Westview Press, 2004).

25. See, e.g., Maureen Dowd, "The Red Zone," *New York Times*, November 4, 2004, A25; and Garry Wills, "The Day the Enlightenment Went Out," *New York Times*, November 4, 2004, A25.

26. Pew Research Center and Pew Forum on Religion in Public Life, "Religion and Politics: Contention and Consensus," Pew Research Center/Pew Forum on Religion in Public Life, Washington, DC, 2003.

27. Green, "The American Religious Landscape and Political Attitudes," 34.

28. Laurie Goodstein, "Falwell to Mobilize Support for Israel," *New York Times*, January 21, 1998, A6; and Megan Rosenfeld, "Prime Minister Meets the Evangelists," *Washington Post*, April 16, 1980, E1.

29. Articles by both Martin, "The Christian Right and American Foreign Policy," and Oldfield, "The Evangelical Roots of American Unilateralism," focus largely on the eschatological argument and given little attention to the alternatives.

30. Deborah Caldwell, *Why Christians Must Keep Israel Strong*, Internet Web site, n.d., http://www.beliefnet.com/story/106/story_10697_1.html (accessed March 17, 2007).

31. These statistics are drawn from a Tarrance Group poll for Stand for Israel, as reported in Todd Hertz, "*The* Evangelical View of Israel?" *Christianity Today*, June 9, 2003, 21.

32. Richard Mouw, "How to Bless Israel," n.d., http://www.beliefnet.com (accessed March 17, 2007).

33. Hertz, "*The* Evangelical View of Israel?"

34. The letter is available at http://campus.northpark.edu/centers/middle/mideast.letter_to_bush.htm. See Caryle Murphy, "Evangelical Leaders Ask Bush to Adopt Balanced Mideast Policy," *Washington Post*, July 27, 2002, B9.

35. The letter is available at http://www.ouramericanvalues.org/press_release_article.php?id=051903 (accessed March 17, 2007).

36. Elizabeth Bumiller, "Bush Admits Mideast Plan Is Stalled and Blames Arafat," *New York Times*, September 18, 2003, A8.

37. Dennis R. Hoover, "Is Evangelicalism Itching for a Civilization Fight? A Media Study," *Brandywine Review of Faith and International Affairs* 2, no. 1 (2004): 11–16.

38. Laurie Goodstein, "Seeing Islam as 'Evil' Faith, Evangelicals Seek Converts," *New York Times*, May 27, 2003, A1.

39. Bill Broadway, "Evangelicals Speak Softly about Iraq," *Washington Post*, January 25, 2003, B9.

40. Hertzke, *Freeing God's Children*. See also Marshall, *Their Blood Cries Out*. He argues that while Christians must pay attention to persecution of members of all groups, they have a special responsibility for halting the persecution of fellow Christians.

41. See the exchange between T. Jeremy Gunn, "Full of Sound and Fury," *Christianity Today*, March 2003, 51 and Michael Horowitz, "Cry Freedom," *Christianity Today*, March 2003, 48. See also Robert Seiple, "Cursing Darkness, Lighting Candles," *Brandywine Review of Faith and International Affairs*, 2, no. 2 (2004): 1–2.

42. Allen Hertzke, "The Shame of Darfur," *First Things* 156 (2005): 16–22.

43. Hertzke, *Freeing God's Children*; and Bumiller, "Evangelicals Sway the White House on Human Rights Issues Abroad."

44. Carl Hulse, "House Adopts Global Plan of $15 Billion against Aids," *New York Times*, May 2, 2003, A9.

45. Buss and Herman, *Globalizing Family Values*.

46. Chris Hickey, "ABC's and AIDS: Condom Nation," *Brandywine Review of Faith and International Affairs*, 2, no. 2 (2004): 47–49. On Rick Warren, see Timothy C. Morgan, "Purpose Driven in Rwanda," *Christianity Today*, October 2005, 32–36, 90–91.

47. Based on content analysis of all 396 articles in *Citizen* magazine from January 1999 to December 2006, as well as 605 Concerned Women for America press releases from January 1999 to August 2006.

48. On evangelical localism, see Melissa Deckman, *School Board Battles: The Christian Right in Local Politics* (Washington, DC: Georgetown University Press, 2004).

49. Green, "The American Religious Landscape and Political Attitudes." It should be noted, however, that over half of even the most traditionalist evangelicals claim that the U.S. government should address the AIDS/HIV epidemic on the African continent.

50. Timothy Weber, "How Evangelicals Became Israel's Best Friend," *Christianity Today*, October 5, 1998, 38.

51. Fineman and Lipper, "A Very Mixed Marriage."

52. http://www.persecutedchurch.org/about/index.cfm.

53. Hertzke, *Freeing God's Children*.

54. David Neff, "Operation Human Rights," *Christianity Today*, October 2004, 106–107.

55. Charles Krauthammer, "When Unilateralism in Right and Just," in *Liberty and Power: A Dialogue on Religion and U.S. Foreign Policy in an Unjust World*, ed. E. J. Dionne, Jr., Jean Bethke Elshtain, and Kayla M. Drogosz (Washington, DC: Brookings Institution, 2004).

56. Bruce Murphy, "Neoconservative Clout Seen in U.S. Iraq Policy," *Milwaukee Journal Sentinel* (April 6, 2003): A1.

57. Paul Wolfowitz, "Remembering the Future," *National Interest* (Spring 2000): 35–49. For Wolfowitz's role on the trafficking issue, see Hertzke, *Freeing God's Children*, 329. For a discussion of the features of "neoconservatism," see Irving Kristol, "The Neoconservative Persuasion," *Weekly Standard*, August 25, 2003.

58. Neff, "Operation Human Rights."

Chapter Eleven

President George W. Bush and Judicial Restraint: Accommodating Religion

Nina Therese Kasniunas and Jack E. Rossotti

President George W. Bush is the first president in over a century to seemingly disregard the balance of religions represented on the Supreme Court. This is puzzling as Bush is one Republican who acknowledges and gives voice to the conservative Christian wing of his party. The only concern of President Bush is that his appointees maintain a jurisprudential posture of judicial restraint. This has been a prime consideration in his nominations not only for the courts but for the Department of Justice as well.

President Bush has not been disregarding religion; in fact, appointing judicial restraintists has been his strategy to provide more accommodation for religion in this country. Placing restraintists on the Court enables more conservative interpretations of the establishment and free exercise clauses as well as on other moral issues such as abortion, affirmative action, and homosexuality.

Selecting solicitors general from the growing pool of Federalist Society members also ensures his administration will pursue litigation that enables restraintist decisions. It enables it to file amicus curiae briefs in cases that could render such decisions. By these actions he is advancing the interests of the conservative Christians without appearing to do so, keeping the religious sector of his party gratified while at the same time not unsettling the moderates.

One of the most quoted lines from President Dwight Eisenhower was in response to a question asking him if he had made any mistakes when he was president. He replied, "Yes, two, and they are both sitting on the Supreme Court" (Abraham 1999, 200). Eisenhower, of course, was referring to his appointments of Chief Justice Earl Warren and Associate Justice William Brennan. The point he was making was that the two were judicial activists, indeed, two of the most activist justices who have sat on the Supreme Court.

Eisenhower is one in a long line of Republican presidents who have intended to appoint justices who would practice a philosophy of judicial restraint, justices, in other words, who would not "legislate from the bench." President Richard Nixon frequently said he would appoint strict constructionists to the Court, justices who "see themselves as caretakers of the Constitution and servants of the people, not super-legislators with a free hand to impose their social political viewpoints upon the American people" (Abraham 1999, 225). President Ronald Reagan, in nominating Judge Robert Bork to the Court, said that "Judge Bork's appointment will mean a Supreme Court that practices judicial restraint as our forefathers intended" (Reagan 1987). President George W. Bush during the 2000 presidential campaign said that he would appoint Supreme Court justices who were strict constructionists (Berke 2000, A28). In nominating John Roberts, initially to be an associate justice, Bush said, "He (Roberts) will apply the Constitution and laws, not legislate from the bench" (Bush 2005).

What exactly did these Republicans mean by strict constructionists who would not legislate from the bench or who would exercise judicial restraint? Let us consider judicial restraint, a term that is easier to use than to put into practical application. It can have several meanings. It can mean originalism or using a textualist approach to analyzing the provisions of the U.S. Constitution. More specifically originalism can be defined as examining the plain meaning of the words in the Constitution as they "would have been understood at the time of enactment" (Stack 2004). A variation of this method is to interpret the words in the Constitution or to try to determine what the draftsmen intended the words to mean (Stack 2004).[1] For example, one may look at context within the Constitution or one may interpret the words in the Constitution by examining an extemporaneous document such as *The Federalist Papers* (Hamilton, Madison, and Jay 1989). Still another method is to take words in the Constitution and to apply them to modern circumstances, for example, the unreasonable searches and seizures provision in the Fourth Amendment in the Bill of Rights. A modern usage of this provision might be to apply it to wiretapping telephones, devices that obviously did not exist in the 1700s. By doing this no wording is changed in the Constitution; existing terminology has simply been applied to contemporaneous circumstances (Jipping 1995). Are wiretaps unreasonable searches and seizures?

Another aspect of judicial restraint, which is particularly important when examining the philosophy of the modern Rehnquist and Roberts

Courts, is for justices to refrain from overturning precedent. But there can be an interesting variation here. Take, for example, the high-profile issue of abortion rights. If the current Roberts Court were to overturn the landmark decision of *Roe v. Wade* (1973), would that be an act of judicial activism or could it actually be an act of judicial restraint? It is possible to consider such a decision an act of judicial restraint because it would reverse an existing activist decision;[2] in other words, it would be like a double negative. In general, judicial restraint takes into account a more passive role for justices, being deferential to existing authority as much as possible and not applying their own independent judgment to what they think some provision of the Constitution (or a statute) should mean as opposed to what it does mean objectively.[3]

Why has the George W. Bush administration made judicial restraint such a central focus? The simple answer lies in the fact that Republicans have dominated the congressional electoral landscape for the past decade and at the presidential level since Richard Nixon was elected in 1968. At the same time, Democrats have been successful in achieving many of their political ends through the courts. In areas such as abortion rights,[4] affirmative action,[5] free speech,[6] the death penalty,[7] homosexual rights,[8] the free exercise clause,[9] and the establishment clause,[10] the Supreme Court has rendered decisions that were consistent with a liberal political agenda. That certainly had to frustrate conservatives because by the time Bush took office in 2001 seven of the nine justices had been appointed by Republican presidents.[11] Therefore, two of the administration's goals had to be to appoint justices who agreed with a restrained approach to judicial decision making and to pursue litigation intended to produce restrained judicial decisions.

By doing these things the Bush administration simultaneously would be able to satisfy religious conservatives without appearing to have a specific religious agenda. For example, a restrained approach to judicial decision making would likely bring establishment clause rulings more in line with allowing certain endorsements of religious activities as opposed to insisting there be a total wall of separation between church and state. The plain wording in the First Amendment speaks of Congress not making a law "respecting an establishment of religion." Restraintists and originalists are not likely to conclude that nativity scenes in courthouses and clerical invocations in public school graduations establish state religions.[12] Similarly, restraintists and originalists likely would conclude that excluding devotional theology degrees from state-sponsored scholarship aid programs do violate the free exercise of religion.[13]

The Bush Administration, Religion, and Judicial Restraint

With respect to religious issues, how well has the Bush administration achieved these objectives? Are the appointments of Chief Justice Roberts and Associate Justice Samuel Alito likely to fulfill Bush's promise to appoint judicial restraintist justices to the Supreme Court? What of the litigation the administration initiated? What of the litigation it has supported as an amicus? First let us consider the role religion has played in the selection of nominees to the Supreme Court.

A Catholic Majority on the Supreme Court

Justice Alito took his seat on the Supreme Court as the 110th justice. Without much fanfare, the religious balance shifted in favor of the Catholics.[14] Justice Alito is the fifth Roman Catholic to join the Roberts Court. Chief Justice Roberts is joined by justices Scalia, Kennedy, and Thomas as the other Catholics on the bench.[15] This is an unprecedented situation for Catholics, who only a century ago were struggling against the tide of nativistic anti-Catholic forces. The treatment of Catholics was not dissimilar to the discrimination faced by the Jewish faithful. Because this posed a barrier to holding high political office for both religious groups, presidents during the twentieth century initiated a practice whereby they would maintain two seats on the Supreme Court: one to be occupied by a Catholic and one to be occupied by a Jew. This tradition was not consistently maintained; no Jew was seated following the retirement of Justice Fortasin 1969 until Ruth Bader Ginsburg was appointed in 1993. Similarly, there was a gap of seven years, 1949–1956, when the Supreme Court existed without a Catholic justice.

Even with the deviation of a couple of presidents, this convention acknowledges the importance of descriptive representation. Descriptive representation concerns who the representative is or what he or she is like rather than what he or she does (Pitkin 1967). Implementing descriptive representation into the process of selecting justices may be crucial in producing a body of government that is seen as "legitimate" by all of the American people, and whose rulings similarly will be respected by all (Perry 1991; Goldman 1979; Brennan 1985). It could be difficult otherwise to produce legitimacy for a branch of government that is undemocratically selected.

That the Supreme Court now consists of five Catholics, two Jews, and two Protestants, certainly negates the consideration of religion in descriptive terms. Of the American populace, 52.2 percent describe themselves as Protestant, 24.4 percent as Catholic, and 3.7 percent as Jewish.[16] Nor does the current Court composition reflect the makeup of the American electorate or those who voted for Bush in 2004 (table 11.1).[17] Although not much notice was given to the shift in the religious balance of the Court, the religious background of the Bush Supreme Court nominees did become an issue during the confirmation process. Questions about nominees' abilities to distill their faith from their reading of the law were raised more than once. The appointees were also questioned extensively on the matter of religious issues such as the separation of church and state.

Historically, the anti-Catholic sentiment in this country stemmed from several sources. Many Protestants harbored hostility emanating from the Reformation, as was evidenced by similar treatment of Catholics throughout Europe (Perry 1992). Others were concerned about the devotion of Catholics to the pope—a foreign prelate of all Romans (Perry 1992). The hierarchical structure of the church was inimical to the spirit of democracy, a belief to which Protestants adhered as passionately as their own religious beliefs. Secular reasons included the threat these European immigrants, who were flooding America, posed to the social and economic well-being of those already settled here. The immigrants, heterogeneous in their ethnicities had one common thread—their religion.

Today those Catholic immigrants are fully assimilated into mainstream American culture, and nativistic sentiment is almost a trace of the past (Tatalovich 1995). Politically, Catholics support both political parties. This is not to say that Bush's Catholic nominees did not face any impediments. Concern surrounding John Roberts's Catholic faith emanated from an unexpected source: Catholic Senator Richard

Table 11.1 Religious Composition of the Roberts, Rehnquist, Burger, and Warren Courts

Religion	Roberts Court (%)	Rehnquist Court (%)	Burger Court (%)	Warren Court (%)
Catholic	55.6	33.3	11.1	11.1
Protestant	22.2	44.4	88.8	77.7
Jewish	22.2	22.2	0	11.1

Durbin. Durbin, in a private meeting with Roberts in the weeks preceding his confirmation hearings, reportedly asked him how he would reconcile the differences between Church teachings and U.S. law. Roberts is said to have replied that he would probably have to recuse himself. This account was the spark that reignited the debate over the extent to which religious faith would distort a justice's ability to decide law.[18]

During the formal confirmation hearings, Senator Durbin did not persist in this line of questioning but his colleague Senator Feinstein did:

> In 1960, there was much debate about President John F. Kennedy's faith and what role Catholicism would play in his administration. At that time, he pledged to address the issues of conscience out of a focus on natural interests, not out of adherence to the dictates of one's religion. And he even said, "I believe in an America where the separation of church and state is absolute." My question is: Do you? (Senate Judiciary Committee Hearings, 9–13–05).

Roberts responded in a somewhat evasive manner, and Feinstein pushed him to directly answer her question. To which Roberts replied, "I do know this: that my faith and my religious beliefs do not play a role in judging. When it comes to judging, I look to the law books and always have. I don't look to the Bible or any other religious source" (Senate Judiciary Committee Hearings, 9–13–05).

Senators Durbin and Feinstein raise real concerns. In an article published on the death penalty, Supreme Court Justice Antonin Scalia wrote about the tension he has felt between his religious beliefs and following the letter of the Constitution. He claims that he even consulted church canon experts on the teachings surrounding the death penalty to learn that the doctrine of the church does allow him to remain a faithful Catholic while still upholding death penalty rulings. Scalia writes that had his religious beliefs been contrary to his reading of the law that he would have had no choice but to retire (Scalia 2002).

Weighing on the minds of others is whether a Catholic would succumb to pressures placed on politicians by the church hierarchy or whether they would be able to dismiss such mandates. The Vatican recently has called on politicians to oppose gay marriage.[19] And certainly few can forget during the 2004 presidential campaign when the Vatican instructed priests to deny communion to U.S. politicians who support abortion rights.[20] Although most Americans think this type of pressure is inappropriate no one can be sure that public officials are immune to it.[21]

In an empirical study examining the factors that influence how judges decide religious disputes, Gregory Sisk and his colleagues found a judge's religion influenced his or her rulings. The study examined district and appeals court cases involving religion from 1986 through 1995, finding that religion was consistently a significant factor impacting how judges decided those cases (Sisk, Heise, and Morriss 2004). The effect of religion might even be more nuanced. Some legal scholars have argued that one's religious faith affects one's jurisprudence. For example, Stanford Levinson, from the University of Texas at Austin, has pointed to a parallel between how religions regard the Bible and constitutional interpretation.[22] Those raised in conservative denominations (as some Protestants) believe in the literal word of the Bible and as such likely will be strict constructionists who believe in the literal reading of the U.S. Constitution. Others, Catholics for example, whose religions are more liberal in their treatment of the Bible and rely on its interpretation rather than its word might be more likely to treat the Constitution in a similar manner. Levinson also suggests an alternate manifestation of the religious influence. Protestants believe in a personal relationship with God and the Bible whereas Catholics look to the church clergy as facilitators of their relationship with God. In this regard, it might be the Catholics who would rely on the Courts' hierarchy to decide constitutional matters and would approach interpretation of the law more conservatively than their Protestant counterparts. And the Protestants then would likely be more open to who could interpret the Constitution, even allowing for congressional involvement. The latter explanation comes close to the concerns of George W. Bush in appointing a justice who would take a seat on the bench and dutifully serve with judicial restraint.

If religion does matter, as it appears to, then why would Bush abandon the practice of maintaining a religious balance on the Supreme Court? Perhaps the answer lies in the problem with attempting to bring representation to a body that is not democratically selected. As Joel Grossman (1965) has indicated, the classic conceptualization of the judge is as an interpreter, rather than a maker of the law. Judicial decisions are products of independent and objective reasoning. Representative considerations are assigned to the legislative branch. Using this conceptualization, it is possible that by bringing representative considerations to the bench, justices will understand and feel compelled to fulfill the role of representative. However this is impossible from the jurisprudential posture of judicial restraint. As has been noted, judicial restraint is the prime consideration of President George W. Bush for his nominations to the courts. Were he to continue the practice of maintaining a representative Court he would be putting judicial restraint in jeopardy.

George W. Bush not only used judicial restraint as a prime consideration in choosing his Supreme Court nominees, but also in choosing appointments to key positions within the Department of Justice. In such a way, Bush in not only ensuring conservative decision making on the courts, but he is also ensuring a solicitor general who will pursue legislation intended to produce restraintist judicial decisions.

Cases Pursued by the Bush Administration

One way to discern the Bush administration's disposition toward the courts in regard to religion is to examine the cases pursued by the solicitor general. The solicitor general determines which cases the federal government will appeal to the Supreme Court, and for which cases the U.S. government will file amicus curiae briefs.

Bush's first solicitor general was Theodore Olson. Bush selected Olson for this position after he successfully represented Bush in the case involving the disputed 2000 presidential election. Olson was also desirable in that he shares Bush's belief in judicial restraint. As with many Bush appointees selected for high political office, Olson is a member of the Federalist Society. The Federalist Society states in its mission: ". . . that the state exists to preserve freedom, that the separation of governmental powers is central to our Constitution, and that it is emphatically the province and duty of the judiciary to say what the law is, not what it should be" (www.fed-soc.org). When Olson decided to resign his post in June of 2004, he was replaced with his deputy Paul Clement, also a member of the Federalist Society.

As Bush chose solicitors general who were so closely aligned with his jurisprudential posture, the cases they choose to pursue will reveal Bush's approach to the religious cases. Table 11.2 lists all of the religious cases on the Supreme Court docket during Bush's tenure treating religion. Here "religious" is identified as any case before the Supreme Court in which religious interest groups filed amicus briefs. Such a broad definition enables an examination of cases that deal not only with separation of church and state and free exercise concerns but also cases that deal with moral matters.

Twenty-four cases have been identified. Each case attracted activity by at least two religious groups that filed briefs on behalf of either party.[23] The issues range from traditional establishment clause and

Table 11.2 Religious Cases before the Supreme Court during the Bush Administration

Year	Case	Subject[a]
2001	*James Alexander v. Martha Sandoval*	Civil Rights Act, equal protection clause, English-only policy, driver's license examination, national origin discrimination
2001	*Good News Club v. Milford Central School*	First Amendment, free speech, school access, religious instruction
2002	*Ashcroft v. ACLU*	Child Online Protection Act, First Amendment, community standards
2002	*Ashcroft v. Free Speech Coalition*	Child Pornography Prevention Act, First Amendment, free speech
2002	*Zelman v. Simmons-Harris*	First Amendment, establishment clause, school vouchers
2003	*Grutter v. Bollinger*	Affirmative action, equal protection clause, Fourteenth Amendment, Title VI of the Civil Rights Act of 1964
2003	*Gratz v. Bollinger*	Affirmative action, equal protection clause, Fourteenth Amendment, Title VI of the Civil Rights Act of 1964
2003	*Lawrence v. Taylor*	Sexual orientation, equal protection clause, Fourteenth Amendment, privacy, criminal law
2003	*Scheidler v. NOW*	Racketeer Influenced Corrupt Organizations Act
2003	*Operation Rescue v. NOW*	(RICO), Hobbs Act, abortion clinics, protests, injunctive relief
2003	*United States v. American Library*	Children's Internet Protection Act, libraries, Internet *Association* access, First Amendment
2004	*Elk Grove Unified School District.v. Newdow*	Pledge of Allegiance, First Amendment, establishment clause
2004	*Locke v. Davey*	First Amendment, free exercise clause, education
2004	*Austria v. Altmann*	Foreign Sovereign Immunities Act of 1976, foreign states, jurisdiction, wrongful appropriation, international law
2005	*Cutter v. Wilkinson*	Establishment clause, Religious Land Use and Institutionalized Persons Act

Continued

Table 11.2   Continued

Year	Case	Subject[a]
2005	Granholm v. Heald	Twenty-First Amendment, importation of beverage alcohol, commerce clause, Webb-Kenyon Act
2005	McCreary County v. ACLU of Kentucky	First Amendment, establishment clause, Ten Commandments display
2005	MGM Studiosr v. Grokster	Copyright law, Internet-based "file-sharing"
2005	Roper v. Simmons	Minimum age for capital punishment, cruel and unusual punishment clause, Eighth Amendment, Fourteenth Amendment
2005	Van Orden v. Perry	First Amendment, establishment clause, religion, Ten Commandments display
2006	Ayotte v. Planned Parenthood of Northern New England	New Hampshire Parental Notification Prior to Abortion Act, standard of review, minor's health
2006	Gonzales v. O Centra Espirita Beneficiente Uniao do Vegetal	Religious Freedom Restoration Act of 1993, Schedule I Hallucinogenic Controlled Substances, international treaties
2006	Gonzales v. Oregon	Controlled Substances Act, physician-assisted suicide, Oregon Death with Dignity Act
2006[b]	Rumsfeld v. Forum for Academic and Institutional Rights	Solomon amendment, equal access, federal funds, institutions of higher education, military recruiters, First Amendment

Notes: [a] The subject was from Findlaw's Supreme Court Center located at http://supreme.lp.findlaw.com/supreme_court/resources.html.
[b] No decision has been handed down yet on this case.

free exercise claims to government attempts to regulate sexual pornography over the Internet. The U.S. federal government was a direct party to six of these cases. In addition to those six cases, the solicitor general filed amicus curiae briefs during the merit phase for an additional 11. The merit phase is the stage after which the Supreme Court has granted review to a case. See table 11.3 below for the cases in which amicus briefs were filed. Amicus curiae briefs offer an opportunity to an interested party that is not directly involved in a case to be able to make an argument on how the Court should decide the case. Filing amicus briefs is a strategy used by hundreds of interest groups in

Table 11.3   Supreme Court Cases in which the United States Filed Amicus Briefs during the Merits Phase

Zelman v. SimmonsHarris (2002)
Grutter v. Bollinger (2003)
Gratz v. Bollinger (2003)
Elk Grove Unified School District v. Newdow (2004)
Locke v. Davey (2004)
Austria v. Altmann (2004)
Cutter v. Wilkinson (2005)
Van Orden v. Perry (2005)
McCreary v. ACLU of Kentucky (2005)
MGM Studios v. Grokster (2005)
Ayotte v. Planned Parenthood of Northern New England (2006)

an attempt to shape policy. This approach is not the exclusive domain of interest groups; presidents and legislators, singularly and in groups, have used it as well. But would President Bush endorse this practice for his administration? Doing so might contradict his belief that legislating is restricted to the legislature.

Such a question can be answered by examining the Bush administration briefs filed during the merits phase.[24] In some of the cases, the Bush administration briefs coincide or make arguments similar to those being made by the religious groups. For example, in *Ayotte v. Planned Parenthood* (2006), the solicitor general makes two arguments. The first is that the application of *Stenberg v. Carhart* (2000) to this case by the court of appeals is erroneous. This same argument is made in the brief submitted by the U.S. Conference of Catholic Bishops and the Roman Catholic Bishop of Manchester. The second argument is that the standards concerning facial challenges that were set in *United States v. Salerno* (1987) were improperly applied. The Eagle Forum Education and Legal Defense Fund make a similar claim in their briefs.

In both of the cases involving the Ten Commandments, *Van Orden v. Perry* (2005) and *McCreary County v. ACLU of Kentucky* (2005), the United States' briefs maintain that the Court has long recognized and repeatedly affirmed that the establishment clause does not require government to ignore the nation's political and legal history that is infused with religious influences. This is the argument promulgated as well by the Family Research Council, the Becket Fund for Religious Liberty, and the National Jewish Council.

Similarly, the United States finds itself in the company of a number of religious groups when it purports in *Elk Grove Unified School*

District v. Newdow (2004) that the Pledge of Allegiance is a patriotic exercise, not a religious exercise, and that it passes constitutional muster. These groups include Focus on the Family, the Catholic League, the Knights of Columbus, and the Rutherford Institute. In all, the Bush administration's briefs parallel those of religious groups in four of the eleven cases. And when they do coincide, the argument being made is not a moral or religious argument but rather a legal argument.

Certainly, by virtue of the action in which the administration chooses to file an amicus curiae brief, Bush is attempting to influence policy. This would seem to counter his belief in judicial restraint. But a close reading of the arguments being made reveals otherwise. These briefs do not advocate a change in how the Court decides the individual cases and thus "legislate" in such a manner. For example, the Eagle Forum Education and Legal Defense Fund and Focus on the Family briefs encourage the Court to abandon the Lemon Test as the standard to be applied to establishment clause cases in their briefs filed in *Van Orden v. Perry* (2005). Had the Bush administration made a similar plea, which it did not, one could easily maintain that President Bush was contradicting his belief in judicial restraint. Yet all of the United States' briefs to date simply recommend which precedents to apply; they do not promulgate any type of policy change.[25]

In addition to the briefs filed during the merits stage, another 11 briefs were filed by the administration during the petitions stage.[26] See table 11.4 for a listing of these cases. This is the phase prior to the Court granting certiorari in which one of the parties is requesting that the Court grant review. These 11 petitions briefs were examined to determine the administration's interests. One thing becomes eminently

Table 11.4 Supreme Court Cases in which the United States Filed Amicus Briefs during the Petitions Phase

Henderson v. Mainella (Director of National Park Service) (2001)
Coalition of Clergy, Lawyers & Professors v. Bush (2002)
United States v. Newdow (2002)
Alameida v. Mayweathers (2003)
Newdow v. United States Congress (2003)
Bass v. Madison (2003)
Gonzales v. O Centro Espirita Beneficent Uniao do Vegetal (2004)
Town of Surfside, Florida v. Midrash Sephardi, Inc. (2004)
Gonzales v. Carhart (2005)
Martha McSally v. Rumsfeld (2005)
American Jewish Congress v. Corporation for National and Community Service (2005)

clear: the Bush administration files a brief when the case being considered concerns a piece of legislation supported and/or passed by the administration, or when the case affects a similar federal policy supported by the president. For example, the Religious Land Use and Institutionalized Persons Act of 2000 (RLUIPA) is the subject of three briefs. This bill was enacted before Bush was elected, but it is a law that he has vigorously attempted to defend. This law "prohibits zoning and landmarking laws that substantially burden the religious exercise of churches or other religious assemblies or institutions absent the least restrictive means of furthering a compelling governmental interest" (http://www.usdoj.gov/crt/housing/rluipaexplain.htm).

A few of the briefs filed also aim to protect federal and state programs that provide scholarship money or school vouchers that enable students to choose private schools that may have a religious affiliation. Such is the issue at hand in *Zelman v. Simmons-Harris* (2002), *American Jewish Congress v. Corporation for National and Community Service* (2005), and *Locke v. Davey* (2004). In these cases the solicitor general defended an Ohio voucher program, the AmeriCorps Education Awards program and a Washington State Scholarship respectively. Certainly Bush was concerned about school voucher programs as he advocated for them in his 2000 presidential campaign.

The Bush administration has also been guarding a piece of legislation that was a triumph for them and their conservative Christian supporters: the Partial Birth Abortion Ban Act of 2003. Protecting this law is the basis for filing briefs in *Gonzales v. Carhart* (2005) and *Ayotte v. Planned Parenthood of Northern New England* (2006). In each brief, whether it concerns abortion or school voucher programs, the solicitor general is stating the administration's interest in protecting a specific law, statute, or policy that already exists.

With 24 cases attracting the attention of religious interest groups who all are actively attempting to shape public policy, there has been ample opportunity for President George W. Bush to follow suit. Certainly administrations past have used the filing of amicus briefs as a means of affecting policy. However, examining the briefs that were filed, it is clear that this is not the intent of the solicitors general, both of who are active members of the Federalist Society and believe in judicial restraint. The Bush administration's policy regarding which cases to pursue does not violate the principle of judicial restraint. Rather the strategy has been to pursue cases that would allow the Court to render a restraintist decision, one that allows for greater accommodation of religion and as such furthers religious interests.

Conclusion

Conservative religious interest groups have become a major force in American politics, and Republican presidents ignore them at their peril. This has become quite clear at the confirmation stage of judicial nominations to the federal bench[27] and by the number of amicus briefs these groups submit for Supreme Court cases.[28] While abortion may be the highest-profile issue associated with these groups, other somewhat less prominent issues are still important to them. These include a host of establishment and free exercise issues such as those we have mentioned. At the same time modern Republican presidents have been consistent in their campaigns in saying they want to appoint restraintist judges and justices to the federal courts. Therefore, there has been a convenient marriage of the two minds. The motivations of the presidents and the groups appear to be quite genuine. The presidents make the argument that democracy is best served by having popularly elected officials make political decisions. The interest groups make the arguments that it was never the intention of the framers to completely root religion out of American public life.

The religious groups have become quite concerned about what they see as the secularization of American culture.[29] Religion has been a part of American society since the first day the settlers landed on the American shores. There were excesses to be sure and therefore the framers of the Constitution wanted to make sure those were prohibited by the First Amendment.[30] But just as the framers wanted to have a president instead of a king, they also wanted to allow some religion but not have another state religion such as that which existed in England.

Religion has always played some role in the appointment of Supreme Court justices, particularly in modern times.[31] Moreover, one can make the argument, as we have here, that religion may be a factor that affects the decision making of a Supreme Court justice. Justice Scalia's Catholicism, for example, may very well be an influence in the literal approach he takes to reading the provisions of the Constitution. Protestant justices, on the other hand, considering their more diverse way of relating to God and the Bible, may allow for more subjective interpretations of constitutional provisions looking toward framers' intent.[32]

Theory aside, the key purpose of our analysis has been to see how religious groups and the Bush administration have worked in common in making their legal arguments before the Supreme Court on religious issues. To begin, the Bush administration has twice chosen as solicitor general, the government's lawyer before the Supreme Court, two men who are members of the Federalist Society, which has as its core principle the practice of judicial restraint, the legal technique the president has publicly espoused.

Of the cases on the merits that we examined there are clear parallels between the activities of interest groups and the government. Both make their arguments not only as parties but also as amici the latter being a technique that by its very nature means to influence decision making. In those cases where the United States was an amicus, the government only recommended which precedents to apply as opposed to promulgating policy change or simply made the restraintist argument to return to the original meaning of the Constitution. In each case in which the government filed a brief at the petitions stage the administration interest was only in protecting a law or policy that already exists, the same arguments made by the conservative religious group parties.

The bottom line on all the cases we examined is that the Bush administration has made it clear that allowing some religion in American life and judicial restraint are often one and the same. That is what some scholars contend the framers of the Constitution intended, and that is what it intends.[33] In short, President Bush, through his judicial activity, has made good on his campaign promises. He is a man who has made religion an important part of his life, has said religion has a place in American public life, and has followed through where he has had the opportunity to reaffirm religion's role in the American legal system.[34]

Notes

1. Stack was quoting Supreme Court Justice Antonin Scalia.
2. Activism also is an imprecise term capable of different meanings. Probably the most easily identifiable activist method is to infer a new right into the constitution. In the case of abortion rights, the word abortion does not appear anywhere in the constitution so inferring that there is a constitutional right to have an abortion can easily be viewed as an exercise in activism. For a useful list of possible activist techniques, see Young 2002, 1139–1216.
3. Of course, judicial restraint and activism can easily be used as substitutes for political and partisan ends. While today activism is usually associated with political liberalism, in the Lochnerian period in American constitutional history (the end of the nineteenth and the beginning of the twentieth century) the Court engaged in conservative activism as it protected private property rights.

4. *Roe v. Wade* (1973).
5. *Regents of the University of California v. Bakke* (1978); *Steelworkers v. Weber* (1979); *Johnson v. Transportation Agency* (1987); and *Grutter v. Bollinger* (2003).
6. *Reno v. American Civil Liberties Union* (1997).
7. *Atkins v. Virginia* (2002); and *Roper v. Simmons* (2005).
8. *Lawrence v. Texas* (2003).
9. *Locke v. Davey* (2004).
10. *Wallace v. Jaffree* (1985); *Allegheny v. ACLU* (1989); and *Lee v. Weisman* (1992).
11. Indeed in late 1991 when Justice Clarence Thomas was elevated to the Court, eight of the nine justices had been appointed by Republican presidents. The sole exception was Justice Byron White, a Kennedy appointee, who ironically was one of the Court's conservatives.
12. Indeed the justices who would most fit the descriptions of being both restraintists and originalists did vote like this in actual Supreme Court cases. In the case of nativity scenes Justice Antonin Scalia voted (in dissent) to allow a nativity scene in a courthouse. *Allegheny v. ACLU* (1989). Justices Scalia and Clarence Thomas voted (in dissent) to allow a clerical invocation in a public school graduation.
13. Similarly Justices Scalia and Thomas voted (in dissent) to allow state-sponsored scholarships for devotional theology degrees. *Locke v. Davey* (2004).
14. Only six articles were written about the possibility of Alito becoming the fifth Catholic justice. All of the articles were written in the few days proceeding a press release by the Associated Press on October 31, 2005. And of the articles written, the journalists took special note that this was only worthy of news because it was not newsworthy as Catholics are generally accepted and not many were concerned about this possibility. This information was attained by searching the Lexis-Nexis database of Northeastern, Southeastern and Western U.S. new sources.
15. Although born a Baptist and raised a Catholic, Justice Thomas regularly attended an Episcopal church until he reclaimed his Catholicism in a speech given at Holy Cross College in Massachusetts in 1996, *USA Today* (Mauro 1996).
16. These are data gathered from the U.S. Census for 2001.
17. According to the CNN exit polls, 54% of the electorate in 2004 was Protestant, 27% Catholic, and 3% Jewish. The same exit poll data reveal that 59% of Protestants, 52% of Catholics, and 25% of Jews voted for Bush.
18. This was reported in an opinion piece authored by Jonathon Turley and published in the *Los Angeles Times*.
19. On July 31, 2003 the Vatican released a 12-page report devoted to homosexuality, gay marriage, and adoption by gays and lesbians. In it Catholic bishops and politicians are instructed to oppose gay marriages.

20. The decree was issued by the Vatican on April 23, 2003. The document was issued to address the abuses of the celebration of the Eucharist of Christ.

21. According to a Pew Research Center poll conducted on August 5–6, 2004, 64% of the respondents indicated that they felt it was improper for Catholic Church leaders to deny communion to Catholic politicians whose views on abortion and other life issues go against the Church teachings.

22. Sanford V. Levinson spoke with *Boston Globe* reporter Drake Bennett (2005). This explanation of Levinson's theory appeared in an article by Drake Bennett in the August 7, 2005 edition of the *Boston Globe*.

23. Religious groups were identified in part by consulting Weber 1994. This reference volume has a comprehensive listing of most all religious interest groups active in the United States.

24. Only the amicus briefs filed during the merits phases are being considered. Excluded are the briefs filed for the six cases in which the United States was either the petitioner or the respondent. In this manner all of the briefs that are examined are amicus briefs allowing for a comparison between the United States and the religious groups.

25. One can also make the argument that taking the position of agreeing to abandon the Lemon Test is restraintist because it means returning to the original meaning of the establishment clause.

26. These petitions concern cases outside of the 24 "religious" Supreme Court cases identified. This is to enable a much larger sampling of Bush administration arguments.

27. For analyses of the activities of these groups during two highly controversial Supreme Court nominations see DeGregorio and Rossotti 1994a; and DeGregorio and Rossotti 1994b, 1–19.

28. Rossotti 1997.

29. For an interesting discussion of this issue see Rosen 2003, SM48.

30. For example, there were mandatory Sunday church attendance laws, and there was considerable discrimination against certain religious minorities including Catholics, Jews, and Quakers.

31. A very recent example occurred when President Bush invoked religion as a factor in the ill-fated nomination of Counsel to the President Harriet Miers to the Supreme Court. See Baker and Babington 2005, A08.

32. These descriptions coincide with Levinson's alternative theories and are more likely accurate in describing how most Protestants and Catholics would look at the Bible today.

33. See, e.g., Pepper 1989, 323–362; and McConnell 1985, 1–59.

34. For a critical analysis of this see Wallis 2003. See also Kengor 2004.

References

Abraham, Henry. 1999. *Justices, Presidents and Senators*. Lanham, MD: Rowman and Littlefield.

Baker, Peter, and Charles Babington. 2005. "Role of Religion Emerges as Issue." *Washington Post*, October 13.

Bennett, Drake. 2005. "Faithful Interpretations: Is There a Catholic Way to Read the Constitution?" *Boston Globe*, August 7.

Berke, Richard L. 2000. "Bush and Gore Stake Out Differences in First Debate." *New York Times*, October 4.

Bush, George W. 2005. "President's Radio Address." July 23.

DeGregorio, Christine, and Jack E. Rossotti. 1994a. "Campaigning for the Court: Interest Group Participation in the Bork and Thomas Confirmation Processes." In *Interest Group Politics 4th Edition*, edited by Allan J. Cigler and Burdett A. Loomis. Washington, DC: Congressional Quarterly Press.

——— 1994b. "Resources, Attitudes and Strategies: Interest Group Participation in the Bork Confirmation Process." *American Review of Politics* 15: 1–19.

Goldman, Sheldon. 1979. "Should There Be Affirmative Action for the Judiciary?" *Judicature* 62: 488–494.

Grossman, Joel. 1966. "Social Backgrounds and Judicial Decision-Making." *Harvard Law Review* 79: 1551–1564.

Hamilton, Alexander, James Madison, and John Jay. 1989. *The Federalist Papers*. New York: Bantam Books (first published in 1788).

Jipping, Thomas L. 1995. "Solving the Madisonian Dilemma: Reflections on Judicial Review." *Essays on Our Times* 36: 1–15. Washington, DC: Free Congress Research and Education Foundation.

Kengor, Paul. 2004. *God and George W. Bush: A Spiritual Life*. New York: HarperCollins.

McConnell, Michael W. 1985. "Accommodation of Religion." *Supreme Court Review* : 1–59.

Mauro, Tony. 1996. "After 28 Years Thomas Reclaims Catholic Faith." *USA Today*, June 18, 4A.

Pepper, Stephen. 1989. "A Brief for the Free Exercise Clause." *Journal of Law and Religion* 7 (2): 323–362.

Perry, Barbara. 1991. *A "Representative" Supreme Court? The Impact of Race, Religion, and Gender on Appointments*. New York: Greenwood Press.

Pitkin, Hanna. 1967. *The Concept of Representation*. Berkeley, CA: University of California Press.

Reagan, Ronald. 1987. "Voluntarism and the Supreme Court Nomination of Robert H. Bork." Radio Address, October 3.

Rosen, Jeffrey. 2003. "How to Reignite the Culture Wars." *New York Times*, September 7, SM48.

Rossotti, Jack E. 1997. "Scaling *Amicus* Briefs as an Ideological Measure of Judicial Activism on Abortion: A Preliminary Analysis of *Roe v. Wade* and *Webster v. Reproductive Health Services*." Paper presented at the annual meeting of the Western Political Science Association, Tucson, AZ, March.

Scalia, Antonin. 2002. "God's Justice and Ours." *First Things* 123: 17–21.

Sisk, Gregory C., Michael Heise, and Andrew P. Morriss. 2004. "Searching for the Soul of Judicial Decisionmaking: An Empirical Study of Religious Freedom Decisions." *Ohio State Law Journal* 65: 491–614.

Stack, Kevin M. 2004. "The Divergence of Constitutional and Statutory Interpretation." *University of Colorado Law Review* 75: 1–58.

Tatalovich, Raymond. 1995. *Nativism Reborn? The Official English Language Movement and the American States*. Lexington, KY: University of Kentucky Press.

Wallis, Jim. 2003. "Dangerous Religion: George W. Bush's Theory of Empire." *Sojourners Magazine*, September/October.

Weber, Paul J. 1994. *US Religious Interest Groups: Institutional Profiles*. Westport, CT: Greenwood Press.

www.fed-soc.org.

www.usdoj.gov/crt/housing/rluipaexplain.htm.

Young, Ernest A. 2002. "Judicial Activism and Conservative Politics." *University of Colorado Law Review* 73: 1139–1216.

Cases Cited

Alameida v. Mayweathers, No. 02-1655 (2003)

Allegheny v. ACLU (American Civil Liberties Union), 492 U.S. 573 (1989)

American Jewish Congress v. Corporation for National and Community Service, No. 05-282 (2005)

Ashcroft v. ACLU (American Civil Liberties Union), 535 U.S. 564 (2002)

Ashcroft v. Free Speech Coalition, 535 U.S. 234 (2002)

Atkins v. Virginia, 530 U.S. 304 (2002)

Austria v. Altmann, 541 U.S. 677 (2004)

Ayotte v. Planned Parenthood of Northern New England, No. 04-1144 (2006)

Bass v. Madison, No. 03-1404 (2003)

Coalition of Clergy, Lawyers & Professors v. Bush, No. 02-1155 (2002)

Cutter v. Wilkinson, No. 03-9877 (2005)

Elk Grove Unified School District v. Newdow, 542 U.S. 1 (2004)

Gonzales v. Carhart, No. 05-380 (2005)

Gonzales v. O Centro Espirita Beneficient Uniao do Vegetal, No. 04-1084 (2004)

Gonzales v. O Centro Espirita Beneficiente Uniao do Vegetal, No. 04-1084 (2006)

Gonzales v. Oregon, No.04-623 (2006)

Good News Club v. Milford Central School, 533 U.S. 98 (2001)

Granholm v. Heald, No. 03-1116 (2005)

Gratz v. Bollinger, 539 U.S. 244 (2003)

Grutter v. Bollinger, 539 U.S. 306 (2003)

Henderson v. Mainella (Director of National Park Service) No. 01-978 (2001)

James Alexander v. Martha Sandoval, 532 U.S. 275 (2001)

Johnson v. Transportation Agency, 480 U.S. 616 (1987)

Lawrence v. Texas, 539 U.S. 558 (2003)

Lee v. Weisman, 505 U.S. 577 (1992)

Locke v. Davey, 540 U.S. 712 (2004)

Martha McSally v. Rumsfeld, No. 05-40 (2005)

McCreary County v. ACLU of Kentucky, No. 03-1693 (2005)

MGM Studios v. Grokster, No. 04-488 (2005)

Newdow v. United States Congress, No. 03-7 (2003)

Operation Rescue v. National Organization for Women (NOW), Inc., 537 U.S. 393 (2003)

Regents of the University of California v. Bakke, 438 U.S. 265 (1978)

Reno v. American Civil Liberties Union, 521 U.S. 844 (1997)

Roe v. Wade, 410 U.S. 113 (1973)

Roper v. Simmons, 543 U.S. 551 (2005)

Rumsfeld v. Forum for Academic and Institutional Rights, No. 04-1152 (2006)

Scheidler v. National Organization for Women (NOW), 537 U.S. 393 (2003)

Steelworkers v. Weber, 443 U.S. 193 (1979)

Stenberg v. Carhart, 530 U.S. 914 (2000)

Town of Surfside, Florida v. Midrash Sephardi, Inc, No. 04-469 (2004)

United States v. American Library Association, 539 U.S. 194 (2003)

United States v. Newdow, No. 02-1574 (2002)

United States v. Salerno, 481 U.S. 739 (1987)

Van Orden v. Perry, No. 03-1500 (2005)

Wallace v. Jaffree, 472 U.S. 38 (1985)

Zelman v. Simmons-Harris, 536 U.S. 639 (2002)

Notes on Contributors

Amy E. Black is Associate Professor of Political Science at Wheaton College. She coauthored *Of Little Faith: The Politics of George W. Bush's Faith-Based Initiatives* (2004). A former APSA Congressional Fellow, she is the author of *From Inspiration to Legislation: How an Idea Becomes a Bill* (2007).

David B. Cohen is Associate Professor of Political Science and Fellow of the Ray C. Bliss Institute of Applied Politics at the University of Akron. His research on the American presidency and other topics has been published in a number of scholarly journals and book chapters, and he is coeditor of *American National Security and Civil Liberties in an Era of Terrorism* (2004) and *The Final Arbiter: The Long Term Consequences of Bush v Gore in Law and Politics* (2005).

William D'Antonio earned his PhD from Michigan State University. He has taught at Michigan State, University of Notre Dame, University of Connecticut (Emeritus Professor). He was CEO of the American Sociological Association from 1982 to 1991. He is the coauthor of seven books and coeditor of four collections. His two upcoming books are on Catholic Americans and Voice of the Faithful (a social movement for reform in the Catholic Church).

Kevin R. den Dulk is an Associate Professor of Political Science and member of the Honors faculty at Grand Valley State University. He is the coauthor of *Religion and Politics in America* (2004), among other writings on the role of religion in domestic and international affairs.

Paul A. Djupe is Associate Professor of Political Science at Denison University. He is the coauthor of several articles and books on religion and politics, including *Religious Interests in Community Conflict: Beyond the Culture Wars* (2007), *The Prophetic Pulpit: Clergy, Churches and Communities in America* (2003), and *Religious Institutions and Minor Parties in the U.S.* (1999).

Michael K. Fauntroy is an Assistant Professor of Public Policy at George Mason University. He is the author of *Republicans and the Black Vote* (2007) and *Home Rule or House Rule? Congress and the Erosion of Local Governance in the District of Columbia* (2003).

He was previously an analyst in American national government at the Congressional Research Service (CRS), where provided research and consultation to members and committees of Congress. Prior to joining CRS, he was a civil rights analyst at the U.S. Commission on Civil Rights.

John C. Green is Senior Fellow at the Pew Forum on Religion and Public Life, a Distinguished Professor of Political Science, and Director of the Ray C. Bliss Institute of Applied Politics at the University of Akron. He is coauthor of *The Bully Pulpit: The Politics of Protestant Clergy* (1998), *The Diminishing Divide: Religion's Changing Role in American Politics* (2000), and coeditor of *The Values Campaign?: The Christian Right in the 2004 Election* (2006).

James Guth is William R. Kenan, Jr., Professor of Political Science at Furman University. He has written widely on the role of religion in American and European politics and is currently studying the impact of religious factors on public attitudes toward American foreign policy.

Ted G. Jelen is Professor of Political Science at the University of Nevada, Las Vegas. He is the author of *To Serve God and Mammon: Church-State Relations in the United States*, and *The Political World of the Clergy*, as well as numerous other books and articles on religion and politics and the politics of abortion. He is the coeditor of the journal *Politics and Religion*.

Nina Therese Kasniunas is a PhD candidate in Political Science at Loyola University of Chicago.

Lyman Kellstedt is Professor Emeritus of Political Science at Wheaton College. He is the author or coauthor of numerous leading studies on the intersection of religion and politics in the U.S.

Douglas L. Koopman is Professor of Political Science and the William Spoelhof Teacher-Scholar in Residence at Calvin College. He is coauthor of *Of Little Faith: The Politics of George W. Bush's Faith-Based Initiatives* (2004), editor of *Serving the Claims of Justice: The Thoughts of Paul B. Henry* (2001), and author of *Hostile Takeover: The House Republican Party, 1980–1995* (1996).

Eric McDaniel is Assistant Professor of Government at the University of Texas, Austin. His work focuses on black politics, religion and politics, and collective action. His current research includes an examination of why and how religions institutions choose to become involved in political matters. He earned his PhD from the University of Illinois, Urbana-Champaign in 2004.

Jacob R. Neiheisel is an undergraduate at Denison University and has coauthored several papers on the role of religious interests in the campaign to ban same-sex marriages in Ohio. His research interests include religion and politics, deliberative processes, and political communication.

Laura R. Olson is Professor of Political Science at Clemson University and the author of many books and articles on religion and American politics. Her book *Women with a Mission: Religion, Gender, and the Politics of Women Clergy* (with Sue Crawford and Melissa Deckman) was published in 2005. Her most recent book is *Religious Interests in Community Conflict: Beyond the Culture Wars* (with Paul A. Djupe, 2007) and Her most recent book is.

Jack E. Rossotti is Assistant Professor of Government at American University. He has published a number of articles and book chapters on judicial politics, interest group politics, and other topics.

Mark J. Rozell is Professor of Public Policy at George Mason University and the author of numerous studies on religion and politics. His latest book is *The Values Vote?: The Christian Right in the 2004 Elections* (2006; edited with John C. Green and Clyde Wilcox), and he is coauthor of the book *Second Coming: The New Christian Right in Virginia Politics* (1996; with Clyde Wilcox). He is coeditor of the Georgetown University Press Series on religion and politics.

Corwin Smidt serves as Professor of Political Science and as Director of the Henry Institute at Calvin College, where he has taught since 1977. He is author, editor, or coauthor of ten books, including *Pulpit and Politics* and *Religion and Social Capital* (2004) , as well as numerous chapters in edited volumes and articles in refereed journals. He has served as Executive Director of the Religion and Politics section of the American Political Science Association.

Adam L. Warber is Assistant Professor of Political Science at Clemson University. An expert on the American presidency and public policy, he is the author of *Executive Orders and the Modern Presidency: Legislating from the Oval Office* (2006).

John W. Wells is the Vice President for Academic Services and Interim President of Young Harris College. Author of numerous articles and essays, he coedited *American National Security and Civil Liberties in an Era of Terrorism* (Palgrave, 2004). He resides in Young Harris, Georgia, with his wife and two children.

John Kenneth White is professor of politics at The catholic University of America in Washington, DC. He is the author of numerous books and articles on the presidency, cultural values and politics, and religion and politics, among other topics.

Gleaves Whitney is the Director of the Hauenstein Center for Presidential Studies at Grand Valley State University. Before his appointment to the Hauenstein Center, he was senior speechwriter and historian for Michigan Governor John Engler. He is also a Senior Scholar at the Center for the American Idea in Houston. He has written, edited, or contributed to several books, including *John Engler: The Man, the Leader and the Legacy* (2002), *American Presidents: Farewell Messages to the Nation* (2002), and the revised edition of Russell Kirk's *The American Cause* (2003).

Index

ABC Good Morning America, 143
ABC News Poll, 17
A Call to Service, 61
Afghanistan, 114
African Americans, 4, 6, 7, 33, 74,
    96, 98, 104–7, 110–12, 145,
    177–82, 184–90, 192–3
Africans, 111–12
Aging with Dignity, 170
AIDS/HIV, 8, 106, 214, 227, 234
Alameida v. Mayweathers, 246, 253
Alito, Samuel, 200, 207, 238
Alliance for Marriage, 143
Alzheimer's, 138–9, 202
American Baptist Churches, 70, 77
American Civil Liberties Union
    (ACLU), 100
American Federation of Labor, 185
American Jewish Committee (AJC),
    102–3
*American Jewish Congress v.
    Corporation for National and
    Community Service*, 246–7, 253
American Nationalities for Nixon-
    Lodge, 53
American Values, 60, 223
AmeriCorps, 247
Angelican Church, 70
Annenberg Public Policy Center, 19
Anti-Catholicism, 32, 42, 58–9
Anti-Defamation League, 100
Arabs, 103, 111–12
Arafat, Yasir, 223
Aristotle, 1
Arizona, 13
Ashcroft, John, 12, 20, 131 (See also
    Ashcroft v. ACLU)
Ashcroft v. ACLU, 243, 253
Austria v. Altmann, 243, 245, 253

Awad, Nihad, 110
*Ayotte v. Planned Parenthood of
    Northern New England*, 209,
    244–5, 247

Bakker, James, 32
Baltimore Sun, 56
Bass v. Madison, 246, 253
Bauer, Gary, 19, 60, 223, 227
Becket Fund for Religious Liberty,
    245
Bernardin, Cardinal Joseph, 197,
    206
Bible, 1, 11, 108, 149, 240–1, 248,
    251 (See also *Old Testament*)
Bible Belt, 11
Bill of Rights, 236 (See also
    Constitution)
Bishop, 55, 61, 64, 245
Bishop of Manchester, 245
Black, Amy E., 6, 255
Black Capitalism, 184–5
Black Church, 4, 104, 106–7, 110,
    118, 189, 193
Black Ministers Association of
    Houston and Vicinity, 182
Black Power, 184–5
Bob Jones University, 14–15, 59,
    145, 148
Bork, Robert, 236
Bowers v. Hardwick, 139
Brennan, William, 235
Bridgeland, John, 169
Brimmer, 185
Brown, Janice Rogers, 201
Brownback, Sam, 203
Buffalo (New York), 53
Bush, George H.W., 3, 9, 59, 63, 76,
    132–3, 199

Bush, George W., 1–5, 9, 11–12, 15, 42, 57, 59, 61–3, 69, 75–6, 84–5, 88, 95, 101, 103, 105–8, 115, 118, 123, 129, 131–3, 155, 160, 163, 180–1, 197–200, 204–5, 213, 215, 221, 228, 235–7, 241–2, 247
Bush, John Edward (Jeb), 203
Bush, Laura, 76, 171

California, 16–17, 25, 48, 101, 203
Callahan, Daniel, 137
Calvin, John, 71
Calvinism, 71
Camden, New Jersey, 61
Campaign for Working Families, 19
Campolo, Tony, 223
Capital Hill, 6, 142, 144, 160, 164, 173
Card, Andrew, 76
Carson, Brad, 132
Carter, Jimmy, 32, 129, 202
Casey, Gov. Robert, 136
Castro, Fidel, 53
Catholic(s), 3, 4, 15, 17, 19, 23–4, 33, 35–8, 47–8, 51–3, 55–64, 73, 78–9, 81, 88, 112, 136, 145, 163, 168, 197, 238–9, 241, 250–1 (See also Catholicism and Roman Catholics)
Catholic League, 59, 246
Catholic University, 58, 136
Catholicism, 14, 32, 42, 54, 56, 58–9, 240, 248, 250 (See also Anti-Catholicism)
Census Bureau, 56, 179
Central Intelligence Agency (CIA), 74
Chafee, John, 58
Chaput, Bishop Charles, 61
Chautauqua Movement, 54
Cheney, Richard, 57, 62, 76, 137,
Chicago, Illinois, 53
Chiles, Lawrence, 170
China, 32, 215

Christian, 1–2, 5–6, 8, 11–21, 23–6, 32–5, 48, 70, 77, 102, 105, 108, 115, 119, 129–33, 136, 138–43, 146–9, 183, 191, 197, 207, 213–14, 216–28, 231, 235, 247 (See also Christianity)
Christianity, 32, 52, 60, 87, 217, 223, 227, 228, 230 (See also Christian)
Christian Church (Disciples of Christ), 70 (See also Disciples of Christ)
Christian Coalition, 12, 15–16, 19, 24, 33–4, 197, 219, 225–6
Christian Federation International, 228
Christian Right, 1–2, 5–6, 11–21, 23–6, 34–5, 48, 105, 115, 129–33, 136, 138–43, 147–9, 183, 191, 213–14, 218, 221, 227, 231
Christian Zionism, 222
Christianity Today, 60, 217, 223, 227, 228, 230
Cincinnati Enquirer, 56
Citizen, 226
Civilian Conservation Corps (CCC), 51
Civil Rights Movement, 74, 107, 184, 189–90
Civil War, 58, 70, 162
Cizik, Richard, 224
Clement, Paul, 242
Clinton, Bill, 3, 19, 59, 76, 129–31, 156, 162, 192, 199, 224
Clyburn, James, E., 105
Coalition of Clergy, Lawers, and Professors v. Bush, 253, 256
Cohen, David B., 5, 255
Coleman, Norm, 101–2
Colorado, 22, 48, 61
Colorado Springs, Colorado, 61
Colson, Charles, 217
Committee on Government Contracts, 186

Concerned Women for America
(CWA), 138, 143, 197, 226
Congregational Church, 71
Congress, 13–14, 18, 25–7, 130,
141, 143, 145, 147–8, 156–7,
160, 162, 165, 167, 171, 180,
182, 205, 206, 214, 215, 223,
228–9, 237, 247
Constitution, 52–3, 111, 140–1,
204, 236–7, 240–2, 248–9
(See also First, Fourteenth,
and Fourth
Amendments)
Coral Ridge Ministries, 223
Cornyn, John, 140
Council on American-Islamic
Relations (CAIR), 110, 116
Craig, Rev. Mark, 76
Crawford, Texas, 205
Crown Heights riots, 99
Culture and Family Institute, 143
Cutter v. Wilkinson, 243, 245, 253
Cuomo, Mario, 58

Daley Machine, 183
Dallas, Texas, 76
D'Antonio, William, 3, 255
Darfur, Africa, 224
Dean, Gov. Howard, 105
Delay, Thomas, 205
Democracy in America, 55
Democratic Leadership Council
(DLC), 162
Democratic National Convention,
52, 139 (See also Democratic
Party and Liberals)
Democratic Party, 4, 5, 45, 57, 63,
69, 74–5, 81, 86–8, 99–102,
106, 110, 114, 118, 132, 135,
145, 162–3, 179, 189 (See also
Democratic National
Convention and Liberals)
den Dulk, Kevin R., 7–8, 255
Denver, Colorado, 61
Department of Health and Human
Services, 137, 158, 182, 200

Department of Health and
Rehabilitation Services, 170
Department of Justice, 8, 165, 235,
242
Department of Labor, 185
de Tocqueville, Alexis, 55
Detroit, Michigan, 64
DiIulio, John, 20, 159, 166, 168
Dionne, E.J., 62
Disciples of Christ, 70, 77
Djupe, Paul A., 4, 255
Dobson, Ed, 31
Dobson, James, 13, 25, 197, 225–6,
246 (See also Focus on the
Family)
Dole, Sen. Robert, 2, 19, 20
Domestic Policy Council, 160,
167, 169
Donahue, William, 58
Dred Scott v. Sanford, 200
Dubuque County, Iowa, 64
Dukakis, Michael, 3
Dunn, Rep. Jennifer, 137
Durbin, Richard, 239–40
Dutch, 71

Eagle Forum Education, 138,
245–6
Eberly, Don, 159
Eckstein, Yechiel, 219
Education Trust, 187
Edwards, Sen. John, 88
Eisenhower, Dwight D., 53, 69,
235–6
*Elk Grove Unified School District v.
Newdow*, 245, 253
Episcopal Church, 70–1, 250 (See
also St. Martin's Episcopal
Church)
Episcopalians, 70, 101
Europe, 217, 239
Europeans, 137
Evangelicals, 2–3, 8, 19, 21–4,
31–45, 47–8, 53, 56, 60–1, 64,
79–80, 84–6, 121, 130, 132–3,
141–3, 148, 190, 207, 213–14,

Evangelicals—*continued*
216–25, 227–30 (See also
Evangelical Protestants)
Evangelical Lutheran Church in
America (ELCA), 70, 77
Evangelical Protestants, 2, 3, 4, 8,
21, 24, 31, 34–6, 40, 43, 45,
47–8, 69, 75–6, 78, 80, 82, 84,
86, 96, 99, 207, 227
Executive Order 11246, 186

Fahrenheit 911, 22
Falwell, Jerry, 11, 16, 133, 138,
222–3
Family Research Council, 138, 142,
225–6, 245
Farrakhan, Louis, 16
Fauntroy, Michael K., 6, 7, 255
Federal Reserve Board, 185
Federalist Papers (See *The Federalist
Papers*)
Federalist Society, 8, 235, 242, 247,
249
Feinstein, Dianne, 240
First Amendment, 237, 248 (See also
Constitution)
First Presbyterian Church, 76
First United Methodist Church of
Midland, 76
Five Pillars, 113
Focus on the Family, 13, 25, 197,
225–6, 246
Fourteenth Amendment, 140 (See
also Constitution)
Fourth Amendment, 236 (See also
Constitution)
Fowler, Donnie, 64
Fox News, 117, 120
Frank, Barney, 145
Free Congress Foundation, 223
Free Muslim Coalition Against
Terrorism, 116
Freeing God's Children, 220
Fried, Bill, 145
Frist, Bill, 203, 205
Fukuyama, Francis, 137

Full Faith and Credit Clause, 140
Fuller Seminary, 222

Gallup Poll, 55
Gaza, Palestine, 223
Georgia, 17, 48, 131
Get Out the Vote, 37, 101
Gibson, Mel, 133 (See also *The
Passion of the Christ*)
Gillespie, Ed, 57
Ginsburg, Ruth Bader, 238
Goldwater, Barry, 180
*Gonzales v. O Centra Espirita
Beneficiente Uniao do Vegetal*,
244, 253
Gonzales v. Oregon, 244, 253
Good Morning America, 143
*Good News Club v. Milford Central
School*, 243, 253
GOP, 1–3, 11–13, 15–19, 26, 31,
33, 37–8, 42, 44, 46–7, 57,
100–3, 132, 142, 146, 162,
163, 168, 177–81, 183,
188–90, 192, 203, 207, 219
(See also Grand Old Party, and
Republican Party)
Gore, Al, 20, 22, 24, 59, 115–17,
162–3, 192
Gould, Louis, 180
Government Affairs at the National
Association of Evangelicals, 224
(See also National Association
of Evangelicals)
Graham, Billy, 53
Graham, Franklin, 223
Graham, Hugh Davis, 186
Graham, Lindsay, 180
Grand Old Party, 31, 180 (See also
GOP and Republicans)
*Grand Old Party: History of the
Republicans*, 180
Granholm v. Heald, 244, 253
Gratz v. Bollinger, 243, 245, 253
Greater Houston Ministerial
Convention, 52
Green, John C., 2, 256

Greer, George, 204
Grossman, Joel, 241
Grutter v. Bollinger, 243, 245, 253
Gumbleton, Bishop Tom, 64
Guth, James, 2, 141, 256

Hagerty, Barbara Bradley, 61–2
Hamas, 223
Hatch, Sen. Orrin, 137
Hatfield, Mark, 170
Henderson v. Mainella, 246, 253
Hertzke, Allen, 220
Highland Park United Methodist Church, 76
Himmelfarb, Milton, 101
Holy See, 220
Horowitz, Michael, 220
House of Representatives, 167, 219
Houston, Texas, 52, 76, 182
Hughes, Karen, 76

Independent(s), 12, 13, 15, 19, 48, 102, 113, 144, 182, 237, 241
Indianapolis, Indiana, 187
Indians, 111
International Day of Prayer, 228
Iowa, 22, 48, 63, 137
Iraq, 34, 40, 63, 77, 84, 103, 105, 114–16, 119, 201, 209, 213, 224, 229 (See also Iraq War)
Iraq War, 84, 103, 115–16, 229 (See also Iraq)
Iron Curtain, 53
Islam, 117–18, 214, 223–4 (See also Free Muslim Coalition Against Terrorism, Muslim, Muslim in American Public Square (MAPS), and Muslim Public Affairs Council (MPAC))
Israel, 4, 99, 100–1, 103–4, 115–16, 218–220, 222–3, 229 (See also West Bank)
Israeli-Palestine conflict, 8, 214, 219, 222–224

Jackson, Rev. Jesse, 99, 104–5, 107
James Alexander v. Martha Sandoval, 243, 253
Jelen, Ted G., 7, 102, 256
Jesus, 1, 54, 60–1, 74, 131–2
Jews, 4, 23, 33, 35–8, 51, 59, 64–5, 82, 88, 96–7, 99–104, 118–19, 216, 219–20, 222, 230, 239, 250, 251 (See also American Jewish Committee, Judaism Orthodox Jews and Russian Jews)
Johnson, Lyndon B, 77, 186
Joint Center for Political and Economic Studies, 190
Jones III, Bob, 148
Judaism, 87 (See also Jews)

Kansas, 48, 203
Kasinunas, Nina Therese, 8, 256
Kass, Leon, 137
Kellstedt, Lyman, 2, 256
Kennedy, D. James, 223
Kennedy, John F., 51
Kennedy, Joseph P., 51
Kerry, Sen, John, 3, 22–4, 37–9, 41–3, 45–6, 57, 60–4, 69, 85–6, 88, 100–1, 106, 108, 116–17, 142, 200
Kevorkian, Jack, Dr., 204
Khrushchev, Nikita, 53
King Jr., Martin Luther, 184
KKK, 107
Knight, Robert, 143
Knights of Columbus, 246
Koerner, W.H.D., 129
Koopman, Douglas L., 6, 256
Kotlowski, Dean, 184
Krauthammer, Charles, 228
Kristof, Nicholas, 215, 231

Ladd, Everett Carl Jr., 54, 65
Lake, Celinda, 136
Lawrence v. Taylor, 243
Lawrence v. Texas, 140
Lebanese, 116
Left Behind, 133

Legal Defense Fund, 245–6
LeHaye, Tim, 133
Lemon Test, 246, 251
Levinson, Stanford, 241
Liberals, 13, 99, 144, 147–8, 201
    (See also Democratic National
    Convention and Democratic
    Party)
Lieberman, Joseph, 162
Liberty Party, 178
Lincoln, Nebraska, 61
Locke v. Davey, 243, 245, 247, 253
Log Cabin Republicans, 21 (See also
    GOP and Republicans)
Lott, Sen. Trent, 135
Lowry, Rich, 11
Luker, Kristin, 207
Luntz, Frank, 188
Lutheran Church, 71, 77

Mack, Sen. Connie, 137
Mainline Protestants, 3–4, 19,
    34–40, 42–3, 47, 69–88, 146
Mainline Protestantism, 70–3, 75–8,
    86
Martha McSally v. Rumsfeld, 246
Maryland, 17
Massachusetts, 3, 24, 48, 57, 203,
    250
McCain, Sen. John, 2, 11
McClellan, Marc, 199
McClellan, Scott, 143
*McCreary County v. ACLU of
    Kentucky*, 245
McDaniel, Eric, 4, 256
Medicaid, 182
Meet the Press, 56
Mehlman, 171, 177
Methodist, 61, 70–1, 73, 76–8, 129,
    149
Mexico City Provision, 199
MGM Studios v. Grokster, 244
Michigan Right to Life Committee,
    15 (See also National Right to
    Life Committee)
Middle Eastern, 111

Midland, Texas, 76
Midwest, 71, 134
Miers, Harriet, 200, 251
Milwaukee, Wisconsin, 192
Mississippi, 17, 48, 134
Mississippi Delta, 134
Missouri, 12, 48, 61, 63, 131
Moral Majority, 15–16, 32
Mother Theresa, 170
Mouw, Richard, 223
Muslims, 4–5, 96–8, 110–19, 224
    (See also Islam, Muslims in
    American Public Square (MAPS)
    Muslims in American Public
    Square (MAPS), 111–12,
    115–16, 120 (See also Free
    Muslim Coalition Against
    Terrorism, Muslims and
    Muslims Public Affair Council)
Muslims Public Affair Council
    (MPAC), 116

Nader, Ralph, 116
National Association of Colored
    People (NAACP), 106
National Association of
    Evangelicals, 56, 190, 216, 218,
    220, 224
National Election Studies, 19, 42,
    77, 78, 80–5, 88, 107
National Jewish Council, 245
National Prayer Breakfast, 60–2
National Review, 11
National Right to Life (NRTL)
    Committee, 14, 17 (See also
    Michigan Right to Life
    Committee)
Nationalities Division, 52
Nazi, 138
NBC, 56
Neff, David, 223
Neiheisel, Jacob R., 4, 257
New Deal, 51, 58, 73, 99, 140, 144,
    179
New England, 12, 17, 132, 178,
    209, 247

New England Colored Citizens
   Convention, 178
New Hampshire, 12–15, 48
New Mexico, 38, 48
New York, 16–17, 48, 54, 58, 101,
   215
New York City, New York, 58
New York Times, 54, 56–7, 215
Newdow v. United States Congress,
   246, 254
Newsweek, 219
Netherlands, 71
*Nixon's Civil Rights: Politics,
   Principle, and Policy*, 184
Nixon, Julie, 56
Nixon, Richard M., 51–2, 56, 69,
   162, 184, 236–7
No Child Left Behind (NCLB), 155
North America, 217
North Korea, 215
Northrup, Ann, 146
NPR, 61

O'Connell, Rev. David, 58
O'Connor, John, 14
O'Connor, Sandra Day, 200
Office of Faith Based and
   Community Initiatives, 20, 158,
   160–1, 165–70, 173, 182, 190
Office of National Aids Policy, 21
Ohio, 17, 23, 48, 61, 63–4, 100,
   192, 247
Oklahoma, 48, 132
Olasky, Marvin, 77, 164
Old Testament, 223 (See also *Bible*)
Olson, Laura R., 3, 257
Olson, Theodore, 242
Operation Rescue v. NOW, 243
Oregon, 48, 132, 204
Orthodox Jews, 4, 100, 103–4, 118
   (See also Jews and Judaism)
Oval Office, 75 (See also White House)
Owen, Priscilla, 201

Pakistani's, 111
Palm Beach, Florida, 192

Parkinson's Disease, 13
Partial Birth Abortion Ban Act, 247
Pennsylvania, 38, 48, 62–3, 100,
   136, 144
Pentecostal, 131
Pentagon, 21, 116
Perot, Ross, 59
Personal Responsibility and Work
   Opportunity Reconciliation Act
   of 1996, 181
Pew Center, 217
Philadelphia, 160, 184–6, 192
Philadelphia Plan, 184–5
Pitney, 188
Plan B, 199
Plato, 1
Polish, 53
Pope John Paul II, 7, 136, 197
Powell, Colin, 105, 181
Prayer for the Persecuted Church,
   227
Presbyterian Church, 70–2, 77 (See
   also First Presbyterian
   Church)
Prison Fellowship, 138
Protestants, 3, 4, 48, 52–3, 55–6,
   58–62, 69–74, 76–7, 81–2,
   85–6, 107–8, 145, 162, 214,
   239, 241, 248, 250 (See also
   Evangelical Protestants and
   Mainline Protestants)
Public Works Administration (PWA),
   51
Puerto Ricans, 101
Puritans, 71

Radical Abolitionist Party, 178
Reagan Administration, 21, 74, 225
Reagan, Ronald, 9, 32, 69, 74, 100,
   129, 134, 162, 199, 236
Reconstruction, 6, 178
Reed, Ralph, 12, 33, 219
Reeve, Christopher, 138
Reformed Church in America,
   70–1, 77
Rehnquist, William H., 200

Religions Land Use and Institutionalized Persons Act of 2000, 247

Religious Right, 4, 13–17, 19–20, 22–3, 102

Rell, Claiborne, 58

Republican National Committee, 52, 171, 177 (See also GOP and Republican Party)

Republican Party, 1, 4, 6, 21, 26, 31, 33, 42, 69, 74–5, 85, 88, 95, 99, 100–2, 104–5, 116, 131, 134, 140, 162, 177–9, 181, 185, 192–3, 203, 230 (See also GOP, Republican National Committee, and The Republican Policy of Liberation)

Review of Faith and International Affairs, 218, 231

Rhode Island, 48, 58

Rice, Condoleezza, 76, 105, 181

Roberts, John, 200, 207, 236

Robertson, Pat, 11–12, 16, 138, 222

Roe v. Wade, 13, 25, 134, 198, 200–1, 207, 237

Roman Catholics, 35–8, 48, 136, 145 (See also Catholics and Catholicism)

Roosevelt, Franklin D., 51, 73

Roper v. Simmons, 244, 250, 254

Rose Garden, 140 (See also Oval Office and White House)

Ross, Mike, 134

Rossoti, Jack E., 8, 257

Rove, Karl, 34, 37–8, 141, 143

Rudman, Warren, 15

Rumsfeld v. Forum for Academic and Instiutional Rights, 244, 254

Russia, 52

Russian Jews, 103

Rutherford Institute, 246

RU-486, 199–200

Saginaw, Michigan, 1

Sanctuary Movement, 74

San Francisco, California, 24

Santorum, Rick, 140

Saudi Arabians, 111

Scalia, Antonin, 200, 249–50

Scammon, Richard M., 56, 58

Scandinavia, 71

Schattsschneider, E.E., 62

Scheidler v. NOW, 243

Schiavo, Michael, 204–5

Schiavo, Terry, 7, 26, 203–5, 208

Schindler, Mary, 204

Schindler, Robert, 204

Scott, Dred, 199–200

Seale, Elizabeth, 168

Seiple, Robert, 218, 223

Senate (See also U.S. Senate), 6, 58, 132, 135, 140, 142, 146, 162, 164, 166, 169, 188, 200, 203, 219, 229, 240

September 11th, 5, 110, 114, 116, 169, 171, 223–4, 226

Sharpton, Al, 16, 105

Sheinkopf, Hank, 101

Shelton, Rev. Louis, 193

Sheridan, Bishop Michael, 61

Shi'a, 111

Sisk, Gregory, 240

Six Crises, 52

Smidt, Corwin, 2, 213, 257

Social Gospel, 72–3

Social Security, 51, 80, 82–3, 143–4, 149, 171, 189, 201

Solomon Project, 102–3

South Asians, 111–12

South Carolina, 13–14, 48, 105, 146, 180

Southern Baptists, 60, 62, 70

Southern Baptist Convention (SBC), 142, 219, 222

Soviet Union, 100, 216, 224

Specter, Arlen, 148

Stand for Israel, 219

Stendberg v. Carhart, 199, 245, 254

St. Louis, 61

St. Matthew's Cathedral, 62

St. Martin's Episcopal Church, 76

Sudan Peace Act of 2002, 215
Sunni's, 111
Super Tuesday, 17
Supplemental Security Income, 182
Swaggart, Jimmy, 32
Swartznegger, Gov. Arnold, 203
Steinfels, Peter, 54
Syriana, 115

Tammany Hall, 182
Temporary Assistance for Needy
    Families (TANF), 181
Tennessee, 20, 48
The Arlington Group, 143
The Federalist Papers, 236
The Passion of the Christ, 22, 133
The Republican Policy of Liberation,
    53 (See also GOP, Republican
    National Committee, and
    Republican Party)
Thomas, Cal, 31
Thomas, Clarence, 200, 250
Thompson, Sec. Tommy, 137, 200
Thurmond, Strom, 146
Times, 32
Towey, Jim, 169–70
*Town of Surfside, Florida v. Midrash
    Sephardi, Inc*, 246
Traditional Values Coalition, 138,
    193
Trafficking Victims Protection Act of
    2000, 215
Tulsa, Oklahoma, 132

United Church of Christ, 70–1, 77
United Methodist, 76
United Methodist Church, 70–1,
    76–8
United Nations (UN), 220, 225–7
United Nations Fund for Population
    Activities, 225
United States, 7, 11, 32, 53, 58,
    69–72, 99–100, 111–12, 114–18,
    136–8, 180, 184, 197, 206,
    208, 213, 216–17, 219, 223–4,
    231, 245–6, 249, 251

United States Conference of Catholic
    Bishops, 138
United States v. American Library,
    243, 254
United States v. Salerno, 245, 254
University of Pennsylvania, 144
University of Texas, 77, 241
Unlevel Playing Field, 158, 166, 169
UN Population Fund, 220
Urban Institute, 187
U.S. Conference of Catholic Bishops,
    245
U.S. News and World Report, 53
U.S. Senate, 58, 200–1 (See also
    Senate)
U.S. Supreme Court, 8, 198–200,
    204
Utah, 39, 48
Utenher, Bishop Kenneth, 55

VanOrden v. Perry, 244–6, 254
Vatican, 60, 220, 230, 240, 250–1
Vermont, 48, 105
Vietnam, 74, 162
Virginia, 15–17, 48, 53, 55
Voice of the Martyrs, 228

Warren, Earl, 235
Warren, Rick, 225
War on Poverty, 77
War on Terror, 8, 84, 146, 214,
    223–4
Warber, Adam L., 3, 257
Washington, D.C., 58, 62, 74, 99,
    155, 160, 187
Washington Post, 11, 56, 62, 194–5,
    228
Watergate, 162
Wells, John W., 5, 257
Wesley, Charles, 129
West Bank (Israel), 103, 223
West Virginia, 48, 53, 55
Weyrich, Paul, 223
Wisconsin, 48, 63, 137
When Work Disappears,
    187, 195

White House, 5, 6, 11, 20, 56, 100,
    130–1, 140–3, 145–6, 149,
    158–60, 165, 167–70, 172–3,
    182, 186, 190–1, 200, 217, 230
    (See also Oval Office)
White, John Kenneth, 3, 258
Willet, Don, 159
Wolfowitz, Paul, 229
World Trade Center, 116

World Vision, 218
World War II, 32, 88
Works Progress Administration
    (WPA), 51

zakat, 113
Zelman v. Simmons-Harris, 243,
    247, 253
Zogby International, 22, 120